"Signal 63/7 to"

Killing Atlanta's Finest!

Harold B. Goldhagen

BOOKLOGIX
Alpharetta, GA

ISBN: 978-1-6653-0505-1

Library of Congress Control Number: 2022912722

⊗This paper meets the requirements of ANSI/NISO Z39.48-1992 (Permanence of Paper)

0 8 1 8 2 2

Dedication

This book is dedicated to Atlanta police officers who were killed in the line of duty, who made the ultimate sacrifice in a violent manner.

And this book is dedicated to those closest to and most affected by that loss . . . their families.

Officer M. W. Rasbury	March 3, 1872
Officer Robert L. Albert	July 13, 1897
Officer Thomas J. Ponder	November 8, 1897
Officer Carl Mills	August 1, 1898
Officer Edward H. Debray	June 20, 1901
Officer Tom Grant	May 16, 1902
Officer Edward Crabtree	May 16, 1902
Officer Hugh Osburn	May 16, 1902
Officer Hans E. Drasbach	October 3, 1903
Officer James A. Manier	December 6, 1907
Officer Henry T. Adams	December 7, 1917
Officer James E. Travis	February 23, 1922
Officer Jonas Aiken	December 13, 1924
Officer John E. McDaniel	August 19, 1928
Officer Aaron B. Roberts	June 18, 1930
Officer William Higgins	January 23, 1932
Officer F. C. Foster	March 15, 1932
Officer J. M. B. Goode	June 28, 1932
Officer E. C. Robertson	August 1, 1932
Officer G. A. Jenkins	August 21, 1932
Officer S. A. Smith	October 24, 1932
Officer C. W. Crankshaw	February 2, 1939
Officer J. Harry McWilliams	November 13, 1946
Officer Marion H. Key	March 3, 1948
Officer W. M. "Tex" Richards	December 2, 1952
Officer William G. Turner	November 29, 1953
Officer Clyde L. Elsberry	July 9, 1955
Officer Fred E. Nunnally	February 11, 1956
Officer G. T. Ward	June 19, 1957
Officer Charles J. Busby	August 28, 1959
Officer Hoyle W. Dye	November 9, 1960
Officer Claude E. Mundy Jr.	January 5, 1961
Officer Joseph F. Porter	October 9, 1961

Officer Pearl Martin	December 15, 1961
Officer Charles R. Dickson	April 14, 1962
Officer Hiram B. Durrett	October 7, 1963
Officer Joe E. Phillips	May 10, 1966
Officer H. A. "Tony" Quave	September 19, 1966
Officer Michael L. Little	February 16, 1967
Lieutenant E. Bryson Mitchell Jr.	May 17, 1967
Officer Kenneth C. Bell	April 4, 1968
Officer Thomas Ramsden III	October 26, 1968
Officer Donald D. Baty	June 3, 1970
Officer Billy M. Kaylor	August 23, 1971
Officer James R. Greene	November 3, 1971
Officer James M. Cannon	June 17, 1973
Officer Larry Barkwell	June 19, 1973
Detective Clarence E. Harris	October 21, 1973
Officer Henry L. Jones	December 12, 1973
Officer R. M. Dale	April 4, 1974
Officer Gregory R. White	July 15, 1974
Detective Sam Guy	January 7, 1975
Officer Cled Neal Wingo	July 23, 1975
Detective Ernest L. Wilson	April 27, 1976
Officer Barry Dean Melear	September 23, 1977
Officer James Crawford	January 14, 1978
Officer Frank Robert Schlatt	May 13, 1978
Officer Roy W. Dooley	December 6, 1979
Officer Alfred M. Johnson Jr.	February 16, 1980
Sergeant James E. Richardson Jr.	July 19, 1980
Officer Philip Bruce Mathis	April 25, 1985
Sergeant Willie D. Cameron	February 6, 1987
Officer Gregory L. Davis	August 26, 1988
Officer Layne B. Cook	January 27, 1989
Officer Joseph E. Davis	June 7, 1989
Officer Niles Johantgen	December 21, 1991
Officer Randy J. Schipani	May 8, 1992
Officer Wyley Hart Shepherd	January 14, 1994
Officer George Dawson	February 25, 1994
Officer Dennis L. Carder	May 9, 1996
Officer John Richard Sowa	October 12, 1997
Officer Russell T. Stalnaker	March 31, 1999
Sergeant Melvin Grigley	July 2, 2000
Officer Allen B. Rogers	July 24, 2000
Detective Sherry Lyons-Williams	April 4, 2001
Officer Mark Cross	April 23, 2005
Officer Peter Faatz	August 3, 2006

Prologue

The trigger is squeezed until the hammer falls, causing the firing pin to strike the primer of the cartridge—there's a thunderous explosion and the muzzle flashes—the bullet travels through the barrel of the gun, exiting at an extraordinary velocity, and slams into the body. Tears flesh and muscle. Shatters bone. Rips apart everything . . . that is in its path.

The circumstances surrounding the killings of Atlanta police officers may be different in each case. But the final result is the same when there's a gun in the wrong hands—the sequence described above ends with another of Atlanta's finest shot and killed in the line of duty.

Throughout the United States, law enforcement agencies—police departments, state police, sheriffs, federal agencies—communicate the need for police response through signals comprising a series of numbers. Signals specify the nature of the response required: "signal 50" denotes "person shot," "signal 48" denotes "person dead." Numbers are also used to communicate other information, such as "rush call" designated as "code 3" or "arrived on call," which is "code 26." These are signals and codes used by the Atlanta Police Department. Each agency in the U.S. uses its own system of signals and codes, but the purpose is the same—a verbal shorthand that communicates rapidly and precisely the nature of the call.

The most dreaded call from the "vocabulary" of the Atlanta Police Department is "signal 63/50/48"—"officer needs help/ person shot/person dead." That signal prompts immediate action from all cops who hear it and who begin fearing the worst—that "person dead" is a fellow police officer.

Introduction

As you enter the lobby of the Atlanta Police Department Headquarters you will see a display case. Behind the glass are seventy-seven brass rectangular plaques, each engraved with the name, the date, and the manner in which an Atlanta police officer was killed in the line of duty.

That's what this book is about. It's about cops in Atlanta—but it is the same for cops everywhere—cops who

. . . know what it's like to be alone while approaching a car pulled over on a dark street in the middle of the night;

. . . respond to a call and knock on a door, not knowing what's on the other side when it's opened;

. . . search a dark, empty building after a break-in;

. . . restrain, without help, a violent or demented person;

. . . face an angry mob;

. . . are involved in a shoot-out.

My name is not on one of those brass plaques. For that I am grateful. For those whose names are on those plaques, I am respectful. Through this book, although it is about the twenty-eight Atlanta police officers who were shot and killed while serving and protecting between 1960 and 2005, I honor all seventy-seven Atlanta police officers who were killed, intentionally or accidentally, while serving and protecting since 1872.

Harold B. Goldhagen
Captain (retired)
1962–1992
Atlanta Police Department

Table of Contents

Atlanta Police Officer

Mark Anthony Cross

He had been keeping up with the NFL draft that day, hoping the Atlanta Falcons would draft players who could produce a winning football team in the fall

Mark Cross was "a teddy bear in a grizzly bear's skin" according to the cops who knew and worked with him. He was big, strong, fast, aggressive, and tough when necessary yet compassionate when he sensed the need to be. His good looks and military bearing while in uniform, if featured on an Atlanta Police Department recruiting poster, surely would have increased the rate of applicants.

Mark Cross was born in 1973 in Lansing, Michigan, where he lived until he was eleven years old, probably the longest stretch he lived anywhere as a youngster. His family moved each time his father, FBI Special Agent James Cross, was transferred to a different field office in the U.S. Whether it was Mobile, Alabama, or Chicago, Illinois, Mark excelled in football at the school he was attending at the time. When the Cross family transferred to Atlanta, Mark received a scholarship to Savannah State College, where again, he was a star football player.

While attending Savannah State, Mark met his future wife, Kanthanaree "Gem" Chaiboon. As students, they both held jobs at the Hyatt Regency Hotel in Savannah. After graduation, Gem returned to her native Thailand. Mark followed Gem, and on their return to the United States, they were married. Later, they had two children: a boy, Thai, and then a girl, Aida.

Law enforcement was a large part of the Cross DNA. Mark's father, James Cross, had a distinguished career as a special agent with the FBI, ending his years of service as a supervisor in the Atlanta Field Office. Mark dreamed of one day playing in the National Football League, hopefully for his beloved Atlanta Falcons, but told his dad he felt a "calling" and decided, instead, to follow him into law enforcement. Mark considered the FBI but joined the Atlanta Police Department instead in 1999. He was assigned to Zone 5 morning watch. His goal was SWAT or Red Dog, because he felt that either would be perfect for him. Four years later he achieved his goal—he became a member of the elite Red Dog Unit.

The mission of the Red Dog Unit was to combat the ongoing problem of street-level drug thugs, the teenage boys and young men who were staking their turfs in Atlanta's city public housing projects, apartment complexes, dark streets, and alleys. These crack-cocaine merchants of the "dime bag" (ten dollars a bag) variety formed gangs who did what they had to, to keep competing dealers from selling on their turfs. The ensuing violence resulted, not only in gang members killing one another, but also in the killing of innocent people, including children, who got caught in the crossfire of the gang shoot-outs and drive-by shootings.

As a Red Dog and the first commanding officer of this new unit, this writer will explain its purpose and how its name evolved: Atlanta Police Commissioner George Napper created in 1988 what was known as the "Overtime Drug Detail," a highly mobile, aggressive, citywide tactical unit that was exempt from answering calls for service and free to give full attention to the escalating violence from the young thugs terrorizing the residents of the housing projects, or wherever they had set up shop. The street-level sale of crack cocaine was an "open secret" that had been ignored by Atlanta police for too long.

The original name, "Overtime Drug Detail," didn't sound appropriate to Commissioner Napper. He wanted a name that reflected the personality of the unit whose tactics included extreme aggressiveness, surprise, speed, and force when raiding a reported drug dealer's location. He chose "Red Dog," at that time a popular football term meaning to go after the quarterback by any means—up, over, through, or around—to tackle him before he could hand off or pass the football. Napper was convinced that "Red Dog" propagated the macho image needed to intimidate the thugs or at the least reflected that the unit was not going to let the thugs continue doing what they had been getting away with. "Red Dog" dripped with testosterone!

Whether he was working Zone 5 or Red Dog, Mark Cross had a serious side—police business he was instructed to do or as situations warranted—as well as a playful side. His tricks and gags on his partners, in turn, made him the butt of pranks. On one occasion, as the Red Dog Unit was gearing up before a raid, Mark bitched that his entry vest (a vest that protects more bodily area than the bulletproof vest that's required to be worn under the shirt) was not right, "It's covering my chin. When I talk, it's in my mouth."

His partners let him complain until they could no longer contain themselves, "Knucklehead, you've got it on backwards!" Embarrassed, Mark nevertheless laughed, a loud and deep laugh, a laugh easily identified in a crowd of laughers.

Another time, while cruising through one of the city housing projects, Mark's Red Dog team came across a parked car occupied by four white males. They were incommunicable, apparently stoned, blitzed on some type of mind-altering substance. One had a huge blond afro, assumed to be a wig. As the guy was being removed from the car, Mark tugged, attempting to remove the "wig." The guy's head responded to the tugging, then his shoulders, and then the rest of his body followed. It was the guy's real hair! Mark fell to his knees. Tears were rolling down his cheeks, he was laughing so hard. That loud distinctive laugh of his alerted everyone who heard it that the "Dogs" were in the neighborhood.

Mark's younger brother, Eric, was assigned to the U.S. Army's 82nd Airborne Division fighting in the rugged terrain of Afghanistan. During the same time, Mark, assigned to APD's Red Dog Unit, was engaged in a different kind of combat on the mean streets of Atlanta.

On April 23, 2005, at about eight thirty in the evening, one of those streets proved fatal for Officer Mark Cross. Earlier that evening, the entire Red Dog Unit had conducted a roadblock at the Bowen Homes housing project on Bankhead Highway in Zone 1. It was routine for the Red Dog commander to call all the "Dogs en masse" to one location for street drug enforcement. Upon completion, all teams were assigned to proceed to the various zones in the city and look for drug activity.

Red Dog team 5—Officers Mark Cross, A. T. Griffin, and F. Watson—headed for Zone 3; having worked this area many times, they were familiar with the hot spots. They checked the McDaniel-Glenn housing project. Not finding any drug-related activity there, they continued on to Adair Park. All during that day and into the evening, Mark Cross had been keeping up with the NFL draft, hoping the Atlanta Falcons would make the draft picks that would result in a winning football team in the fall.

Brandon Leon Williams, black male, age nineteen, was an ex-con and a convicted killer. At age fourteen, he and two other juveniles had beaten a homeless man to death with boards and rocks. He had recently been released from serving a five-year sentence for manslaughter.

Earlier on that April twenty-third day in 2005, the same Brandon Williams was driving down Metropolitan Parkway. He was pulled over by an Atlanta patrol car. After the officer checked his driver's license, tag registration, and insurance card, he was released without charges and with a warning to fix his inoperable brake lights.

(The main thoroughfare on Atlanta's south side, now known as Metropolitan Parkway, was once Stewart Avenue and it had a shady reputation and a history for violent crime. Stewart Avenue was where you went to look for drugs, for hookers, for trouble—all you had to do was cruise up and down Stewart Avenue for a few minutes and you would find what you wanted. The cops knew this and would stop cars for the slightest traffic violation, such as a broken taillight, brake lights not working, or a blown-out headlight. Any legitimate reason to submit the driver's name through NCIC [the National Crime Information Center, available to law enforcement personnel for the purpose of checking the status of persons who were wanted from anywhere in the U.S.]. These stops resulted in the arrest of scores of wanted fugitives. If everything was in order, the driver was released with a warning to fix whatever was on the vehicle that had prompted the stop.)

After Williams was released, he drove to the 700 block on Lexington Avenue and visited a female acquaintance who lived in one of the houses across from Adair Park. He told her that he was pulled over and complained about being pulled over several times in the recent past. He said, "I'm tired of being messed with. I spent five years in prison, and I'm not going back." Brandon Leon Williams then told her, "I'm going to shoot the next police that stop me!" Just before eight thirty PM, Williams left the house and went to his car, a 1980 white Chevrolet Malibu. Robert Clark, black male, age thirty-nine, approached the car and asked if he could get a ride home. Williams agreed. Clark got into the passenger seat.

At about that same time, Red Dog team 5 turned on to Lexington Avenue from Metropolitan Parkway. Griffin was driving, Cross was in the front passenger seat, and Watson was in the right rear seat. As they slowly drove by, they saw the white Malibu parked at the curb in front of 742 Lexington Avenue. The car was occupied by two black males. The one in the driver's seat was observed to be reaching down for something under his seat. Griffin stopped the patrol car and shined a spotlight on the driver as Cross got out and approached the driver's side of the Malibu. Watson had gotten out and taken up a covering position at the right rear of the parked car. Griffin backed up the patrol car a few feet and got out.

As Cross approached the door on the driver's side, the occupant in the driver's seat—without a word spoken between him or Cross—shot Cross in the forehead just above his eye. Cross went down. Griffin was between the cars to the rear, the driver shot him in the face. Griffin went down. Watson returned fire, striking the shooter several times and killing him. The passenger was hit once in the arm by one of Watson's bullets.

Although shot in the face, Griffin got on the radio and called for help: *"Signal 63* [officer needs help]*, 762 Lexington Avenue, we got an officer down, signal 63!"* [A wounded Griffin gives the location as 762 Lexington, when in fact it's 742 Lexington Avenue.

Radio acknowledges: *"Copy, signal 63, 762 Lexington Avenue."*
Griffin again: *"762 Lexington Avenue, officer down, I've been 50* [shot] *to the face, start a 4* [ambulance] *and Fire Rescue, code 3* [rush call]*!"*
Watson: *"We have an officer down, got another one 50, start a 4!"*
Radio: *"I copy. Can you advise how many officers have been shot?"*
Watson: *"Two, radio!"*

Radio: *"Any car near 762 Lexington Avenue, signal 63* [officer needs help], *two officers down, signal 50/4* [person shot/ ambulance on the way] *code 3* [rush]*!"*

Watson: *"Step up that 4, officer down, step it up, we need it code 3. We need it like yesterday, radio!"*

They came from everywhere—flashing blue police lights, flashing red fire department lights, red ambulance lights, sirens screaming, air horns bellowing—patrol cars, motorcycles, detective cars, wagons, vans, and a police helicopter overhead to light up the scene. The two wounded officers were quickly loaded into the ambulances and left with a police escort. The route was set up to have a police officer at every main intersection between the 700 block of Lexington Avenue and Grady Memorial Hospital.

In the midst of all the chaos, with the EMTs tending to the wounded and more and more police units responding, Watson took charge of the .38 caliber revolver on the lap of the dead shooter and placed it on the roof of the Chevy Malibu. As the crowd grew larger, police established a perimeter to keep people away from the immediate crime scene.

During this time, Watson never took his eyes off that pistol until he could turn it over to Homicide. He knew it would be a key piece of evidence.

The shooter was identified as Brandon Leon Williams. The .38 caliber revolver was found by Watson on Williams's body as he lay dead across the front seat of his car. A small amount of crack cocaine was also found in the car. Robert Clark received a superficial gunshot wound to his arm and was treated by EMTs at the scene. It was later determined that he was not involved in the police shootings, however, he was arrested for possession of marijuana and a violation of probation.

Officer Andrew T. Griffin was treated for the gunshot wound to his face and was released from the hospital later that night.

He was lucky, just another inch . . . "I remember the intense burning as the bullet seared across my cheek, spun me around, and knocked me down," said Griffin. "I had dropped my gun and was feeling for it on the ground as blood was filling my mouth and also dripping down the side of my face. I heard multiple gunshots and realized it was Freddy [Watson] shooting at the perp."

Officer Mark Cross died of the gunshot wound to his forehead shortly after being admitted to Grady Memorial Hospital. The Grady Hospital Emergency Room Trauma Unit had performed many miracles on shooting and stabbing victims but not this time. The massive trauma to his brain was too severe for the doctors to save the life of Atlanta police officer Mark Anthony Cross.

Another one of Atlanta's finest gone! Mark's widow, Kanthanaree, and their two small children, Thai and Aida, went back to her native Thailand. The whole Cross family, a loving family, was disseminated by the actions of someone with a chip on his shoulder and a gun in his hand.

Soon after this shooting, the Red Dog Unit became disappointed, perhaps worse, dissatisfied with the APD top brass. The Red Dogs felt let down that neither of the two commanders, those at the very top of the APD, didn't take the time or show any interest in stopping by during one of the roll call sessions to see how everyone was doing in handling the stress and coping with the loss they had just suffered.

Red Dog officers heard the talk going around from some of the cops in the different precincts in the city—even the recruits at the police academy—who were doing a lot of second-guessing about the incident. There were those who felt that the only way the incident could have ended differently was if the Cross/Griffin/ Watson team. had continued down Lexington Avenue without stopping to investigate whatever suspicions they may have had about that Chevy Malibu. But that was not what the Red Dog Unit was about; it was the mission of the Red Dog Unit to investigate suspicions of drug activity.

Mark Cross had been working toward an associate degree through the Georgia Military College. He was awarded an honorary degree posthumously. His two children will be offered full scholarships to the Georgia Military College when they come of age, should they choose to accept and attend.

The Atlanta Police Foundation and Peachtree Presbyterian Church partnered to provide a one hundred thousand dollar life insurance policy for all sworn Atlanta police officers. The insurance policy is one way the community is showing its support to the officers of the APD who "answer the call" and go to work, putting themselves in harm's way for the community each and every day.

The partnership to purchase the life insurance policy was established in January 2006 to honor the memory of APD Red Dog Officer Mark Cross who was killed in the line of duty by a drug suspect on April 23, 2005. Former Atlanta Police Foundation board member Scott Wilfong, president and CEO of the Atlanta Police Foundation Dave Wilkinson, president of Turner Enterprises Taylor Glover, and Dr. Vic Pentz of Peachtree Presbyterian Church were instrumental in putting together this benefit to families of fallen officers.

Three years of funding for the insurance premium was provided by members of Peachtree Presbyterian Church and numerous other donors of the Atlanta community.

The one hundred thousand dollar CHUBB life insurance policies provide one hundred thousand dollars to the beneficiary of an Atlanta police officer killed in the line of duty. In addition, the policy provides benefits for APD officers who suffer dismemberment in the line of duty. This policy is provided at no cost to all sworn APD officers. It is a "blanket" accident policy and, as such, individual applications and health screenings are not required.

In the event the benefits are needed, the beneficiary designation is the name the officer has on file with the APD. This information would only be provided to the insurer when a claim is made. The Atlanta Police Foundation is the policy holder.

RED DOG OFFICER
MARK ANTHONY CROSS
"SHOT WHILE INVESTIGATING A SUSPICIOUS PERSON"
APRIL 23, 2005

Atlanta Police Detective

Sherry Lyons-Williams

Every day that scar on his face reminds him there is no promise of tomorrow . . . live each day as though it is your last

During the one hundred years before the early 1970s, all Atlanta police officers who were street cops were men. Not long after, the Atlanta Police Department began hiring significant numbers of female police officers as street cops. They were assigned to do the same work as their male counterparts. That meant the female officers were subjected to the same risks and the same daily hazards as the male officers. Nevertheless, it wasn't until thirty years later that an Atlanta police officer killed in the line of duty was not a male.

The first female Atlanta police officer killed in the line of duty was narcotics detective Sherry Lyons-Williams.

Narcotics enforcement is a dangerous world. It's inhabited at the top by drug czars of the international cartels and at the bottom by teenage thugs selling "dime bags" on the streets. What is common among them, and at every level in between, is the violence they freely inflict—whatever violence is necessary to stop anyone from interfering in what they do.

Sherry Lyons grew up in Zebulon, Georgia, fifty miles south of Atlanta. In high school, she competed in many sports. She was best in basketball. She continued to star in basketball while attending Gordon College in Barnesville, Georgia, and after that at the University of Georgia in Athens. In 1988, she joined the Atlanta Police Department. Just as she did in school sports, Sherry worked hard to be the best she could be during her training at the police academy, in all her precinct assignments after the academy, and then as a member of the narcotics squad.

Sherry was noticed. The big brass recognized how easily she would acknowledge them when simply passing through the halls of the headquarters building. In the same simple, easy way that she acknowledged the brass, she greeted her peers in the squad. Sherry was noticed and liked by all. This, at a time when not everyone liked that women were being accepted as cops into police departments throughout the nation.

Successful undercover narcotics detectives must be like chameleons. They must change from one appearance in the environment of one drug dealer to a completely different appearance in the environment of some other drug dealer. Sherry Lyons-Williams was able to do that—to pull it off, regularly, successfully. She was tall, willowy, and attractive. She could buy dope posing as one of the beautiful people out to score a stash for some big bash on one end of the drug-addicted social spectrum. And on the other end, she could pose as a pitiful malnourished crackhead in dire need of a dime bag.

12

Sherry worked with several different partners once joining the narcotics squad. One night, she and her partner Detective Stacie Gibbs were out cruising the areas known for street drug sales looking to make a marijuana buy. Sherry was driving and stopped at a street corner where several young black males were hanging out. One of the males approached the car, looked in, and seeing two women, one white and the other black, he said, "I know you bitches are the police so get the fuck out of here before I blow your shit away!" The detectives looked at each other and drove off knowing that they had been "made as narcs."

Within a block, Sherry stopped the car and said to Stacie, "We can't let that scumbag talk to us like that. We're the police, the good guys. Let's go back and jack him up."

A cooler head prevailed, and Stacie replied, "Why go back and get ourselves hurt or be forced to shoot someone over a bag of weed?" They drove off to try another location. But that was Sherry, headstrong and determined not to be intimidated by anyone.

Stacie Gibbs and Sherry worked as partners for almost a year. Stacie knew how tough and fearless Sherry could be, but she also got to know Sherry's softer side. During the many boring hours on surveillance or just riding around when there was nothing going on, they talked about their private lives. Sherry revealed that although she had no children of her own, she was a sort of godmother to eight kids. She became aware of these different children over time. They were children living in fatherless homes (more likely housing project apartments) with a mother who was working two or more jobs. She made sure that these kids were not disappointed at Christmas or on their birthdays when she got them a cake and a present. Sherry also made sure that they had what they needed for school, and she seemed to have a sense of the many little things that meant a lot to them.

In Lieutenant Stacie Gibbs's Zone 5 office today, there is a photo of Sherry holding Stacie's baby in her lap. Between some partners, a bond sometimes emerges from their friendship, mutual understanding, and respect in their private lives that grows into a force that binds them in their work in the world of street cops and detectives. So it was with Sherry and Stacie.

As time goes on, things change and so do partners as personnel get promoted or transferred to other assignments. Sherry Lyons-Williams and her new partner, Thaddeus "TJ" Chambers, a fifteen-year veteran, formed this same kind of bond. They had both worked seven years in narcotics. They crossed racial and gender barriers, a black female cop and a white male cop, working as partners. Sherry and her husband attended Chambers's wedding. And they visited Chambers and his family at his home in the north Georgia mountains, occasionally spending the night.

Sherry and Chambers would often lunch together at Manual's Tavern, a cop lunch spot and watering hole. Manual's Tavern is a colorful local spot located at North Highland and North Avenues, one block from historic Ponce de Leon Avenue. It's a throwback to the '50s and '60s, inhabited by a kaleidoscope of cops, lawyers and lawyer types, media people, politicians, young professionals, workers with blue collars, with white collars, college kids, and a few of the neighborhood locals.

On the job, Sherry and Chambers were always the first two through the door when the team served a narcotics warrant, those initial moments when nonverbal communication was essential and every nuance between the two was perceived and understood by the other.

They were the best examples of yin and yang, a perfect fit . . . they were partners. They were good at finding the dope, confiscating drug money, and taking the guns from the bad guys as they put them out of business. Sherry's highest individual professional achievement was when she busted a dealer with 750 pounds of marijuana. Chambers's highest was his bust of six kilos of methamphetamine and a quarter of a million dollars in cash. They had it going their way until the day when things went wrong.

April 4, 2001, started out like it was a usual day for the day watch members of the APD's narcotics squad team 3. It was a cloudy but warm day in the Lakewood Heights neighborhood of southeast Atlanta. The target was 1855 Lakewood Terrace S.E., an old, dilapidated, shabby-framed house. Several previous cocaine buys had been made there by the team's CI (confidential informant). On this day, Detective W. T. Weems was issued a search warrant for the location. The seller in the house was described as a black male, called "Mike," who was between twenty-five and thirty years of age, heavy set, medium complexion, 5'8" to 5'10", approximately 180 pounds with a very close haircut, almost bald.

Detective W. T. Weems was issued a twenty dollar bill by the City of Atlanta. The serial number on the bill was recorded by the police for purposes of identification. Weems had also written his name on it for further identification. The CI was given that twenty dollar bill and sent to the house to make an additional buy. The CI returned shortly with a small black plastic baggie that appeared to contain crack cocaine. Team leader Sergeant E. Brown requested several uniformed officers from Zone 3 to assist with the execution of the warrant. Within thirty minutes, they hit the house.

Weems and Detective W. N. Gilmore took the burglar bar door and the front door down with a pry bar and sledge hammer. TJ Chambers was the point man and first to enter the house with Sherry Lyons-Williams directly behind him. Once in the house, the team started to clear the rooms. The Zone 3 uniforms covered the outside rear and sides to cut off possible escape. They observed a black male open a rear basement door and quickly duck back inside, closing and locking the door behind him. Using his radio, one of the Zone 3 cops reported to the detectives in the house what they had just seen. Chambers immediately descended the stairs to the basement, Sherry a few steps behind him, while the others continued to clear the rooms on the main level.

As Chambers reached the foot of the stairs, he saw a door close at the end of the narrow hallway. Chambers approached the door. The moment he kicked it, a black male came out shooting. Chambers grabbed the shooter's arm and returned fire. They were shooting simultaneously at each other at point blank range. Chambers fell to the floor, the shooter lying on top of him. He pushed the shooter off and turned around to see if Sherry was okay. He saw her lying face down, not moving.

Alerted by the gunshots, the others rushed down to the basement and found the three had been shot. The shooter had fired seven rounds from his .45 caliber semi-automatic. Chambers emptied his gun of thirteen 9mm rounds. Sherry never got off a round. They could not get Sherry to respond. Chambers had been hit in the knee and face. The shooter was hit multiple times in the torso; he was not moving.

Zone 3 police unit: *"We're out with a narcotics unit at 1855 Lakewood Terrace serving a warrant and hear signal 25s* [discharging firearms] *on call."*

Narcotics unit: *"Signal 63 at 1855 Lakewood Terrace S.E., two officers shot, need two signal 4s* [request for ambulance] *and Fire Rescue, right away!"*

Detective radio dispatcher (on all frequencies): *"Any car near 1855 Lakewood Terrace S.E., signal 63/50/4* [officer needs help/person shot/ambulance on the way]*!"*

Zone 3 dispatcher: *"Units on Lakewood Terrace, we have two ambulances and Fire Rescue responding code 3* [rush call]. *"*

As always, they responded from everywhere with sirens screaming, lights flashing, air horns blowing, and the whup-whup of the rotor blades from the two police helicopters hovering overhead.

Police unit: *"Is there a lookout on the shooter?"*

Detective unit: *"Negative, he's still in the house and looks to be signal 48* [person dead]. *"*

Air unit: *"Have to get some of these patrol cars and a fire truck moved. They're blocking the street. The ambulances will not be able to get through when they arrive."*

Dispatcher: *"Copy that, get vehicles moved."*

Unit 500 (from Zone 5, downtown): *"We'll have the streets blocked off from the Edgewood Avenue exit of the downtown connector to Grady Hospital. Advise us when those signal 4s are on the connector, and we'll shut the streets down."*

Police unit: *"The 4 is leaving the scene now, transporting the first wounded officer, be advised he is shot in the leg and the face."*

Dispatcher: *"How about the other officer?"*

Police unit: *"They are still working on her."*

Detective supervisor: *"Cancel the signal 63. Put everything back in service. Homicide is on the scene and will keep a couple of Zone 3 units here."*

Dispatcher: *"All units code 4* [cancel] *the signal 63, all Zone 3 cars, code 7* [back in service]."

Detective TJ Chambers was hit three times by .45 caliber bullets: in the knee; in the side of his face; and in "center mass," the middle of his chest. The bulletproof vest he was wearing saved his life. The knee wound was his most serious injury, requiring two surgeries and months of painful physical therapy. It was seven months before Chambers was able to return to duty, assigned to electric surveillance in the confines of police headquarters. His knee has not returned to 100%, and it is doubtful that he will ever return to street duty.

Sherry Lyons-Williams didn't make it alive to Grady Memorial Hospital. She was pronounced DOA (dead on arrival).

During the shoot-out, Sherry was directly behind Chambers in that narrow hallway. Some of the bullets that missed Chambers hit her. She was hit by four rounds: one, apparently the first, hit the shoulder strap of her vest, which stopped penetration, but the force of the bullet twisted her sideways; another round, likely the second, entered her side just under the armpit, where there was no vest protection, and pierced her heart, killing her; she was also shot in the side of the head in the vicinity of her ear, directly below her helmet, another potentially fatal shot; and the fourth hit her in the hip.

The shooter was dead. He was identified as the drug dealer Michael Moran Thompson, black male, thirty-one years of age. He had been shot by Detective Chambers multiple times in the chest and stomach. A search of the house confirmed that 1855 Lakewood Terrace S.E. was Thompson's legal residence. Also found in the house were the drugs that he was selling: more than fifty hits of crack cocaine; some white powder, possibly cocaine or heroin; and a large amount of marijuana. The marked twenty dollar bill with the matching serial number and Weems's signature was found in Thompson's pocket.

Almost a decade later, as he looks in the mirror every day while shaving, TJ Chambers sees the scar on his face. Every day that scar starts to replay, over and over in his mind, what happened "the day we lost Sherry." He says of that day, "What I learned was there is no promise of tomorrow. Live each day as though it is your last!"

A small irony is that Detective TJ Chambers and Michael Thompson were both originally from York, Pennsylvania (they had not known of each other previously).

Detective Sherry Lyons-Williams was thirty-nine years old and a thirteen-year veteran of the APD. Seven years prior to her death, she earned her gold detective badge. That was when she was assigned to Narcotics. She had an infectious smile and a good word for everyone as she went about her daily job of doing the dangerous grunt work for society. Sherry stayed away from the politics and went after the dopers with a passion.

Sherry Lyons-Williams was the first female Atlanta police officer killed in the line of duty.

INVESTIGATOR
SHERRY LYONS WILLIAMS
"SHOT WHILE SERVING NARCOTICS WARRANT"
APRIL 4, 2001

Atlanta Police Officer

Russell T. Stalnaker

A brief, routine encounter

When a heavy rain falls on cool evenings in Atlanta, it can cause the road surfaces to become slick, leading to more traffic accidents than usual, although most are fender benders. On this dismal rainy evening, at about seven, March 31, 1999, Officer J. J. Daigle, assigned to the Zone 5 Precinct, which includes downtown and midtown, working car 3525, was patrolling southbound on Spring Street. At the intersection of Spring Street and Linden Street, he observed a pickup truck, none of its lights on and no driver, blocking a lane of traffic on Spring Street. Daigle stopped his patrol car behind the pickup, flipped on his blue flashing lights, and because it appeared to be stalled, he called for a wrecker. As he walked toward the vehicle to investigate, he saw a man approach carrying a car battery. When Daigle told the man that a wrecker was on the way, the man said that replacing the battery would start the pickup and he would get it moving and out of the way. Daigle cancelled the wrecker.

It was nothing more than a brief, routine encounter.

On December 8, 1974, Russell Travis Stalnaker was born at Northside Hospital in Atlanta, Georgia. His family started calling him "Rusty," which he responded to before he could crawl. As his personality developed, those who were close to him or those who became close called him "My Rusty."

At an early age, he learned responsibility through looking out for his younger siblings. Their father, who worked in the construction business, sustained a brain injury from a fall out of a second-story window while on a job. Larry Stalnaker was in the hospital for two months, most of that time in a coma. Rusty's mother, Linda, spent most of her time at the hospital doing what she could for her husband, leaving eleven-year-old Rusty to act as father to the other kids in the family. Larry Stalnaker had a long convalescence. When he was able to return to work, Rusty was there with him when he didn't have to be at school or doing homework.

Rusty was often at the home of his Uncle Ronnie and Aunt Donna. He idolized his Uncle Ronald Travis Shaw, who was an Atlanta police officer. He liked to watch as his uncle prepared to go to work, putting on his police uniform with all the leather gear and hardware that went with it. Ronnie often took Rusty to visit different police precincts and to parades where Rusty got a seat up front.

After graduating from Stockbridge High School, Rusty Stalnaker had to decide what he would do next. If he followed his father into the construction business, he would have to ride its highs and lows—money coming in when there was work and struggle through the times when no work meant no income. His uncle, as a police officer, received a paycheck every two weeks no matter what was happening in the construction business. Besides the regular pay, Rusty was influenced by what he perceived as the glamour and adventure connected with police work. He had made up his mind. He would follow his Uncle Ronnie.

But his uncle and aunt were not happy with his decision and tried to discourage "My Rusty" from becoming a police officer. It wasn't the danger inherent in police work, which Ron Shaw was all too familiar with, that concerned them. They were concerned that their nephew would not be using all that he had to offer. People tended to gravitate to Rusty Stalnaker. They tended to follow his lead. That was pretty clear from watching how his classmates, the members of the clubs he belonged to, or even how his friends. behaved around him. Despite hours of discussion, Ronnie and Donna could not get Rusty to see that, and how he had leadership potential. How his leadership skills could grow throughout his life, benefiting not only himself but others as well. But to no avail.

After a long career, Captain Ronald Shaw retired from the APD in 1995. About the same time, Russell Stalnaker joined the Atlanta Police Department. Once he completed the police academy, he was assigned to Zone 5 evening watch.

The rain persisted on the evening of March 31, 1999, as the driver inserted and connected the battery in the stalled pickup truck. He put the gear in neutral as he attempted to get it started. The pickup slowly rolled back toward Officer Daigle's patrol car, but the engine started just short of hitting it. The man shifted out of neutral and the pickup lurched forward with a "jackrabbit" start. Its wheels spinning on the wet pavement and almost ran over Daigle's foot. The pickup crossed three lanes of Spring Street traffic with no headlights and no taillights and then turned on to Pine Street. Daigle followed and found the pickup stalled again. The driver jumped out, trying to push it. Daigle called for a wrecker. He asked the man for his driver's license and was handed a learner's permit.

(The following is from a transcript of the communication between radio [APD's communications center], Officer Daigle, and the responding patrol cars after the call for the wrecker.)

Unit 3525: *"3525 to radio."*

Dispatcher: *"Go ahead."*

Unit 3525: *"3525, hold me at Spring and Pine on GA tag 990PWY, it's the same 81* [stalled vehicle] *as earlier."*

Dispatcher: *"Received."*

Unit 3525: *"3525 to radio, go ahead and start me an 85* [wrecker]*."*

Dispatcher: *"3525, I copy."*

Dispatcher: *"Okay, 3525. That's gonna be Pine, and what's the cross street with it?"*

Unit 3525: *"Think it was Spring and Pine."*

Unit 3525: *"Can you raise 3593* [sergeant]*? Go to S1."*

Unit 3593 (sergeant): *"I copy."*

(S1, or the surveillance channel, provides the ability to talk one-on-one by switching over to a separate frequency that does not go through a "repeater" controlled by the communications dispatcher. It does not require radio procedure and allows for more informal dialogue, such as over the telephone dialogue, and cannot be monitored by anyone not on that narrow frequency.)

Surveillance channel:

Unit 3593: *"3593 I'm on S1, go ahead."*

Unit 3525: *"Hey, Sarge. The 81* [stalled vehicle] *I had earlier, okay the driver showed up, he got cranked up, I was standing by the window talking to him and stuff and he just rolls off, nearly runs over my foot. I come to find out he only has a learner's permit, no proof of insurance, I'm gonna go ahead and code 10* [impound] *it."*

Unit 3593: *"3593, I copy, he's got a learner's permit, no adult with him, gonna 23* [traffic ticket] *him on a copy and code 10* [impound] *the vehicle, is that what you are advising?"*

Unit 3525: *"Affirmative."*

Unit 3593: *"I copy."*

Daigle told the man to wait in his truck while he returned to his patrol car to write the citations. By that time, the man had pushed the pickup halfway into the intersection.

The man approached the patrol car and started screaming at Daigle. "Fuck this shit! It shouldn't take no damn thirty minutes to write a ticket. Either give me a ticket or let me go." Daigle told him to calm down and get back in his truck. Instead, the man continued to push the truck.

Zone 5 traffic:

Unit 3525: *"You got a unit that can come by?"*

Dispatcher: *"3525, yeah, Gilmer and Butler?"*

Unit 3525: *"Negative radio, I'm gonna be at West Peachtree and Pine right now."*

Dispatcher: *"West Peachtree and Pine, copy."*

Dispatcher: *"Calling 3504* [Stalnaker].*"*

Unit 3504 (Stalnaker): *"I'm en route, I'm close by."*

Unit 3506: *"3506, I'm right around the corner doing a 17* [report], *I'll hold my paperwork for a second and go there."*

Unit 3593 (sergeant): *"3593 to 3525, can you 62* [switch channels] *to S1 and advise me?"*

Surveillance channel:

Unit 3525: *"Are you still here?"*

Unit 3593 (sergeant): *"You having a problem?"*

Unit 3525: *"I got a 24* [demented person], *I'm gonna 23* [arrest] *him, he's a kind of big guy, I might need a hand out here."*

Unit 3593 (sergeant): *"3593, I copy, I'll also be en route."*

Unit 3515 (paddy wagon): *"3515 en route too."*

Unit 3504 (Stalnaker): *"3504, I'll be coming up 26* [arriving].*"*

Unit 3504 (Stalnaker): *"3504 to 3525, where're you at?"*

Zone 5 traffic:

Unit 3515 (paddy wagon): *"I'm gonna be en route to 3525's location, and then I'll come back and pick up that Ponce de Leon."*

Dispatcher: *"3515, okay, copy that."*

Unit 3593 (sergeant): *"3593, have the first unit 26* [arrived] *with 3525 and give me an ETA."*

Unit 3506: *"3506, I should be there in about thirty seconds."*

Dispatcher: *"Copy that."*

Unit 3506: *"3506 to 3525, are you on Pine or West Peachtree?"*

Unit 3525: *"We're on Pine right down the hill, over here."*
Unit 3506: *"I copy."*
Unit 3506: *"3506, I'm 26 [arrived] with him."*
Dispatcher: *"3506, 26 I copy that."*
Unit 3504: *"3505, 26."*
Dispatcher: *"3505, 26."*
Unit 3593 (sergeant): *"3593, units with 3525, advise."*
Dispatcher: *"3593, can you advise which units are 26?"*
Unit 3593 (sergeant): *"3593, 3506, 3505 and 3504 advised they're 26."*

Several patrol cars arrived as Daigle was attempting to get the man to come out of the truck. Daigle opened the driver's door, which held on by a rusty hinge that gave way, and the door fell off, dangling by the other hinge. The man started screaming, "You broke my fucking door!" and proceeded to get out of the truck. Daigle grabbed him, attempting to lead the man toward the patrol car. The man resisted, broke loose, and forced Daigle to the ground. That's when the other officers intervened. Stalnaker, Wiskerman, and Price wrestled the man down onto his stomach, attempting to handcuff him. The man twisted free from their collective grasp, rolled onto his back, and started firing a pistol. Stalnaker was shot in the head. The first round hit him.

The others rolled off the man but held their fire because Stalnaker was still lying on him, not moving. The man kept shooting, hitting Price's radio battery (which saved him), then jumped up and ran to Daigle's patrol car. Once the shooter was clear of Stalnaker, the officers returned fire and at least one bullet struck the man in the leg. Nevertheless, he was able to get in the patrol car and drive away toward Peachtree Street.

Unit 3525: *"3525 signal 63 [officer needs help], signal 63, we got a perp, be advised he got my car."*
Unknown: *"Officer down!"*
Unknown: *"He's at Peachtree and Pine, radio."*
Dispatcher: *"Peachtree and Pine signal 63, Peachtree and Pine signal 63!"*

Unknown: *"Start a 4* [ambulance] *code 3* [rush call] *and a supervisor."*

Dispatcher: *"Signal 4, code 3, copy."*

Unit 3593 (sergeant): *"3593, I copy."*

Dispatcher: *"3525, can you advise?"*

Unit 3525: *"3525, I lost them."*

Unit 3525: *"Check with 3508 or 3506, I think he's following him."*

Dispatcher: *"Copy that."*

Unit 3548: (sirens) *"3548, give me a direction of travel, I'm 26 with the vehicle, give me a direction of travel."*

Dispatcher: *"3520, 3506, can you advise 3525?"*

Unit 3506: *"3506, we're on the call now, trying to find him, he wrecked the car* [Daigle's] *at Pine and Peachtree, I didn't see a direction of travel."*

The radio traffic on the Zone 5 frequency was frantic, two immediate concerns being addressed at the same time. Officer Stalnaker was lying on the sidewalk and seriously wounded with a gunshot wound to the head. He was not moving and nonresponsive. Officers with him were trying desperately to get an ambulance to the scene for medical help. The other officers were searching for the shooter, who was fleeing on foot after he wrecked the patrol car he had stolen. The shooter ran into the parking lot of St. Luke's Episcopal Church at 435 Peachtree Street where he attempted to carjack a woman. Her screams scared him off and alerted a security guard who chased him into the church.

Unit 3593 (sergeant): *"3593 is standing by at the corner of Peachtree and Pine."*

Dispatcher: *"Copy, Peachtree and Pine, the 4 is en route Peachtree and Pine at this time."*

Unit 3548: *"3548, be advised that subject is 69* [armed] *with a weapon, he is somewhere between the parking lot at Peachtree and Pine on the corner—"*

Unit 3575: *"3575, we got him in the church, he's inside the church."*

Dispatcher: *"3575 inside the church."*

Unit 3575: *"3575, we're inside the church, we got the subject secure."*

Unit 3525: *"3525, can you get an ETA on the 4?"*

Unit 3593 (sergeant): *"3593, raise 3591* [lieutenant]*, go ahead and start Homicide and ID to this location and Fire Rescue. ASAP."*

Dispatcher: *"Fire Rescue, 4 en route, ID's* [crime scene unit] *gonna be en route."*

Unit 3593 (sergeant): *"3593, have the 4 come in off Williams Street."*

Unit 3591 (lieutenant): *"3591, I copy, I'm 26."*

The chaos in the Zone 5 radio traffic continued—one unit cutting off another, 3593 (Sergeant J. Chesney, Stalnaker's immediate supervisor) pleading for an ambulance and Fire Rescue for Officer Stalnaker. Stalnaker still had not responded or moved. His head wound looked serious. Fire Rescue got there first and began administering CPR. When the ambulance arrived a few minutes later, Stalnaker was immediately loaded into the ambulance. It departed with a police escort, running code 3. All intersections were blocked by police so the ambulance and accompanying vehicles never had to slow down. When they arrived at Grady Memorial Hospital, Officer Stalnaker was pronounced DOA.

The perpetrator, identified as Kimani Atu Archie, a black male, twenty-eight years old, was in custody. He had been shot in the leg as he ran toward Daigle's patrol car. Attempting to flee after he wrecked the patrol car, he ran into a church during a candle light service attended by 150 parishioners. He ran down the main aisle into a room where the pursuing security guard locked the door, trapping him inside, until police arrived. He was taken to Grady Hospital under heavy police security.

Rusty Stalnaker came to the aid of a fellow officer. Cops anywhere have done, and will do, the same. It is the genetic code of the police profession, the Eleventh Commandment. Whether the words over the police radio are "Start me another car" or "Do you have another car near my location?" or "I need another car right away," cops working patrol cars in the area will start that way immediately, they will start before their next heartbeat. Rusty Stalnaker was one of those cops on that evening.

Atlanta police officer Russell Travis Stalnaker was twenty-four years old, respected by his peers, and recognized by supervisors as having the "right stuff" for a successful career in the police profession.

The words that Ron Shaw had cautioned his nephew with have haunted him since the night Rusty was killed—"Rusty, don't put too much faith in that vest, take care of your head!"

The killer, Kimani Atu Archie, was spared the needle when he entered a plea of "guilty while insane." He had a long history of various mental illnesses, including a severe case of paranoid schizophrenia. There was no trial, the court accepted his plea and sentenced him to life without parole.

Rusty Stalnaker was married to Dana Stalnaker for a year and a half, they had moved into their second home just three months prior to his death. They had no children.

Each year on March 31—the anniversary of Rusty's death—Larry Stalnaker places a floral wreath at Pine Street and W. Peachtree Street on the spot where his son, Officer Russell Stalnaker, was killed.

OFFICER
RUSSELL T. STALNAKER
"SHOT WHILE STRUGGLING WITH AN ASSAILANT"
MARCH 31, 1999

Atlanta Police Officer

John Richard Sowa

A quiet Sunday night can turn out to be as deadly as a busy Friday or Saturday night

Zone 2. Sunday night. The evening watch cops were catching their breaths from the usual activity from the previous Friday and Saturday nights. Those two nights in the Buckhead area had become raucous and rowdy, mostly in the Buckhead Village—those few square blocks where there was a concentration of too many clubs, bars, and other "joints."

Once only unpleasantly loud and boisterous, this area was becoming increasingly violent—fights, stabbings, and shootings, some resulting in death, occurred regularly. Not only did the Zone 2 cops always have to be on the alert for these problems, and then deal with them when they occurred, they always had to deal with the certainty of the hundreds of revelers cruising up and down Peachtree Road, a major thoroughfare, causing enormous traffic jams.

For any cops in any area in any city such as Zone 2 in Atlanta, working a Sunday evening is a relief from working the previous Friday and Saturday evenings. Sunday nights can seem easy, peaceful, pleasant . . . they can lull cops into thinking they can relax their sense of security. Any Sunday night can be as deadly as any other night. Anything can happen. At any time.

Atlanta police officer John Sowa, assigned to Zone 2 evening watch, was on duty Sunday night, October 12, 1997. Sowa, twenty-eight years old, had been a sworn officer of the APD for three years. Like many Atlanta cops, he was born and raised somewhere other than in Atlanta, not even in the state of Georgia.

John Sowa was born in Germany on July 22, 1969, the son of a military family. When they returned to the U.S., the family settled in Fulton, New York (near Syracuse). When John was seventeen years old, he moved to Plymouth, Massachusetts. While there, he studied criminal justice at a community college, worked part time in a liquor store, and worked in security for a supermarket chain that had him traveling around Massachusetts. John Sowa's career goal was to be a police officer. He applied at various law enforcement agencies in Massachusetts as well as in other states. At the time, none were accepting applications. This was in 1987, around the same time when he met Danielle Sheehy. They were good friends at first, but within several months, they began dating.

In 1994, John received a reply to one of his inquiries from Atlanta, Georgia. The Atlanta Police Department was not only accepting applications, they were hiring. He went to Atlanta, worked his way through the application, the testing, and hiring processes. In December 1994, he became Atlanta police officer John Sowa, badge number 4824. He was assigned to Zone 2 evening watch. Danielle moved to Atlanta to be with him. They were married in May, 1996.

The Zone 2 Precinct, located behind the Lindbergh Plaza off Piedmont Road between Morosgo Drive and Sidney Marcus Boulevard, is responsible for police services in the Buckhead area and most of Atlanta's north side.

When the cops on the evening watch reported for duty at three PM, Sunday, October 12, 1997, they were told that Communications was having trouble with the Zone 2 radio frequency. They were told that it had been operating intermittently during the preceding day watch and that it would be fixed shortly. As afternoon turned into evening, radio traffic was slow and occasionally the Zone 2 dispatcher could not communicate with the patrol units. The cops in the patrol cars compensated by using the surveillance channel to communicate with the precinct and one another. The surveillance channel provided the ability to talk one-on-one by switching over to a separate frequency that did not go through a "repeater" controlled by the communications dispatcher. It also did not require radio procedure and allowed for more informal dialogue.

A police officer is assigned to a given precinct to monitor and handle all local and more informal radio traffic to and from the units within that precinct. However, by not going through Communications, many resources are lost, such as controlling and accounting for the movements of the patrol cars on the street at any given time, connection with the 911 operators and other zone dispatchers, and the recording of all radio transmissions. It was not the most efficient way to communicate, but it was the best they could do under the circumstances—an example of military field expedience, "Do the best with what you've got!"

Gregory Lawler, white male, age forty-four, lived at 2453 Morosgo Way, apartment B, with his girlfriend Donna Rodgers, white female, age forty-two. This location was around the corner and down the street from the Zone 2 Precinct. Lawler left his apartment at about six on that October Sunday evening to go to his favorite hangout, the Sand Bar and Grill on Piedmont Road, just a few blocks away. At about seven thirty, Donna Rodgers decided to join him. They had drinks at the bar. She became intoxicated.

They left shortly after nine PM and started to walk the short distance back home. Rodgers was literally "falling down drunk." She fell several times, each time Lawler helped her up. Then came a fall when a Glock 9mm handgun fell out of her handbag. He got angry and started yelling at her for taking one of his guns out of the apartment. The 911 operator received several calls of a disturbance, a woman screaming, and a man beating a woman.

Officer John Sowa, car 3225, and Officer Patricia Cocciolone, car 3210, were assigned to the area. The following is a summary of the relevant radio transmissions between the precinct dispatcher and Officers Sowa and Cocciolone:

2117 hours (9:17 PM): Radio dispatches Cocciolone (3210) to a disturbance at the bowling alley on Piedmont Circle. Sowa (3225) volunteers to back her up.

2118 hours (9:18 PM): Zone 2 Precinct. Officer Thomas (3219) calls from the precinct and asks the dispatcher to switch to channel 2 and gives the dispatcher the information on a man beating a woman at the Exxon station at Piedmont and Lindbergh. Thomas also gives descriptions of a white male and a white female. It's later learned that they were descriptions of Gregory Lawler and Donna Rodgers.

2120 hours (9:20 PM): Cocciolone arrives at the bowling alley and tells Sowa to cancel coming to the bowling alley. Sowa, having monitored the "man beating woman" call given on channel 2, volunteers to pick up the Exxon call.

2121 hours (9:21 PM): Sowa arrives at the Exxon station and asks radio to repeat the descriptions. Cocciolone pulls back in service [meaning available to receive additional calls]. from the bowling alley call.

2122 hours (9:22 PM): Sowa tells radio that he has located "them" at the pawn shop.

2125 hours (9:25 PM): Sowa asks Cocciolone to meet him at the pawn shop.

Cocciolone asks if he is at the pawn shop by Zesto's.

There are no radio transmissions from Sowa or Cocciolone during the next seven minutes.

2132 hours (9:32 PM): In an excited voice, Cocciolone says only, "2456 Morosgo Way!" [The wounded Cocciolone gives the address on Morosgo Way as 2456 instead of 2453].

2134 hours (9:34 PM): Radio advises that a "person shot and injured" call has come in from Morosgo Way via 911.

2134 hours (9:34 PM): A garbled voice can be heard mumbling, struggling to say what sounds like "Please . . . Please . . ."

No further transmissions from Sowa or Cocciolone.

Sergeant R. G. Adams and Officer M. M. McCain were at the precinct when they heard these radio transmissions. They immediately put out a "signal 59 [meet an officer, ASAP] right away" that was upgraded by the Zone 2 dispatcher to a signal 63 (officer needs help). Adams and McCain left the precinct and less than two minutes later were the first cars to arrive at the Morosgo Way location. They found Officers Sowa and Cocciolone lying on the ground in front of 2453 Morosgo Way, apartment B. Sowa was not moving and nonresponsive. Cocciolone was barely able to talk. Both were bleeding from apparent multiple gunshot wounds.

Here's what happened before the shooting: Officers Sowa and Cocciolone confronted Lawler and Rodgers behind the Zesto's on Piedmont Road. Evaluating the situation, they were convinced that although they were in a heated argument, Lawler was not assaulting Rodgers and that she was on the ground because she was so drunk she could not walk for long before falling down. The two officers let Lawler continue on his way. Rodgers was put into

Cocciolone's patrol car to be taken the two blocks to her apartment. Sowa followed in his car. When they arrived at 2453 Morosgo Way, Sowa and Cocciolone helped her from the car and toward the front door of apartment B. As the trio approached the entrance, the front door was flung open by Gregory Lawler. He grabbed Donna Rodgers, yanked her into the apartment, and started firing a rifle at the two officers. He shot both several times. They went down. He came out from the doorway, stood over Cocciolone, who was wounded and helpless, and shot her again. Then he retreated back into the apartment.

Responding to the "signal 63," police units came pouring into the area from all directions and set up a perimeter around the building. Sergeant Adams looked through the front window of apartment B. He saw a woman sitting on the living room floor, leaning against the wall. He tried the front door. It was open. He went in and quickly approached the woman. She said her boyfriend had just shot the cops with a rifle and was now upstairs in the apartment. Sergeant Adams could hear the movements of someone above while he was dragging the very drunk Donna Rodgers out of the apartment.

Fire Rescue personnel and EMTs administered first aid to both officers, then loaded them into ambulances for the code 3 (rush call) trip to Grady Hospital with police escort and blocked intersections all along the way.

Officer Patricia Cocciolone was rushed into emergency surgery.

Officer John Sowa was DOA.

Officer Sowa was shot five times: two to his back (the fatal shots), two to his side, and one to his buttocks. All five wounds were back to front, indicating that he saw the rifle and turned to seek cover as the shots were fired. Officer Cocciolone was shot three times: one to her head, one to her arm, and one to her buttocks.

At Morosgo Way, the SWAT team had arrived and had relieved the patrol officers on the inner perimeter. A command post was established across the street in the Lindbergh Plaza. Hostage negotiators made contact with Lawler and were trying to get him to come out and surrender. The siege was on! SWAT sniper teams reported numerous times that they had clear shots as they watched Lawler move around inside the apartment. The orders from the command post were, "Hold your fire. Continue negotiating." At about four AM, seven hours after it started, Gregory Lawler surrendered and was taken into custody by SWAT officers.

A search of the premises yielded a large number of firearms: automatic weapons, rifles, semi-automatic handguns and pistols, and thousands of rounds of ammunition. There were also many books and magazines on anti-government subjects, survivalist skills, bomb-making manuals, soldier-of-fortune information, and other right-wing literature. Lawler was a member of an organization called "Citizens for Safe Government" and a member of the National Rifle Association. Gregory Lawler was originally from New Jersey and well-educated with a master's degree from Emory University in Atlanta. He had been arrested in the past for driving under the influence in Atlanta and for aggravated assault in DeKalb County, Georgia. At the time of this shooting, he was employed as a furniture installer.

Officer John Sowa was killed because Gregory Lawler was anti-government, anti-authority, and capable of murder. Officer John Sowa was killed because he was capable of doing what he could to help others. When "signal 58 [man beating woman]" was dispatched to the beat car that covers Piedmont and Lindbergh, the officer acknowledged the call but responded that he was on the other end of the beat and that it would take him a few minutes to get to the location specified. Sowa heard and advised radio that he was thirty seconds away; he would handle the call. He didn't have to do that. But Sowa was the kind of cop, the kind of person, who was conscientious, dependable, and always willing to help. Sowa and Cocciolone went "above and beyond" when they put Donna Rodgers in the patrol car to get her home safely. They didn't have to do that. They could have easily charged her with public drunkenness, called for a wagon, and sent her to jail.

Gregory Lawler was tried in Fulton County Superior Court for the murder of Officer John Sowa and aggravated battery for the shooting of Officer Patricia Cocciolone. He was found guilty and sentenced to death. It's been ten years (at this writing) since the sentence was imposed and Lawler still sits on death row while the appeal process slowly works its way through the courts.

Officer Cocciolone survived the shooting but life for her since has been in and out of hospitals. She's endured over sixty painful surgeries and many sessions of difficult therapy, both physical and psychological. And she had to learn to walk, talk, and read all over again. She suffered from post-traumatic stress disorder and survivor's guilt, beating herself up with such regularly recurring thoughts as "If I had done this" or "If I had not done that, maybe John would be alive" and "Why is John dead and not me!" What made things still worse for her were the workman's compensation officials. They denied her the needed medications for severe headaches and other brain disorders. Cocciolone had to retain an attorney and go to court to fight for approval of the medications that she was entitled to receive. The judges ruled in her favor in each case.

Patricia Cocciolone grew up in Michigan, just north of Detroit. On completing her schooling, she joined the U.S. Army and later was honorably discharged at Fort McPherson, Georgia. She remained in Atlanta where she joined the Atlanta Police Department in 1987. She was a ten-year APD veteran when she was shot by Gregory Lawler.

A decade after the shooting, Pat Cocciolone said, "Lawler was such a loser that when he stood over me and shot me again, he couldn't even kill me!" Asked if she wants to be a witness to his execution, she answered promptly, "Yes, I want to see him die!"

John Sowa's wife, Danielle, remembered clearly, years later in 2008 that she tried to get John to stay home that Sunday night, to call in sick. She had a premonition, an uneasy feeling in her gut that something might happen. Sowa's response to her was, "We're already shorthanded. If I stayed home and something happened to one of the cops, I'd never forgive myself." John went to work. He called Danielle at nine PM, told her that everything was fine, and that he would see her later. She said she loved him and that he should be careful. He replied, "Always, because I have to come home to you."

Thirty minutes later another of Atlanta's finest, Officer John Sowa, would be dead.

When she went to the front door to answer the bell, Danielle saw half a dozen uniforms, several of John's police buddies, the Zone 2 commander, and the police chaplain. She knew why they were there before they even tried to speak. She was taken to Grady Hospital where she saw John. Her first reaction, understandably, was hopeful, because he appeared to be sleeping. But when she touched him, she knew he was dead.

John Sowa's body is buried in Randolph, Massachusetts.

Asked if she also, like Pat Cocciolone, wants to be a witness to the execution of Gregory Lawler, Danielle answered without hesitation but with strength, passion, and determination:

"This thing they call 'Gregory Lawler' is nothing but a sorry excuse for a human being. He took not only my husband, my best friend, but a caring and good cop. The bastard got a judge and a jury, what did my husband get? Death! Lawler played God that day; he played judge, jury, and executioner. Nothing can bring John back. But I can be there when they take Lawler. And I will look him in the eye as they administer the lethal injection. I pray he feels all the pain for what he has done. There is no forgetting or forgiveness for what he has done, only justice in my eyes. My last thought is that he will burn in hell for all eternity!"

OFFICER

JOHN RICHARD SOWA
"SHOT ON DOMESTIC CALL"
OCTOBER 12, 1997

Atlanta Police Officer

Randy J. Schipani

Unrelated events in Los Angeles, California, and Boynton Beach, Florida, merge in Atlanta

*I*n 1992, almost three thousand miles away from Atlanta, a black suspect named Rodney King was arrested by several white Los Angeles cops and was beaten by those cops as they arrested him. An onlooker who was close enough to witness what was happening from his apartment window captured it all on his video camera. The tape was broadcast on TV news and on commentary shows often during the weeks that followed. The white Los Angeles cops were tried on criminal charges for their actions during the arrest and were ultimately acquitted. The black community was inflamed by that verdict and major riots erupted in Los Angeles. Because of the violence, the burning, and the looting in Los Angeles, police departments in major cities across the United States went on high alert. The fear was that what was happening in Los Angeles would quickly erupt in black communities elsewhere.

On Friday, May 8, 1992, the Atlanta Police Department cancelled off days and vacation time for all sworn personnel, putting all police officers on twelve-hour shifts. That Friday was supposed to be an off day for Officer Randy Schipani according to his schedule of regular off days. He was ordered to work, along with many other officers who were required to forgo vacation days or off days. In Zone 3, the zone where Schipani regularly worked, there were more cops than patrol cars that day, so they were doubled up two cops to a car. (In Atlanta, as in many other cities, it's normally one cop in a patrol car.) Officer W. A. Vaughn was assigned to work with Schipani in car 2301, Schipani's regular car. Vaughn grabbed the car keys and announced that he would drive. There's no rule about who drives but cops accept that the officer regularly assigned to a specific car drives. Schipani called Vaughn on this, but Vaughn would not yield. Schipani let it go, not looking to start a twelve-hour day with a minor disagreement that could escalate into an argument.

On Thursday, May 7, 1992, in Boynton Beach, Florida, not so far from Atlanta, Bradley M. Perry, a fifteen-year-old white male, was making plans to run away from home. He had a Smith & Wesson .38 caliber revolver that he had stolen in a burglary a couple of weeks prior. What he needed was a car. So Bradley Perry watched and waited outside a Publix supermarket on that Thursday morning. Colleen Morell exited the store and headed to her car. When she was close enough to her car, Perry approached Morell and pulled aside his shirttail to reveal the Smith & Wesson tucked into the waistband of his pants. "I need your car, and you're coming with me. But don't worry, I won't hurt you."

She replied, "Here are the keys, but I'm not going with you."

Lulled by Perry's cherubic looks and nonthreatening manner, the would-be carjack victim engaged the teenager in a short conversation and convinced him to join her inside a nearby restaurant for a cup of coffee. Inside the café, Morell tried to reason with him. But Perry told her that he had been suspended from middle school and that he had gotten into other trouble. He said, "I gave life a try. It didn't work out. Now I'm going to see how it is to die." Perry told Morell that he wanted to drive a car before he died. Then he startled her by saying, "I hate police, and I want to kill a cop!" Perry got up from the table, leaving Morell still sitting there, left the restaurant with her keys, and stole her car, a 1990 black Honda Accord with dark-tinted windows. He drove off heading north. His final destination would be Atlanta, Georgia.

Randy Schipani was born in New York City and was raised by his father after his parents divorced. He attended Wiley Post, a small college on New York's Long Island. While there, he did some undercover work for the Nassau County Police Department as a CI (confidential informant) making drug buys from various drug dealers. Randy had been thinking about leaving New York for some time, but he wanted to wait until he completed college. He'd had enough of the snow and ice and the bitter cold winters. He wanted to live in a warm climate where he could feel comfortable all year long. Randy had mixed emotions about leaving his father and his Manhattan home, but he had made up his mind. After completing college in 1979, he packed his personal belongings into his car and left, driving through the tunnel from Manhattan and then south on the New Jersey Turnpike. He ultimately stopped in Birmingham, Alabama, where he rented an apartment. He wanted to go to law school and decided on the Birmingham School of Law. To sustain himself through law school, he took a variety of jobs: restoring furniture, clerking for a law firm, transporting expensive jewelry for a jeweler, and working with the Auxiliary Birmingham Police Department. He often rode in a patrol car with a regular Birmingham cop, assisting when necessary.

In 1983, while still in law school, he met Denise Scoggins who had just graduated from high school. Denise sensed something special in Randy, something different from the other boys that she had known. And before long, they fell in love. After dating for over two years, they were married. After graduating from law school, Randy started to reconsider his future. He expressed his concerns to Denise, "I don't want to defend criminals so criminal law is out!" As he reviewed the different types of law practices he could pursue, he half-heartedly said to Denise, "I guess I could be a plaintiff's attorney or even a divorce lawyer."

The more Randy thought about the various career paths in law, the more he became convinced that he did not want to be an attorney. He began thinking about law enforcement, about the work he had done in New York with the Nassau County Police and with the Auxiliary Birmingham Police Department. "I want to be a cop," he told Denise. When he went to the Birmingham Police Department, Randy was dismayed to learn that applications for jobs as cops were not being accepted. He discovered that in neighboring Georgia, the Atlanta Police Department was hiring. He applied and was accepted by the APD. Shortly after being hired, Randy and Denise moved to Atlanta where Officer Randy Schipani began his career with the Atlanta Police Department. The year was 1987.

As he settled into his Zone 3 assignment, Randy made friends easily and hooked up with several cops who rode their personal motorcycles while off duty. He became interested, learned to ride, and got his own motorcycle. He and Denise did a lot of riding with that group. Randy loved riding his "Harley."

Officers Randy Schipani and W. A. Vaughn stood for roll call at six thirty on Friday morning, May 8, 1992, at the Zone 3 Precinct. Before seven, they were out on the streets patrolling car 2301's beat. Fate had put them on a collision course with an emotionally twisted fifteen-year-old juvenile from Boynton Beach, Florida. Car 2301 was northbound on I-75/85, keeping pace with the normal rush-hour traffic, when the officers observed a black Honda Accord with Florida tags speed past them. Schipani and Vaughn went after the car as it weaved in and out of the traffic, getting behind it just south of the University Avenue exit, where they turned on their car's flashing blue lights and siren. They followed the Honda off the exit ramp and stopped on University Avenue and Pryor Road.

Vaughn, who was driving, got out of the patrol car and approached the driver's side of the Honda. Schipani took up a covering position at the right rear. Because of the heavily tinted windows of the Honda, Schipani could not see into the interior to determine whether any other occupants were in the car. To get a clear look inside, he walked around to the front of the car and approached the driver's window, which the driver, Bradley Perry, had lowered. Vaughn asked Perry for his driver's license and proof of insurance. Perry reached toward his rear pocket, seemingly for a wallet, but instead, his hand came forward with the Smith & Wesson revolver in it. Perry fired through the open driver's window, striking Schipani in his right temple. Schipani fell to the ground. Vaughn returned fire, striking Perry multiple times and killing him instantly.

(The following is from a transcript of the radio communication between Officer Vaughn, other police units, and the police radio dispatcher after the shooting. Radio traffic becomes chaotic whenever a help call is broadcast as responding units overload the frequency for updated information.)

Male officer: *"Signal 63* [officer needs help], *63—Pryor and University, Pryor and University, officer down, officer down!"*

Dispatcher: *"Pryor and University, signal 63, got an officer down, 100 University, I got an officer down!"*

Male officer: *"Signal 4, code 3—4, code 3."*

Dispatcher: *"All right, signal 4* [ambulance], *code 3* [rush call], *100 University, got a signal 63, got an officer down, first car on the scene advise. 2393* [sergeant]*?"* (The dispatcher is asking for confirmation from car 2393 that a supervisor has received the transmission.)

Unit 2393 (sergeant): *"2393 copy."*

Dispatcher: *"First car on the scene, advise."*

Unit 2393 (sergeant): *"2393 received."*

Male officer: *"180 University! 180 University!"* [address corrected].

Dispatcher: *"I got a car coming up, 180 University, it's going to be at 180 University, 180—"*

Unit 2393 (sergeant): *"2393, I'm 26 [arrived]—"*

Female officer: *"Is the 4 code 3?"*

Dispatcher: *"Okay, the 4 is code 3, Fire Rescue is code 3. Can you give me any more information? First car on the scene, can you update the information?"*

Unit 2396: *"2396, I'm 26."*

Dispatcher: *"2396 is 26."*

Unit 2396: *"Need Homicide and ID* [crime scene unit] *at this location!"*

Dispatcher: *"Homicide and ID, start Homicide and ID."*

Unit 4 (deputy chief): *"Unit 4, what do you have up there?"*

Dispatcher: *"Unit 4, just got a 63, officer down, Homicide and ID on the way. Unit 2396, Unit 4 is on the air, can you advise?"*

Unit 2391 (lieutenant): *"2391, if we need a lookout, have a lookout placed immediately."*

Unit 2326: *"2326, perpetrator dead, officer 48* [dead] *also. Slow anything else on the way."*

Dispatcher: *"Okay. Cars en route, any other cars en route, slow down, code 4* [cancel]. *Unit 4, did you receive, officer 48, perpetrator 48?"*

Unit 4 (deputy chief): *"Unit 4 received, notify unit 1* [chief]*—"*

Dispatcher: *"Yes sir!"*

Dispatcher: *"Calling 2396, can you give me the unit number on the officer?"*

Unit 2396: *"2301."*

Unit 2393 (sergeant): *"Any other suspects . . . ?"*

Unit 2391 (lieutenant): *"2391 raise 2399."*

Unit 2399: *"2399* [the police officer assigned inside the precinct to monitor the radio, answer the telephone and general office duties]*."*

Unit 2391 (lieutenant): *"Notify unit 13* [Zone 3 commander] *and unit 300* [assistant Zone 3 commander]*."*

Unit 2399: *"13 has been notified."*

Unit 2396: *"2396, repeater is off . . . can you give me the officer's name, please?"*

Male officer: *"Officer Schipani!"*

Female officer: *"Schipani!"*

Unit 2393 (sergeant): *"2393, any other suspects?"*

Male officer: *"No other suspects."*

Dispatcher: *"Cancel the signal 63; all cars en route to University and Pryor code 4* [cancel]*."*

As responding police units and other emergency vehicles flooded into the already blocked intersection of University Avenue and Pryor Road, traffic had to be rerouted and the University Avenue exit off-ramps closed. Although the signal 63 was canceled, the cops kept coming. That happens each time a help call is dispatched. The urgency to arrive on the scene increases when cops learn a police officer is shot.

Ambulance personnel and Fire Rescue did all they could for Officer Schipani and the shooter, Bradley Perry, but both were beyond help. They were DOS (dead on the scene). There was an eerie silence around the immediate crime scene. The silence extended throughout the intersection where dozens of cops milled around, a few crying, others in glassy-eyed, dazed shock. A helpless feeling lingered over all the cops. It took awhile to dissipate, but one by one they got back into their patrol cars to return to their respective beats.

On the day he was killed, Officer Randy Schipani was a five-year Atlanta police veteran and would have turned thirty-five years old on his next birthday. Randy Schipani was one of those police officers who come along every now and then. A cop who was well-liked and respected by all, including other cops he worked with, the supervisors he worked for, and the general public that he had contact with. He would arrive at the Zone 3 Precinct an hour or so before roll call to socialize with other cops and to make himself available for any urgent matter that needed attention. The cops who were close to him—and there were many—described him as single-minded and said, "He just wanted to be a good cop!"

Superior officers referred to Schipani as "energetic, self-confident, and assertive."

Communication with the Boynton Beach Police Department confirmed that the 1990 Honda Accord driven by Perry was the one carjacked there the day before. They also confirmed that the Smith & Wesson .38 caliber revolver used in the shooting of Officer Schipani was stolen in a residential burglary a week prior to the carjacking. Bradley Perry was positively identified as the perpetrator in both crimes.

This senseless tragedy was a classic case of "victim-precipitated homicide," or as in cases like this, it is known as "suicide by cop." The victim has a death wish and wants to die but is unable to kill himself. He believes that if he shoots at the police, they will return fire, exercising his suicide for him. Bradley Perry accomplished that, and in so doing, he also took the life of Officer Randy Schipani.

The week after he was killed, Randy Schipani was scheduled to take the test for the ATF (Alcohol, Tobacco, and Firearms), a federal law enforcement agency. The contrast between Randy Schipani and W. A. Vaughn is striking. Corrupt, crooked, and dirty, Vaughn disgraced his uniform and the badge pinned to it. He was already a "rogue cop" on the day fate assigned him to work in the same car with Schipani. However, nothing about Vaughn's darker side is to imply that he was in any way responsible for Schipani getting killed. Vaughn did act appropriately when he immediately returned fire and killed the shooter. Vaughn was a corrupt cop the last five of the seven years he was with the APD. He stole money and drugs from drug dealers, shaking them down for monthly protection money. He was part of a gang consisting of five other corrupt Zone 3 cops doing the same thing. Vaughn and the others were arrested and tried in federal court in 1996. They were found guilty of the charges. Vaughn was sentenced to four years and seven months in a federal prison and was ordered to pay eleven thousand dollars in fines and restitution.

Unlike Vaughn in every respect, Randy Schipani was honest, hard-working, and caring. One of the best of "Atlanta's finest"! A tree was planted at University Avenue and Pryor Road as a memorial to Atlanta police officer Randy Schipani.

Randy is buried in Birmingham.

Atlanta Police Officer

Niles Johantgen

They called him "the Russian"!

𝒜tlanta police officer Niles Johantgen was not Russian. He was not born in Russia. He was not born in any foreign country. Niles Johantgen was an American—a red, white, and blue American. He was born and raised in Jackson, Michigan. He was a big, burly man with Slavic features, and he always had a crew haircut. Niles's ancestry was Norwegian from the sturdy bloodline of the ancient Vikings. However, everyone in the Thomasville Heights housing project referred to him as "the Russian."

Thomasville Heights was one of more than thirty low-income city housing projects in Atlanta. It was made up of hundreds of apartments, most accommodating poor, black, and disadvantaged families. There were usually many single mothers with children of various ages living in them. It was not uncommon for the biological father of the children to be long gone. That gap was occupied, unfortunately not filled, by the mother's current boyfriend, who was usually unemployed and simply hanging out. The mothers were often not home because they were out working, in some cases working two jobs. Their children, without proper adult supervision, would gather with their peers and raise one another in the ways of the streets. Once children formed into groups to play, they grew into teenagers who formed into gangs because they'd learned that there was safety in numbers.

Each of these teenage gangs became a society unto itself, each member accountable to no one but the others in his or her own gang. The main force that drove a gang was money, the kind of money that can be made from selling drugs—a lot more money than can be earned from flipping hamburgers in fast food joints. The established drug distributors—those who purchased crack cocaine in bulk from the cartels as the drugs were moved from Mexico and South Florida to the big cities in the north—moved into Atlanta's housing projects. The distributors formed like franchises in the different projects, using the teenage gangs for retail distribution (street-level sales). In each project, hierarchies within a gang were formed—at the bottom level were the twelve-year-old lookouts who watched and warned when the police were coming; at the mid-level were the teenage boys and young men who were on the streets selling; at the upper level was an enforcer who ensured that the young dealers were not skimming drugs or drug money, at the same time the enforcer protected the distributor's investment, and more so, prohibited, in whatever way, other gangs from moving in.

It became necessary for the gang that was obviously making a lot of money selling drugs to arm its members.

Thomasville Heights, like the other Atlanta housing projects, became a dangerous and violent place to be. Drive-by shootings, drug deals gone badly, and sounds of gunfire were common within the project.

The distributor, the one who put up the money to obtain the drugs from the cartels, established rules about who sold what drugs, for how much, and where. He also decided how much of the money from selling the drugs went to the gang members according to hierarchy. The enforcer in Thomasville Heights who maintained the discipline and made sure these rules were followed was Norris Speed.

Norris Speed, a black male, was a product of the Thomasville Heights housing projects. He lived there sometimes with his grandmother. When he wasn't crashing in her apartment, no one knew exactly where he was staying at any particular time. He was likely staying with one girlfriend or another around southeast Atlanta.

By the time he was twenty years old, Speed was high enough in the hierarchy to have teenage boys selling crack cocaine for him. He was netting fifteen hundred dollars a week. The young sellers who worked for Norris Speed feared him. They had heard that "Norris had killed a couple of guys that tried to fuck him out of his money!" One of the young sellers reported, "I was jumped on by three of Speed's muscle guys," who broke his arm, "because he [Norris] said I disrespected his old lady."

These kinds of things, some were true maybe, some maybe not, were said about Norris. True or not, they circulated credibly up and down within the gang, creating fear and respect for Norris Speed. A few of the gang members said that Speed had told them he was going to kill the Russian.

Thomasville Heights was located within the jurisdiction of the APD's Zone 3 Precinct, which covered many of Atlanta's city housing projects. Zone 3 was often referred to by the media as "the combat zone" because of the frequent violent criminal activity within its boundaries. The evening watch (three PM to eleven PM) cops in this zone responded to one call after another after another, having barely enough time in between to grab a bite to eat or a quick cup of coffee.

Atlanta police officer Niles Johantgen was assigned to Zone 3 evening watch, working car 3309. The Thomasville Heights housing project was on his beat, and he welcomed it. Four years in the United States Marine Corps, plus attending a military school, had prepared him for the assignment.

Johantgen was one of those cops who would enter a known dangerous housing project even when not responding to a call. He would drive deep into the center, park his patrol car, and walk around, chatting with residents who would chat with him. He was popular with most of the people in the Heights, the people who liked seeing the Russian walking around, making conversation with them. He was not popular with the gang members or with the crack dealers. They didn't want any Atlanta police officer strolling on their turf. Not only was his presence bad for business, it diminished their intimidation, their control over the projects.

However, this was Johantgen's beat and therefore his turf too. He dropped by the Heights every working day, making sure he was seen by all the thugs on Henry Thomas Drive. He would be there every day he was on duty, they could count on it. Most of the time, Johantgen was alone—because of APD's one-man car policy— although sometimes several adjoining beat cars would show up with him. In one of these cars was Officer B.C. Williams, Niles Johantgen's best friend. They formed a strong bond, just as any partners will do, even though they worked separate but adjoining beat cars. When you saw one, you saw the other.

One evening, Johantgen and Williams were doubled up in one car because of a shortage of cars. They made a run to Jonesboro South, another Zone 3 housing project. There were ten or twelve drug merchants there selling within their "exclusive open-air market." The moment "Joe" and "B.C." arrived and got out of their patrol car, the sellers scattered in different directions. Each partner chased, caught, and handcuffed a fleeing "entrepreneur," then walked him back to the parked patrol car.

The patrol car was not in the same condition that they had left it in only moments earlier. All four tires had been slashed, every window had been broken, and the blue light bar on the roof had been smashed. After dispatching their prisoners to the city jail and the wrecker had hauled off what was left of the patrol car, both cops spent the rest of their watch doing paperwork explaining the "damage to city property."

It was time for the cops to assert their authority, no more Mister Nice Guys. Johantgen and Williams let it be known in Jonesboro South that until they had the person responsible for trashing their patrol car, there would be no business as usual in Jonesboro South. They made it very difficult for anyone who was coming to buy drugs from the sellers there. They told the gang sellers that there would be patrol cars regularly circling within Jonesboro South and that the high visibility of uniformed cops there might make it seem like the cops were taking up residence in the project. None of this was any good for the business of selling drugs. The pressure was on. Within a week, a guy presented himself to Johantgen and Williams to tell them that he had been the one who had damaged their patrol car. He looked like he had just taken a pretty good beating. He told the two cops, "They whipped my ass every day and was going to keep doing it until I confessed to 'the Russian' that I did it."

On another occasion, Johantgen, Williams, and several other Zone 3 evening watch cops hit Shorty's Place, a joint on Moreland Avenue known for selling drugs and other illegal activities. After a lot of shouting and a few brief scuffles, several men were arrested for a variety of offenses. Johantgen was leading a handcuffed prisoner out to the paddy wagon when out from under the crowd appeared a midget, a three foot tall adult midget. The midget angrily grabbed Johantgen around one knee. Then reaching upward, he started to punch Johantgen in the testicles. Williams and the other cops saw what the midget was doing to Johantgen, and they were frozen by what they were seeing—Niles Johantgen 6'3" tall and 235 pounds was holding a handcuffed prisoner about the same size as him with one hand, and his other hand was trying to swat away the midget as though swatting at a bee. Williams, stifling his laughter, snatched the midget from Johantgen's leg and handcuffed him. After the wagon left on its way to the city jail with the prisoners, including the midget, the cops finally let loose their restrained laughter. Johantgen also laughed while trying to hide his embarrassment about being hit in the balls by a midget.

Amusing incidents like this one, and those not amusing but bizarre, are still susceptible to danger around the corner. Nevertheless, they are the stuff of the work of a street cop, "war stories" told again and again. But now and then, the unexpected happens. Danger comes from around the corner, and what seems to be routine, amusing, or even bizarre, ends in tragedy.

It was four days before Christmas, the twenty-first day of December, 1991, when Officer Niles Johantgen drove car 3309 into the Thomasville Heights housing project parking lot. Christmas lights and decorations were displayed on some of the apartment windows and over the entrance doors. He parked on Henry Thomas Drive, usually the center of drug-dealing activity. He got out and started to walk around among the boys who were, up to that point, open for business and spreading a little holiday cheer "rock by rock" (the street name for crack cocaine) in little dime bags. It was about five thirty on that cold Saturday evening, dusk had just turned to darkness, when Johantgen's ears were assaulted by the sound of rap music blaring from a parked car where four young guys were sitting. The decibel level was so high that the bass notes rattled Johantgen's back teeth. He told the one sitting in the driver's seat to turn the music down to a reasonable level; the driver complied right away. They all knew the Russian meant business.

Johantgen then saw two men leaning against a parked car nearby, the same two he had recently arrested for possession of drugs and handguns. He told them to put their hands on the car and was searching both of them when Norris Speed appeared and demanded to know why the two were being hassled. Johantgen told Speed that it was none of his business and to move on. Speed walked away into the darkness, but he did not leave. Instead, he peered out from behind the corner of a nearby building, watching intently as Johantgen patted down the two guys. Speed moved closer, behind a dumpster between two of the buildings where his car was parked.

Speed went to his car, got his gun from under the car's seat, and then moved quietly, quickly, to stand behind Johantgen. Without a word, Speed struck Johantgen in the back of the head with the gun, sending him face down to the ground onto his stomach. Johantgen lay there stunned. He didn't move as Speed started shooting, missing him each time. Norris Speed then knelt down with his knee in Johantgen's back, placed the gun to the base of Niles Johantgen's skull, and pulled the trigger—killing him. Norris Speed ran back to his car, jumped in, and sped away. There were many witnesses to the shooting. Some of them had had friendly chats with Johantgen at one time or another. All the witnesses knew Norris Speed, who he was, and what he did in the Heights.

911 operator: *"Atlanta 911, what's your emergency?"*
Caller: *"The police been shot, get an ambulance out here quick."*
Operator: *"What's the location?"*
Caller: *"Henry Thomas Drive in Thomasville."*
Second caller: *"Norris Speed just shot the Russian."*
Operator: *"Is that on Henry Thomas Drive?"*
Second caller: *"Yes, in Thomasville Heights."*

Operator: *"An ambulance is on the way."*

Zone 3 dispatcher: *"Any car near Henry Thomas Drive in Thomasville Heights, signal 63/50/4* [officer needs help/person shot/ambulance on the way]. *It's been reported that an officer has been shot."*

Police cars poured into the Heights. The cops found Officer Niles Johantgen on the ground. They knew he was beyond help. He appeared to be DOS (dead on the scene). He was rushed by ambulance with police escort and blocked intersections to Grady Hospital where the ER staff could not revive him.

All resources of the Atlanta Police Department were rapidly deployed to locate and apprehend Norris Speed. This was the number one priority for all cops. Speed's photo was shown on every TV newscast and on the front page of the newspapers. Two days later, veteran fugitive detective Richard Brown received a call from one of his informants. The informant told Brown, "the guy you are looking for, the one that shot the police the other day" was holed up in a motel in Smyrna, an Atlanta suburb.

At eight thirty PM on December 23, 1991, members of the Atlanta Police Fugitive Squad and Metro Fugitive Squad, along with uniformed police from the Smyrna Police Department, surrounded the Best Western Vantage Motel at 1200 Winchester Parkway in Smyrna, Georgia. They knocked on the door of room 305. The door was opened by a black male who was instantly recognized as Norris Speed. He insisted that his name was Kevin Walker. After a brief scuffle, he was wrestled to the floor, handcuffed, and taken to the Atlanta PD Homicide Squad Office where he was questioned by homicide detective Mike Greene, the lead detective in the case. After the initial interview at Homicide, Speed was taken to Grady Hospital to be treated for the injuries he had suffered during the "brief scuffle" at the motel.

Norris Speed was tried in Fulton County Superior Court for the murder of Atlanta police officer Niles Johantgen. He was found guilty and sentenced to death.

Since that sentencing, Norris Speed still lingers on death row. His food, clothing, shelter, and medical care are paid for by the state of Georgia—that is, by the people who pay taxes in Georgia—while the glacier-like movement of appeals oozes from one court to the next.

Niles's wife of eleven years, Gwen, now a widow, looks back at that day so very long ago in Jackson, Michigan, when they first met. Gwen Trumble was working in a Frosty Boy (similar to a Dairy Queen) when Niles came in for a drink. She had filled the cup mostly with ice and very little soda. He paid and left, only to return a few minutes later complaining that his drink was all ice. That conversation sparked an interest in each other that eventually led to Niles and Gwen getting married in 1980.

Niles Johantgen joined the United States Marine Corps at the age of twenty-one. When his enlistment was up four years later, he received his honorable discharge and returned to Jackson to enter the construction business. Two years later in 1986, Niles and Gwen, along with good friends from the USMC, relocated to Atlanta and opened a security company. In 1988, Niles Johantgen became an Atlanta police officer.

Niles and Gwen Johantgen had two children, both boys, ages six years and four months when thirty-two-year-old Atlanta police officer Niles Johantgen was murdered. Gwen and the children returned to Jackson, Michigan.

It's 2009, and it's been more than seventeen years since that tragic December evening. Gwen Johantgen remembers the man she married:

"He was a man of many trades. In his short life, he worked construction, served his country [USMC], business owner, police officer, and most important, a father. I believe his greatest accomplishment in his life would be his two sons. He was a hands-on father that loved to spend time with his sons. Even on his day off when he had to appear in court, he would take his sons with him. He wanted to show his sons by example what a father and man should be."

Niles Johantgen is buried in Jackson, Michigan.

Atlanta Police Officer

Joseph E. Davis

"I'll get your money back for you." A few moments later, four gunshots

That money was seven dollars! Atlanta police officer Joseph E. Davis was killed as he attempted to retrieve seven dollars during a street robbery. Although, there was the possibility that it might not have been a robbery, it might have been a drug deal gone bad. But that doesn't matter. What matters is that Officer Davis was shot to death with his own gun in a wooded family cemetery overgrown with weeds.

Zones 1 and 4 are adjoining zones divided by I-20 that cover the west side of Atlanta. Zone 4 is responsible for police services south of the interstate and Zone 1 to the north. Officer Joseph

Davis, a twelve-year APD veteran, was assigned to the morning watch in Zone 4, which covered the southwest quadrant of the city. Davis was well-known and well-respected by most of the people he had contact with on his regular assignment, 408's beat, where the City of Atlanta adjoins unincorporated Fulton County.

(The numbering system for identifying APD beat cars is a four-digit number. The first number denotes the watch according to the 24-hour cycle: morning watch is 1, day watch is 2, evening watch is 3. The second number indicates the zone, one of the six APD jurisdictions in the city. The last two numbers denote the beat or geographical area within a zone.)

Joe Davis played football in college. He learned to take a few hits and to give a few back. Joe could be tough when he had to be, which meant there were times when he had to suspend the pervasive kindness that was always in him. He served in the United States Army prior to joining the Atlanta Police Department. He treated everyone the same—it didn't matter to him that they were the affluent in the Cascade Heights section of Zone 4, the unemployed hanging out on street corners, or anything between. He was the best example of community policing. [When not on call, park the patrol car, walk around and get to know the people on the beat. People who knew Davis on his beat addressed him as "Officer Joe."

It was between three and three thirty in the early morning hours of June 7, 1989, a warm muggy night with intermittent showers, when Davis was patrolling a quiet, peaceful Martin Luther King Jr. Drive. He was approaching Bolton Road when he saw three men running. One lagged behind the other two. The lagger anxiously gestured to Davis to stop and said, "I've just been robbed of seven dollars by those two guys running." Officer Davis made a quick U-turn, caught up with them, jumped out of his patrol car, grabbed one of the two, Darryl Styles, and quickly pushed him into the backseat of the patrol car. (Styles was considered restrained in the backseat because the rear doors and windows were inoperable from the inside, and the screen between the rear and front seats was impossible to penetrate, although you could see through it.) The other guy continued running, disappearing into the woods of the old cemetery nearby. Davis went into the cemetery to look for him. Unsuccessful, he returned to his patrol car a few minutes later. The robbery victim, Terrence Young, had caught up to the patrol car. Davis instructed him to remain at the car and to keep an eye on the guy in the backseat. "I'll get your money back for you," Davis said as he went back into the dark woods of the cemetery.

Zone 4 radio:

Unidentified police unit (Davis): *"I'll be on Bolton Road, signal 44* [robbery] *pedestrian."*

Dispatcher: *"What unit advised on Bolton Road, 44 pedestrian?"*

Unidentified police unit (Davis): *"Standby, I'll be at Bolton and MLK."*

(The intersection of these two main surface streets, with I-20 crossing overhead, is where Zone 1 and Zone 4 meet.)

A few minutes later, the robbery victim, Young, who was still standing by the patrol car, heard from the woods, "I told you to get down and put your hands behind you back, I told you to get down!" Moments later he heard four gunshots. Then he saw the man who, he said, had robbed him, come out of the woods and run down MLK Drive. The man looked back twice at the patrol car. Young said, "I got in the car and said on the radio that a police had been shot and where it was. Then I flagged down a car and told him what happened and for him to call 911."

Unidentified police unit (probably Davis): *"Officer down!"* [from his portable radio]

Unidentified police unit: . . . *open mike* . . . (No voice transmission, probably Davis.)

Whenever a transmission from an unidentified unit is broadcast on a given frequency (in this case, on Zone 4 radio), the dispatcher will call each Zone 4 unit currently on the street and request a reply. Any unit that fails to reply is likely the unit that needs assistance.

Dispatcher: *"Zone 4 units stand by for roll call, 1401?"*
1401: *"1401."*
Dispatcher: *"1402?"*
1402: *"2."*
Dispatcher: *"1420?"*
1420: *"1420."*
Dispatcher: *"1422?"*
1422: *"22 okay."*
Dispatcher: *"25?"*
1425: *"25 okay."*
Dispatcher: *"445?"*
1445: *"45."*
Dispatcher: *"1403?"*
1403: *"1403."*
Dispatcher: *"1404?"*
1404: *"4."*
Dispatcher: *"1406?"*
1406: *"6."*
Dispatcher: *"1407?"*
1407: *"7."*
Dispatcher: *"1408?"*
(No answer.)
Dispatcher: *"Radio calling 1408."*
(No answer.)
Dispatcher: *"Calling car 1408."*
(No answer.)
Dispatcher: *"1430?"*
1430: *"430."*
Dispatcher: *"440?"*
1440: *"40."*
Dispatcher: *"17?"*
1417: *"17."*

911:
911 operator: *"911 emergency, may I help you?"*

Caller: *"Yes, uh, this customer came in and said, uh, he think, uh, a security officer came in and said, uh, he think a police had been shot or something and running behind somebody in the woods. It's on, uh, MLKing, he say under [I-] 20, the bridge under 20, on MLKing, I guess by Bolton Road, right pass Bolton Road on MLKing, bridge over 20. He was running behind some guys, uh, he say the car is parked in the street. He chased somebody in the woods, something like that."*

911: *"Hold on a minute, hold on a minute."*

Caller: *"I think Officer Joe. I think he the one that was running, uh, Joe Davis."*

911: *"Hello."*

Caller: *"Yes."*

911: *"Okay, Bolton Road and Martin Luther King."*

The Zone 1 dispatcher hears the conversation between the 911 operator and the caller and immediately alerts the Zone 1 cars to the situation at that location, shared by both zones.

Zone 1 radio:

Dispatcher: *"Any unit at Bolton and MLK?"*

Dispatcher: *"1109, go by Bolton and MLK, possible signal 63* [officer needs help] *there."*

1196 (sergeant): *"Who called it in? Let's have a roll call, radio."*

Zone 1 had a roll call of all its units. Everyone was accounted for. Zone 4 continually called car 1408 (Davis) but each time received no response.

Zone 4 dispatcher: *"Cars start for MLK and Bolton Road, signal 63, possible signal 50* [person shot], *try to locate unit 1408."*

Zone 1 dispatcher: *"Be advised that Zone 4 units are responding to a signal 63 at MLK and Bolton Road, cars head that way, one of their units is missing."*

Zone 1 unit: *"1102, I'm en route."*

Zone 1 unit: *"1110, I'll start out there also."*

Zone 4 unit: *"1405, I'm 26* [arrived] *at Bolton and MLK."*

Zone 1 unit: *"1108, 26."*

Zone 1 unit: *"1110 coming up 26."*

Zone 1 unit: *"1106 to radio, the missing Zone 4 unit is 1408."*

Zone 4 unit: *"I'm at Bolton and MLK. We got about four Zone 1 units out here."*

Zone 1 unit: *"1106 to radio, citizen advises officer went in the woods at this location after perpetrator. He heard him stop the perpetrator, he heard 25s [shots fired], officer hasn't returned."*

Zone 1 unit: *"1108, get a signal 4 [ambulance] out here, code 3 [rush call], signal 50 [person shot] to an officer."*

Zone 1 unit: *"1109, officer shot, start Fire Rescue, get somebody out here quick!"*

Dispatcher: *"1109, they're already en route."*

Zone 1 unit: *"1195 [sergeant], 26."*

Zone 1 unit: *"1195, you'll want to start Homicide and ID [crime scene unit], it's going to be a signal 48 [person dead]."*

Zone 1 unit: *"1191 [lieutenant], what you got out there?"*

Zone 1 unit: *"1195, we got a 50/48 [person shot/person dead] on a police officer."*

Dispatcher: *"1195, is it a Zone 4 or a Zone 1 officer?"*

Zone 1 unit: *"1195, going to be a Zone 4."*

Zone 4 unit: *"Zone 1 has located the officer, he's signal 50."*

Dispatcher: *"Possible signal 48."*

Officer Joe Davis was found face down, dead, in that dark wooded cemetery. His open handcuffs and flashlight were on the ground next to his body. His service revolver was missing. It was later determined to be the murder weapon.

Sean Reynard Patmon, a black male, nineteen years old, was unemployed and a regular hangout among the others on the street. He was known on the street as "Too Fresh." Patmon was a violent thug who made his money by selling fake, or "slum" dope, as it's known on the street. It's nothing more than pieces of soap cut up to look like crack cocaine. He sold that phony stuff outside Grad-Flows, a neighborhood store on Martin Luther King Jr. Drive, where there was a phone booth he found convenient to use. In the adjacent parking lot there was always plenty of activity, buyers who came day or night to "cop some dope." Too Fresh sold a baggie of his slum for seven dollars to Terrence Young, then immediately walked away. Young saw that it was fake dope and started after Too Fresh, yelling that he wanted his money back. Too Fresh and Darryl Styles, another two-bit street dealer who also sold drugs and slum, started to flee. Young ran after them. This was the chase that was happening as Officer Joe Davis came cruising down MLK Drive. Young flagged Davis down and told him that he had been robbed.

Sean Patmon was identified by Young as the subject who emerged from the cemetery immediately after he heard the gunshots. Young was still standing by Davis's patrol car, as Davis had instructed him to do, when he saw Patmon come out of the cemetery. From information supplied by the first arriving patrol cars, a "lookout" for Patmon was broadcast citywide over all APD channels, including the Fulton County PD channels. Patmon's photo and description were shown on the early morning local TV news. Both were published on the front page of the newspaper later in the day.

The massive manhunt was on!

Immediately after the shooting, "Too Fresh" Patmon made his way to his cousin's house at the Kimberly Courts Apartments where he spoke with Darrell Ferrell, telling him, "I just shot a chump police," and he showed him Davis's gun. He remained at the Kimberly complex for the remainder of that night instead of on the streets where he would have been easily spotted because there were not many others out. Ferrell hooked him up with Steve Mathews, a security guard at the complex, and Patmon paid Mathews five dollars to drive him to a drug house. Once there, Too Fresh sold Officer Davis's gun for thirty dollars to a guy who was known by the street name of "Bucket." Bucket later sold the gun to another guy known only as Tony.

When daylight came and he felt he could move about unnoticed because of the activity on the streets, Too Fresh went to an apartment on Hilltop Circle in the Eagan Homes housing projects belonging to an acquaintance, Lewis Jackson. Jackson was not home, so Too Fresh forced open the front door and went in. Once inside, he saw his own face and heard his name on every TV news show. He decided to stay holed up there until the excitement died down and the police were no longer looking for him. Jackson was visiting a friend nearby and also saw on TV that Too Fresh was wanted for killing a police officer. Jackson went to his apartment, opened the back door slightly so as not to disturb anyone who might be inside, saw Too Fresh, who didn't see him, and rushed back to his friend's house and called the police.

Patrol cars swarmed into Eagan Homes. They entered the apartment on Hilltop Circle where they found Sean "Too Fresh" Patmon. He was street-smart enough not to offer any resistance; he had had enough experience dealing with cops to be able to read the dark mood emanating from them.

He was arrested without incident for the murder of Atlanta police officer Joseph E. Davis.

Security guard Steve Mathews, who worked with and assisted the police when he could, knew Officer Joe Davis and said he had talked to him just forty-five minutes before he was killed. He learned that it was Tony Walker who had Davis's gun. After locating Walker, Mathews told him that the gun he had bought belonged to the officer who was killed in the cemetery on MLK Drive. Walker gave the gun to Mathews, who then turned it over to police. Detectives were able to track the sales of the gun as it went from one person to another for money or drugs, originating with Sean "Too Fresh" Patmon.

Fulton County district attorney Lewis Slaton declined to go to trial seeking the death penalty. However, on behalf of the people of the State of Georgia, Slaton agreed to a guilty plea from the killer of Joe Davis. The judge accepted the plea and sentenced Sean "Too Fresh" Patmon to spend the rest of his life in prison.

Atlanta police officer Joseph E. Davis left behind a widow, Evelyn, with a twelve-year-old son to raise alone.

Atlanta Police Officer

Layne B. Cook

In the middle of the street he was an open target . . . the shooter came out from behind a tree

Atlanta police officer Layne B. Cook worked in a tough neighborhood encompassing Bankhead Highway and Hightower Road in northwest Atlanta. Cook was assigned to car 1107 morning watch (commonly known as the graveyard shift by those who worked in the munitions and armament factories between the midnight and eight AM shift during World War II) out of the Zone 1 Precinct. This was a high-crime area, and as in most low-income and high-crime areas, a lot of domestic violence occurs, usually severe violence.

Ms. Nancy Hunter was one of the representatives from the Domestic Crisis Intervention Unit for the City of Atlanta. So it was not unusual for her to accompany police officers responding to calls reporting domestic violence. Nor was it unusual for her to be immediately available where experience indicated it was reasonable to expect that kind of violence. That was part of her job.

She was with Officer Cook from the start of his morning watch on January 27, 1989. Shortly after midnight, car 1107 received a signal 29 (disturbance) at 2533 Bellview Avenue NW. The 911 caller reported gunshots at that location. That prompted signal 25 (gunshots). Car 1106 was dispatched as backup.

The following is from the Atlanta 911 Emergency Communications Center:

911 operator: *"Atlanta 911, what's your emergency?"*

Caller: *"Could you send me a car, police, out to 2533 Bellview?"*

911 operator: *"What's the problem?"*

Caller: *"My baby's daddy's in the house shooting."*

Operator: *"He's in the house shooting?"*

Caller: *"Yes, he just shot in the house."*

Operator: *"Wait a minute, he shot in the house, or he—"*

Caller: *"Yes, I think he on cocaine 'cause he's been with some friends of his."*

Operator: *"Okay. Wait a minute, ma'am, hold on. Is he in the house shooting or he shot—"*

Caller: *"Yes, he just shot in the house, and he ran—"*

Operator: *"Ma'am, listen to me for a minute, okay? I got to get this information. Did he shoot in the house or he's inside?"*

Caller: *"He shot in the house. It scared my sister and my baby and them out the house."*

Operator: *"Okay. So who's in the house now, just you?"*

Caller: *"Yes, I'm here by myself 'cause he told me he was going to shoot me, but he went outside. He's somewhere 'round in the house, in the backyard."*

Operator: *"What's he look like?"*

Caller: *"Oh, he's kind of short, about 5', let's see, I'm 5', he's around 5'2" weight about, like 180."*

Operator: *"What's he wearing?"*

Caller: *"He wearing a cap, it's—to the back, and I think he got on some jeans and, like a sweatshirt."*

Operator: *"What color sweatshirt?"*

Caller: *"Grey I think, but see, he been—I think they on cocaine, he been on that stuff, that cocaine."*

Operator: *"Okay."*

Caller: *"Thank you."*

Operator: *"Okay, where's he at now, you say he's in the back?"*

Caller: *"Yes, he's somewhere around in the back or on the side of the house. I'm scared to go outside 'cause I think he's—"*

Operator: *"Okay."*

Caller: *"Thank you."*

It might seem like that call took a long time and that the 911 operator should have reacted more quickly, but in any call like that one, the 911 operator tries to squeeze as much information as possible out of the caller within seconds. The idea is to provide sufficient information to the responding patrol cars so they will not be arriving "blind." The information is passed to the Zone 1 radio dispatcher who then dispatches the call to the appropriate car or cars:

Zone 1 radio dispatcher: *"Cars 1106, 1107, signals 29/25* [disturbance/gunshots] *inside of a house, supposed to be domestic related, 2533 Bellview Avenue."*

Police patrol unit: *"1195* [sergeant], *I copy."*

Patrol unit: *"1107* [Cook], *that's 2533 Bellview?"*

Dispatcher: *"That's correct."*

Patrol unit: *"1107* [Cook], *received."*

Patrol unit: *"1106, 1107 code 26* [arrived on call]."

Dispatcher: *"Cars 1106, 1107 code 26. Your perpetrator will be a black male, 5'2", 180 pounds, wearing blue jeans and grey sweatshirt. Signal 69* [armed] *handgun."*

Patrol unit: *"1107* [Cook], *be advised 1106 is taking the*

17 [report], *but continue to hold me out on Bellview. I'll be in the area checking for the perpetrator. He's 69 with a handgun."*

Patrol unit: *"1106* [Harris], *need a reporting area for 2533 Bellview . . ."*

When they arrived at the location, Officer B. C. Harris, car 1106, Officer Layne Cook, car 1107, and DCI's Nancy Hunter questioned Shelia Leath, who had called 911 a few minutes earlier. She told them that her common-law husband, Jimmy Fludd, had come home with a handgun and had shot at the ceiling. Then he had pushed her down to the floor, put the gun to her head, and threatened to shoot her. He then left the house without another word. Leath said she thought that Fludd would still be somewhere outside waiting for the police to leave. Cook left the house to look around outside, Hunter remained in the house with Harris as he took the report. Cook returned shortly to get Hunter and told Harris he was going to look for Fludd farther up the block.

Driving slowly down Bellview Avenue, his patrol car's lights off, Cook observed a man walking down the sidewalk who matched the description of Fludd. Cook got out, instructing Nancy Hunter not to leave the car. Cook walked toward the man who suddenly ducked behind a large tree. Cook, with nothing in the immediate vicinity to provide cover, was an open target in the middle of the street. He drew his gun as the man came out from behind the tree firing. He struck Cook once in the abdomen. Cook returned fire as he fell, his bullets hitting the base of the tree.

Nancy Hunter recalled later what had happened:

We were driving, looking for the guy. Layne [Cook] had his lights off. We came down Bellview and saw a guy walking that fit the description. We were coming west on Bellview at Woods, when we saw him walking west on the right side of the street down Bellview. Layne stopped the car just west of the intersection at Woods Street and told me to stay in the car. He got out and walked in the same direction as the guy. The man evidently heard the car; he turned back a little bit and looked but kept walking. As he walked past a tree, he sidestepped behind the tree and was out of my sight. I don't know if he was out of sight of Layne or not. At this point, I noticed that Layne had his gun out, by his side. The gun was straight down, but I can't say when Layne pulled it. Layne was still walking toward the tree. The next thing I saw, the man whirled out and around from behind the tree and his arm came up toward Layne. My impression was that it was very rapid that the guy turned to face Layne. I couldn't tell about a weapon. I heard shots, saw fire from both guns. Layne fell to the ground. I don't know what the guy did, but he didn't come in my direction. When I saw Layne fall, I got out of the car. As I was getting out of the car, I called in a signal 63. My mind blanked as to where we were, so I went back a few steps and got the names from the street signs. Then I went up to Officer Cook and attended him until help got there.

When she saw Cook fall, Hunter got on the radio and, in a very excited voice, gave her assigned radio number—8504.

At this point, all radio transmissions over the Zone 1 frequency become chaotic. Patrol units, detective units, supervisors, and special operations units were all attempting to transmit at the same time: "repeat the location," "directions to the location," "need an ambulance right away," "lookout on the shooter." Some police units were not identifying themselves by radio number before they transmitted as required. This frantic scenario will usually occur whenever a police officer is shot, when the adrenaline is pumping, and rage is building in the responding cops.

The following is a transcript of the Zone 1 radio frequency starting with the first help call. The designation "unit" is any police field unit that should identify itself by radio number before transmitting:

8504: *"Signal 63* [Nancy Hunter reporting officer needs help].*"*

Dispatcher: *"What unit signal 63?"*

Patrol unit: *"1107, 6—3* [Layne Cook identified himself via his car number and is on the ground wounded, trying to call for help].*"*

Dispatcher: *"1107, your location?"*

Dispatcher: *"1107?"* (Dispatcher waiting for Cook to respond, giving his location.)

Unit: *"1105, we hear some 25s* [gunshots] *somewhere close."*

8504: *"Bellview and Woods* [Hunter giving the location]. *2533 Bellview."*

Dispatcher: *"At Bellview, 2533 Bellview, signal 63. Signal 63, 2533 Bellview."*

Unit: *"——"* (Likely Cook, but audio is unintelligible and unreadable

Dispatcher: *"Okay, signal 63, 2533 Bellview."*

Unit: *"1105, I'm 26* [arrived] *on Bellview."*

Dispatcher: *"1105, okay."*

Unit: *"——"* (Transmission unreadable unknown unit, again, probably Cook trying to transmit.)

Unit: *"Locate Bellview* [unknown responding car asking for directions].*"*

Dispatcher: *"Catch it off Woods Drive, off Bankhead. Be advised—25s."*

Dispatcher: *"Calling 1107? Cars on the way to Bellview be advised there are 25s in the area."*

Unit: *"1105, we'll be at 2554 Bellview, in the woods, one black male."*

Unit: *"1110, 1107 has been hit. Start a 4* [ambulance], *code 3* [rush call]. *Immediately!"*

Dispatcher: *"Signal 4, code 3."*

Unit (unknown): *"26."*

Unit (unknown): *"What block of Bankhead does Woods Drive run off of?"*

Dispatcher: *"Off 2502 Bankhead."*

Unit (unknown): *"Start Fire Rescue."*

Dispatcher: *"Copy, start Fire Rescue."*

Unit: *"1110, I think I got the perpetrator, signal 25s, start me a supervisor."* (Car 1110 shot at the perpetrator and that requires a supervisor, however, the perpetrator was not hit.)

Dispatcher: *"Signal 25s, need a supervisor."*

Unit: *"1195* [sergeant] *on the way."*

In response to the signal 63, patrol cars streamed onto the location. The officers in those cars knew that a Zone 1 officer had been shot. They knew by his radio number who he was. Their adrenaline was pumping, their emotions boiling. Some officers went directly to Cook, who was still lying in the middle of the street, and began administering CPR to him. In any situation like this, an ambulance never seems to arrive quickly enough, although most respond immediately after the call. This one was taking way too long. Other officers went after the shooter who was located in the woods nearby.

Unit: *"1105, the person that shot, we got him covered."*

Unit (unknown): *"1105's location?"*

Unit: *"1195* [sergeant], *26."*

Unit: *"1104, 26."*

Unit: *"Raise 1105* [meaning raise or call 1105 on the radio and have him respond]."*

Unit: *"1105, we'll be, I can't tell you the exact street address. We'll be behind a brick house, be a white light on."*

Dispatcher: *"ETA of the 4* [ambulance] *for the officer is 6 minutes."* (At this point into the incident, an ambulance should have arrived in half that time. This responding ambulance was a private contract ambulance. A Grady ambulance probably would have arrived sooner.)

Unit: *"1105, what's your location?"*

Unit: *"Give me an ETA on that 4. He's going to be 'low sick'* [very serious]."*

Dispatcher: *"I'm on hold now."* (It is unacceptable for an ambulance dispatcher to put a police or fire dispatcher on hold when a police officer or firefighter is seriously injured.)

Unit: *"1105, what's your location?"*

Unit: *"1195 [sergeant], did someone say they had the perpetrator?"*

Dispatcher: *"ETA of the 4 for the officer is 6 minutes!"*

Unit: *"To 1195, can you advise the condition of the officer, we need to get a—"*

Unit: *"Cars, don't block the street, back up, that unit that— back up so the 4 can get in!"*

Dispatcher: *"Cars, clear the street so the 4 can get in, units on Bellview, clear the street."*

Unit: *"1101, I'm 26 at Woods and Bankhead. I'm going to stand by for the 4."*

Unit: *"1195 [sergeant]. Where is that ambulance? We need it now!"*

Dispatcher: *"1111, they're coming. They're going very slow. They need to code 3 [rush]."*

Unit: *"1111, advise the units the 4 just turned the corner down the street. It's coming in the back way off Bellview."*

Unit: *"The 4 is 26 [ambulance has arrived]."*

Officer Cook was not responding. The ambulance had finally arrived, much later than expected, than wanted, than needed. Cook was placed into the ambulance. It left immediately for Grady Hospital, the main intersections blocked all the way. Upon arrival at the hospital ambulance ramp, doctors and nurses were waiting to rush him to emergency surgery.

Officer Layne B. Cook died several hours later from a gunshot wound that caused major internal damage to his abdomen.
The unanswered question thought by all the cops on the scene— would a quicker response time from the ambulance have made a difference?

Layne B. Cook was born February 27, 1951, in Jasper, a small northwest Alabama town where he grew up. After finishing high school there, he joined the United States Army, serving for three years. Shortly after his honorable discharge in 1973, he applied to and was accepted with the Atlanta Police Department. Layne Cook worked for several years as an Atlanta police officer and then resigned in order to devote his full time and attention to a very difficult divorce, a divorce that threatened him with financial ruin, along with other related personal matters. With the divorce final, and his other affairs taken care of within a year, Layne Cook was reinstated to the APD and assigned to Zone 1 morning watch.

Officer Woody Tripp also worked the morning watch out of Zone 1 in an adjoining beat car. Because he and Cook worked so near to each other, they became close professionally, often depending on each other for backup. The professional closeness became personal closeness. Tripp and Cook became good friends. Most of the calls they responded to were routine, others dangerous, some bizarre. One night during a heavy rainstorm, Tripp received a signal 24/29 (demented person/disturbance) to Bankhead Highway and Hightower Road. He and Cook had just taken a break at an all night coffee joint. Tripp took off, Cook right behind him. When they got to the location, they observed a man in the middle of the intersection, jumping up and down, screaming and cursing, causing traffic to skid around him on the slick streets. They got him to the sidewalk, wrestled him to the ground, and handcuffed him. By that time, they were soaking wet from the heavy rain. They put the wild man in Tripp's patrol car but not before he had spit on both of them. They decided to drive to a nearby closed gas station where they parked under the overhang to get out of the rain. On the way there, the man kept spitting through the open metal screen between the back and front seats. Tripp put his clipboard behind his head to protect himself from the barrage of spittle.

While waiting for the paddy wagon to arrive, Cook and Tripp decided to mete out a little payback—street-cop style. Cook unloaded his weapon, giving all the bullets to Tripp to count. He also had Tripp check the weapon to make sure it was completely empty. Cook pulled the man out of the car, pointed the gun at him, and told him that he was going to shoot him for spitting on them. Tripp, hiding around the other side of the patrol car, had a firecracker. At a prearranged signal, Tripp ignited the fuse on the firecracker so that Cook could figure out very nearly when it would go off. That was when Cook pulled the trigger. The timing was perfect. But instead of the man almost having a heart attack and peeing his pants, which is what the cops expected, he calmly looked at Cook and said, "You missed me, dude!"

On the night Layne Cook was killed, Tripp, by then, was a narcotics detective. He responded to the help call. He knew a cop had been shot, but he did not know it was Layne Cook. Tripp followed several officers into the woods after the shooter, who had fallen to the ground. When the cops got to the shooter, he got up fighting. Tripp was knocked out of the way in the melee by the other cops who rushed to subdue the shooter. Tripp went to see about the cop who had been shot. And found out it was his friend, Layne Cook. Several cops were trying to help Cook, who was unable to talk. While anxiously waiting for the ambulance to arrive, the cops around Cook observed a tear running slowly down his left cheek. The tear started to fall when Cook looked up at Officer Tripp and Officer Maxine McGrath, both close friends, kneeling beside him, each holding his hand.

Tripp rode in the ambulance to Grady Hospital.

After some of the cops vented their rage on the shooter, Jimmy Fludd, he also had to be taken to Grady Hospital by ambulance.

Jimmy Fludd, black male, then forty years old, was a career criminal with a record of many arrests in Georgia and South Carolina, including repeated incidents of domestic violence against Sheila Leath, his common-law wife of twelve years. It was the latest of these episodes that led to the killing of Layne Cook.

His record since 1968 reflected the violent nature of Jimmy Fludd a/k/a Jimmy Floudd, a/k/a John Henry Jones, four different dates of birth on various records. In South Carolina, John Henry Jones was charged with the murder of a man over "who was going to wear the green hat?" The murder charge was later reduced to manslaughter. Jones/Fludd was also arrested in South Carolina for assault and battery with intent to kill. Jimmy Fludd's arrest record in Georgia was not quite as dramatic, but it did include arrests for aggravated assault on a police officer, several DUIs, among other traffic charges.

Jimmy Fludd appeared in Fulton County Superior Court and pleaded guilty to the murder of Atlanta police officer Layne Cook. He was sentenced to life in prison without the possibility of parole.

Layne B. Cook was thirty-eight years old when he was killed. He was divorced, and he left behind two young children, a son, age seven, and a daughter, age four.

He is buried in Jasper, Alabama.

OFFICER
LAYNE B. COOK
"SHOT BY ASSAILANT"
JANUARY 17, 1989

Atlanta Police Officer

Gregory L. Davis

"If I go, I'll take him with me!"

They were Slick Rick and Shorty Pimp—drug dealers, pimps, thugs, and gang bangers—on the streets of Zone 6. However, in the Zone 6 Precinct they were Atlanta police officers Stanley L. Williams and Gregory L. Davis, respectively, undercover cops who roamed the dark streets looking for criminals who were wanted or criminals in the act of or about to engage in illegal activities. They watched. Then they made arrests, providing sufficient evidence in order to prosecute.

For several nights, Slick Rick and Shorty Pimp had been searching for the subject of a "lookout." (A *lookout* is police talk for a description of someone wanted for a crime or a series of crimes.) Not only were Williams and Davis working as undercover cops to locate the subject, but a lot of uniformed cops on their beats in patrol cars were also looking for the same subject—a black male riding a red bicycle with white handlebars turned upward.

From Little Five Points—an area of Atlanta where what was funky, outrageous, and bizarre elsewhere was accepted as normal behavior in the adjoining Zone 6 neighborhoods, and the nearby middle class, residential, and staid city of Decatur—this bicycle rider regularly appeared briefly from out of the night and then disappeared out of sight, only to reappear and disappear back into the night.

Atlanta police wanted to talk to this bicycling night rider about the homicide of a white female who was killed in an apparent random shooting in Little Five Points.

In the neighborhoods around Little Five Points there were reports of a cat burglar, someone who entered houses through open windows during the night while the occupants were sleeping.

In nearby Decatur, homes were entered at night, burglarized while occupants were home, and in several cases where a woman was home alone, the burglary escalated to sexual assault.

Witnesses in both jurisdictions told police they observed a black male riding a red bicycle with white handlebars turned upward. Some witnesses noticed him just before the time of a reported home entry; some saw him not long after a reported home entry.

The Atlanta Police Department's Zone 6 was responsible for police services and criminal activity that occurred in the eastern part of the city, including a bubble that extended into DeKalb County. The major portion of Atlanta was in Fulton County. The pressure was on Zone 6 to stop this ongoing problem of home entries and burglaries during the night. To address the problem, several unmarked Zone 6 cars driven by police officers in plainclothes patrolled the quiet, dark streets from eleven PM to seven AM looking for the man on the bicycle, who was believed to be the cat burglar and was considered a suspect in the Little Five Points homicide.

Atlanta police officers Gregory L. Davis and Stanley L. Williams were plainclothes cops in one of those unmarked cars. They had been partners for three years. The most important thing a police officer wants is the right partner, a partner who can be trusted to anticipate, whose reflexes will prompt immediate action, a partner who understands on all levels and in all ways what is needed of him or her.

Davis and Williams were partners.

Gregory L. Davis, an eight-year veteran of the APD, was born October 5, 1950. The youngest of three brothers, he spent his first nine years in the south Georgia town of Quitman, just twenty miles from Valdosta and near the Georgia-Florida state line. The family moved to Atlanta where Gregory finished his elementary schooling and went on to graduate from West Fulton High School.

Greg Davis joined the United States Army during the Vietnam War, serving four years but not in Vietnam. His two older brothers were in the United States Marine Corps, both served in Vietnam. The army decided against sending Greg there because they didn't want three brothers in Vietnam at the same time. When his four-year tour of duty was up, Greg joined the Atlanta Police Department in 1980. On completing the academy, Atlanta police officer Gregory L. Davis, badge number 3456, was assigned to the Zone 3 Precinct and three years later reassigned to Zone 6. He worked a patrol car for the next couple of years, until he was detailed to the Zone 6 Plainclothes Unit, where he and Stan Williams began their three-year partnership and a three-year friendship.

They were both scheduled to be off that Friday morning, August 26, 1988. Although not on duty, Davis showed up at the precinct sometime after midnight. He said he had been at the movies and thought he would just drop by, say "Hi," and see what might be happening. About that time, an anonymous telephone call came in reporting that a black male on a red bicycle with white handlebars was riding slowly up and down Connecticut Avenue in the Lake Claire area. (Lake Claire is in that bubble of the City of Atlanta that extends into DeKalb County.) Davis grabbed the keys to his assigned unmarked car, told Sergeant J. E. Hughey that the caller had just described the guy they had been looking for, and he quickly left the precinct.

Sergeant Hughey broadcast the lookout to the rest of the Zone 6 cars: *"Cars in the vicinity of Connecticut Avenue in Lake Claire start for that location and 59 [meet] with 1631, it was reported that 'the bicycle burglar' is riding around there."*

A short time later at about one AM, Officer Gregory Davis came on the radio:

"1631, hold me at Southerland Terrace and MClendon Avenue on a signal 54 [suspicious person] and cancel any other cars that are headed to this location."

Dispatcher: *"Copy 1631, Southerland Terrace and MClendon on a signal 54. Any car on the way to Southerland Terrace and MClendon, code 4 [cancel]."*

Then, less than one minute later:

Unknown unit (very faint, barely readable): *". . . I've . . . been . . . shot . . ."*

Sergeant Hughey shouted into his radio as he ran out of the precinct: *"Send a 4 [ambulance] to Southerland Terrace and MClendon, and start some cars, that's 1631 [Davis] trying to call!"*

Dispatcher: *"Any car near Southerland Terrace and MClendon, signal 63/50/4 [officer needs help/person shot/ambulance on the way]."*

Police unit (on the scene): *"Give the 4 a code 3 [rush call], we have an officer shot!"*

The responding police units found both Davis and the bicycle rider lying in the middle of the street, not more than the distance of a car length from each other. The sleeping residential neighborhood had been awakened, first by the sound of gunfire, minutes later by the sirens, flashing lights, loud police radios, and louder voices.

The bicycle rider was DOS (dead on the scene) with a gunshot wound to the head.

Officer Gregory Davis was barely breathing and had a slight pulse. He tried to talk but couldn't. He died moments later before the ambulance arrived. He was shot once in the chest, the bullet struck his heart.

There were no witnesses to the shoot-out.

Stan Williams was at home in a deep sleep having a vague dream about Davis when he was sharply awakened by the incessant ringing of his telephone. He answered, still in bed and still groggy from sleep, but woke instantly when the voice on the other end said words that chilled his blood, words he'll never forget . . .

"Your partner's been shot and killed!"

Williams jumped out of bed, threw on some clothes, and went directly to the scene of the shooting. Later, he did what he had to do—what every cop hopes never to have to do but must do when it happens—he notified his partner's family of his death.

The bicycle rider was identified as Timothy Riley, a black male, age twenty-three, who owned a lengthy arrest record under many aliases. He had been arrested numerous times for burglary, auto theft, theft by taking, carrying a weapon in the commission of a felony, theft by receiving, criminal trespass, and failure to appear. Each time he was arrested, he gave a different name—among them, Akiyele Uomo, Rashed Ahmad Jalal, and Tim Marigna—and a different date of birth with each name. Timothy Riley was a one-man crime wave, the cat burglar who had terrorized the peaceful residential neighborhoods of the Zone 6 portion of Atlanta and adjoining Decatur.

The motive for the murder of the female in Little Five Points, two days before Riley was killed, was never determined. The gun used in that homicide was the same gun that killed Officer Davis.

Atlanta police officer Gregory L. Davis ended the career—the life—of a dangerous and violent criminal who preyed on society. It would have been so much better for society if Timothy Riley's life had ended and Officer Davis's life had not. But that did not happen.

The late night/early morning Zone 6 and Decatur residential burglaries stopped.

Many times as Gregory Davis and Stan Williams rode together in their unmarked car down the dark, quiet streets, Greg would say, when talking about a confrontation with a bad guy, "If I go, I'll take him with me!"

Gregory Davis left behind two young daughters, Tracy and Erin, from a previous marriage. As a memorial to him, the plaza at Moreland Avenue near MClendon Avenue in Little Five Points is officially named the "Gregory L. Davis Plaza."

Atlanta police sergeant

Willie D. Cameron

"Why don't you just leave so I don't have to arrest you"

*E*xtra jobs . . . it doesn't matter whether they are referred to as second jobs, off-duty jobs, moonlighting, or perhaps as supplemental jobs, part-time work, or as simply extra jobs, they are common to police officers in the largest cities and the smallest towns throughout the United States. These extra jobs are an economic necessity for most police officers everywhere. The income from these jobs is needed to supplement their police income so that they can maintain a middle-class standard of living.

A police officer cannot work an extra job without first applying for and receiving the okay from the Atlanta Police Department.

The Atlanta Police Department approves most requests from its cops to work an extra job. To be approved, an extra job must meet certain criteria, such as not working inside clubs and bars, although outside, directing cars to parking spots or directing traffic flow in and out of the parking lots of the clubs and bars, is okay. Working any extra job, an APD cop is required to enforce only criminal laws and not permitted to enforce house or company rules. A police officer must always enforce the law when witnessing illegal activity, whether or not on the property of an extra job. When the APD grants a cop approval, implicit in that approval is also the authority and the power of arrest while working that extra job, the same as though that cop were on duty.

Sergeant Willie D. Cameron had that approval for the three extra jobs he worked: one extra job was as security, a uniformed presence for Sears in the West End Mall of Atlanta; another extra job was as a security guard in an Atlanta police uniform for a bank across the street from the mall; and still another extra job was on Sundays handling traffic for a church. He worked four jobs—three extra jobs! And his regular job as a cop in the APD!

Some cops take an extra job because they have to, even though they may not like the work or circumstances surrounding the extra job. For Sergeant Cameron, Sears was a pleasant extra job; it was out of the weather and among friendly store employees and mall staff. The uniformed police presence was a deterrent against shoplifting, among other illegal activities—it certainly deterred disruptive behavior.

Sergeant Cameron worked that pleasant, uneventful extra job for twelve years. It came to a violent end one cold, rainy afternoon, the sixth day of February 1987.

He was not scheduled to work at Sears that day; that day was the day he worked at the bank. He left the bank. And on his way to attend a banquet later that evening, he stopped by Sears to check on a new extra-job cop. Several Atlanta police officers also worked extra jobs at Sears under the direction of Sergeant Cameron.

Two days prior, February 4, Clarence Eugene Smith, a black male, fifty-one years old, with an extensive arrest record, was in Sears harassing customers for money. This was routinely reported to mall security, which responded, and without incident escorted him out of the mall. The next day, Smith was back doing the same. Sergeant Cameron was working at Sears that day. He responded to the call to mall security. After observing what Smith was doing, Sergeant Cameron ordered Smith to leave the mall and to not return. Cameron cited Smith with a criminal trespass warning, which meant that he would be arrested if he appeared within the premises of the mall again.

At 5:45 PM on February 6, 1987, Sergeant Cameron interrupted his trip to the banquet to go to Sears for no other purpose than to check on the new off-duty extra-job cop working there. He was notified that Smith was back in the store harassing customers. Cameron responded, accompanied by Atlanta police officer Vanessa Hamilton. They caught up with Smith at the catalog order section. Cameron said sternly to Smith, "I thought I told you to stay out of here!" After a few moments, he followed that with a softer approach, "Look, why don't you just leave so I don't have to arrest you."

Smith just stood there, staring at Cameron. Then, keeping one hand in his pocket, he reached forward and ripped the clip-on tie from Sergeant Cameron's uniform shirt. Smith then withdrew the hand that was in his pocket. It came out holding a gun. As soon as they saw Smith's gun appear, both Cameron and Officer Vanessa Hamilton drew their guns but did not fire. Smith ripped the badge from Cameron's shirt with one hand and with the other fired his gun, shooting Sergeant Cameron once in the forehead. Cameron went down so fast he didn't have a chance to squeeze the trigger of his own gun.

Officer Hamilton stood there, frozen. She did not return fire. Customers and employees screamed and ran for cover while Smith calmly walked to the escalator, stood there for a few seconds, then got on it and went up to the next level. Hamilton did not go after

Smith. Instead, she asked to use a phone (this was before cell phones were common and readily available), saying repeatedly, "I have to get backup. I have to get backup!" Someone found a key to a locked room where there was a phone. She used the phone to call for help but calls had already been made to 911 during the time she searched for a phone. Help was already on the way before she made her call.

Police dispatcher: *"Any car near Sears in the West End Mall, signal 63/50/4* [officer needs help/person shot/ambulance on the way]*!"*

Police dispatcher: *"Cars on the way to Sears in the West End Mall. It's been reported that a police officer has been shot, and the shooter is still somewhere in the mall."*

Patrol cars from Zones 3 and 4 responded, their sirens screaming as they fought their way through rush-hour traffic made worse by the heavy rain.

Officer Vanessa Hamilton returned to where Sergeant Cameron lay on the floor—dead! Someone had already covered him with a blanket. She made no attempt to go after or locate Smith.

The responding cops rushed into Sears, were directed to where Sergeant Cameron lay, apparently DOS (dead on the scene). When the ambulance arrived, DOS was confirmed by the EMTs.

The cops were informed that the guy who shot the police officer was in the mall headed in the direction of the Sunshine Department Store. Their focus shifted to the Sunshine Department Store where the police officers caught up with Smith. They ordered him to "put your hands up where we can see them and get on the floor." Instead of complying, Smith pulled a gun out of his pocket and fired at them. The cops returned fire hitting him multiple times and killing him instantly.

Sergeant Cameron's badge was found under Smith's body.

Willie D. Cameron was born in LaGrange, Georgia, on September 8, 1947. Don Cameron, as he was called by family and friends, spent his first eighteen years in LaGrange. He played football in high school, well enough to earn a football scholarship at Morehouse College in Atlanta. He played football at Morehouse until injuries he suffered in an auto accident prevented him from playing. After Morehouse, Don attended John Marshall Law School in Atlanta for more than two years.

Don Cameron became active in his community, working as a mentor with kids, sort of a "big brother" helping to put them on the right path. His experience doing that work helped him to decide that he could do some good as a police officer. He joined the Atlanta Police Department in 1968. This was during the civil rights era, a time when black Atlanta police officers were demanding to be treated equal to and given the same opportunities as their white counterparts. Don Cameron became a member of the Afro-American Patrolman's League, an organization of black Atlanta police officers dealing with these and similar issues. He was heavily involved during the five weeks of intense negotiations to draft a consent decree ordered by a federal judge. Several lawsuits had been filed in federal court by parties claiming racial discrimination and reverse discrimination by the City of Atlanta. The consent decree agreed upon by the parties was accepted by the judge and signed into law, averting a trial. Don Cameron eventually became the president of the AAPL.

Don Cameron met Gloria Corbin at a house party given by Gloria's mother, who had invited an Atlanta police officer, a good friend of the Corbin family. Her mother asked that police officer to bring along several of his buddies. Don Cameron was one of those buddies. Gloria worked at Grady Memorial Hospital in an administrative position where she saw Cameron from time to time. They dated for a while and were married in 1971. They had been married for sixteen years when Don was killed by Smith.

It was the end of her workday that day. Gloria had already left Grady Hospital and was on her way home when she heard on her car radio that an Atlanta police officer had been shot at the West End Mall and was being transported to Grady Hospital. She knew that Don was not working at Sears; this was the day he was working his extra job at the bank. She thought that the cop who was shot might be one of the officers who worked for Don at Sears.

Gloria returned to Grady Hospital where she felt she might be able to help the cop's family members who would be brought there. When she arrived and started asking questions, she could not get answers from anyone. They were being evasive. The Atlanta police chaplain arrived and asked her to accompany him to the family room—that was when she knew. That was the moment when she realized it was Don who had been shot. The family room was where bad news was broken to the next of kin.

Officer Vanessa Hamilton was a coward who committed the unpardonable sin of the police profession—she ran out on her partner in the face of danger! By her own admission, she had her gun drawn and was standing fewer than ten feet from Smith when he ripped the tie from Cameron's shirt. When Hamilton saw Smith grab Cameron's badge with one hand while his other held a gun pointed at Cameron, why didn't she fire? If she had fired at Smith, she might have prevented him from shooting and killing Sergeant Cameron—her partner at that moment. When asked why she didn't shoot the gunman, Hamilton said the training at the police academy had taught her not to fire her weapon when bystanders were present. But she said she would have fired if she had had a clear shot with no one in the way. No one in the way? She was fewer than ten feet from Smith. If she couldn't hit a grown man at that close distance, she had no business being in a police uniform or carrying a gun.

Worse, after Sergeant Cameron was shot, Smith strolled away to the escalator, and before getting on, he stood there for almost thirty seconds. Instead of going after Smith, Hamilton ran in the opposite direction looking for a phone to call for help. By the time she got through a locked door to a phone, 911 had already received several calls indicating what had just happened. She found a blanket, but when she returned to where Sergeant Cameron lay dead on the floor, there was already a blanket covering his body. During that time, Hamilton still made no attempt to locate and apprehend Smith, the person who had shot and killed Cameron.

The shooting happened so quickly that she might not have been able to do anything to save Sergeant Cameron's life. But by not going after Smith, she allowed him to escape, creating the possibility that he was moving through the mall randomly shooting other people. In addition to running out on Cameron, Vanessa Hamilton abdicated her responsibility as a police officer.

Instead of being fired by the APD, she was given time off with pay—after all, she was "traumatized" by the experience at Sears. Hamilton was sent back to her assignment at the Airport Precinct after it was determined she was no longer traumatized. She remained there until she resigned from the APD. No police officer would work with her on the streets.

Sergeant Willie Don Cameron, an eighteen-year veteran of the Atlanta Police Department, was six months shy of his fortieth birthday when he was killed. He left behind a widow, Gloria, and three children—two boys, one thirteen years old, the other twelve, and a girl of seven—to grow up without a father.

SERGEANT
WILLIE D. CAMERON
"SHOT BY ASSAILANT"
FEBRUARY 6, 1987

Atlanta Police Officer

Philip Bruce Mathis

Going back down was not as easy as going up. It was impossible. So they were stranded on the roof

tlanta police officer Philip Bruce Mathis, a sixteen-year veteran, was assigned to the Zone 2 Precinct, which covered most of the north side, including the affluent Buckhead section of Atlanta. Buckhead wasn't exactly Beverly Hills, California. Nor was it as bad as South Central Los Angeles. But, Buckhead was a world away from the high-crime areas of Atlanta.

Lenox Square, in the Buckhead section of Atlanta, was and still is what most shoppers consider a high-end shopping mall. Serving as anchors were two big department stores, Rich's and Davison's, both since taken over by Macy's. Within his first year as a cop, Officer P. B. Mathis started an APD approved extra job as security with Rich's-Lenox Square and continued to work that extra job for fifteen years. It was mostly a quiet and routine extra job interrupted regularly by shoplifting in one part or another of the store. Officer Mathis had made a considerable number of arrests during his fifteen years at Rich's.

Philip Bruce Mathis was born in Atlanta on February 4, 1947. He grew up and lived entirely within the Atlanta area and that made him sort of different within the Atlanta Police Department— a native of Atlanta, unlike most other APD cops who were from somewhere else. Bruce was an Eagle Scout. He played the clarinet in his high school band. And he worked at Rich's part time while in high school. A strong sense of patriotism motivated him to join the National Guard when he was eighteen years old. He played golf, and during the season, hunted deer.

While a youngster, Bruce Mathis had a police scanner, which is a radio receiver that can monitor police radio traffic if the internal chip is tuned to the APD frequency. They are widely used by the media and perfectly legal. What he heard on it generated his interest in police work. He rode around in a patrol car with a good friend, an Atlanta cop, when his friend was authorized to take along a civilian. It was those rides that got Mathis hooked on becoming a police officer.

He became Atlanta police officer Philip Bruce Mathis after college in 1969. As a rookie, he was assigned to driving a paddy wagon. One day while stopped at a traffic light, he gestured to the driver in the car next to his paddy wagon to pull over. The driver was Florence Holmes. He explained to her that he just wanted to chat with her. And so they did for a few minutes. From those few minutes, a friendship began that grew over the next four years, leading to Bruce and Florence getting married.

Through his years with the APD, Bruce Mathis always worked the northernmost beat of Zone 2, which was, statistically, the least active, except for the heavy traffic there during the morning and afternoon rush hours and the hours in between. Mathis alternated between the day watch (seven AM to three PM) and the morning watch (eleven PM to seven AM), which allowed him to work his extra job at Rich's in the evenings. Officer David Mulkey worked an adjacent beat in Zone 2. It wasn't unusual for them to respond together to the same call. Supplying backup for each other formed the basis for that special bond between cops that transcends friendship.

Late one Sunday night the police radio was quiet, both beats were "dead," no activity in either. On quiet, boring nights like this, Mathis and Mulkey would meet at a pond near Chastain Park. With some makeshift fishing gear, they would do some fishing. Mathis received a call that did not require any backup, just some paperwork. Mathis left the pond, and Mulkey continued fishing.

On completing his paperwork, Mathis radioed Mulkey, "Have you caught any of those subjects yet?"

Mulkey replied, "No, but they are still under surveillance."

Later, when their sergeant asked them about that radio transmission, they had no good explanation, so they had to "fess up."

In the serious and deadly business of police work, Huck Finn kind of relief is not only helpful, but it is no-cost therapy, especially when a cop can laugh at himself or herself with the others present. For example, on a bitterly cold January night, Mathis received a signal 7 (burglar in a building). Mulkey heard the call and also responded. The location was a one-story building. A quick check of the premises indicated that every door and window had not been disturbed. So that meant the cops needed to check up on the roof for a possible entry. Without the benefit of stairs or a ladder, Mathis and Mulkey climbed up the outside of the building, grabbing onto anything that would hold them as they made their way upward. For footholds on their ascent, they stepped on ledges and even into the gaps in the outside wall where bricks were missing. The roof checked out okay, no entry evident there either. So this was a false alarm. All was okay. But when they tried to go back down, they realized it was not going to be as easy as it was going up. It was worse than not going to be easy—it was going to be impossible. They were stranded on the roof. Mathis called for the "light truck"—that's the maintenance truck that has a bucket from which traffic lights can be serviced. Mulkey was wearing his "long johns" underwear under his uniform, although he had left his uniform jacket in the car so it would not encumber his climb up the building. Mathis wore his jacket on the way up, but he was not wearing long johns. It was a very long twenty minutes or so before they were rescued from the cold on the roof and made it back to the warmth of their patrol cars.

Shoplifting is a crime defined in the Georgia Criminal Code as "theft by taking." Any theft of an item valued over five hundred dollars is classified a felony. Most shoplifting cases fall under the five hundred dollar threshold, which makes those crimes misdemeanors. Whether the theft is a felony or misdemeanor, retail stores are the victims that suffer losses because of shoplifting.

Misdemeanor thefts are usually committed by a kleptomaniac—someone who has the compulsion to steal an item, whether needed or not. There are also the teenagers and college students who tend to shoplift either on a dare or some type of initiation. What they steal is likely to be a small inexpensive item.

And of course there are the thieves who will steal anytime, anywhere, anything, that is valued above or below five hundred dollars.

The felon who steals merchandise from out on the floor in the presence of employees and customers is commonly a repeat offender. This kind of store thief later sells the stolen items, usually for whatever they will bring.

The retail store thieves at the top of the tier are referred to as "boosters." This thief does not steal from the floor but sneaks undetected into a stockroom, knows the way in and out, and leaves with a large amount of merchandise. The booster, a career criminal, later sells the stolen items to a professional criminal "fence" who then sells the "goods" to others, or the booster directly sells to others who are known to want those particular stolen goods.

Regardless of the category any of these thieves fit in, they usually tend to be nonviolent.

Charles J. Edward, a black male, a/k/a Rick Vinson, a/k/a Richard Fleming Vinson, a/k/a Ricky Harris, a/k/a Slim, a/k/a Po Bird was a known booster in Atlanta. He had a long criminal record, including multiple thefts, burglary, aggravated assault, and escape. He also dealt in stolen credit cards. Edward frequented two black nightclubs—the Scatz Club at 2006 Campbellton Road SW and the 131 Club at 131 North Avenue NE. He was known as "Rick," using the Ricky Vinson alias, in both clubs where he sold stolen goods. Most of the stolen goods he sold had the store tags still on them.

One night while at the Scatz Club, Rick Vinson and some friends heard a report on the radio about the arrest of a shoplifter at a local department store. Vinson startled his friends when he said, with a hard look on his face and coldness in his voice, "If one of them ever catch me up in the mall or store, that he was going to have to lay down and let me get away. If he bucks, I will have to blow him away!"

Walker Kemp, a black male, a/k/a Wilbert O'Dell Brooks, a/k/a Roscoe, a/k/a Colorado, a/k/a Denver was another known Atlanta booster who also had a long criminal record with multiple thefts, burglaries, and aggravated assault. Although Rick Vinson and Kemp were not friends, the two were acquainted with each other and with what the other did. Kemp, like Rick, also let it be known to friends that he would not allow himself to go to jail again. That he would do whatever he had to do if caught.

Both Vinson and Kemp were known to carry handguns.

On April 25, 1985, at five thirty PM, Officer Bruce Mathis arrived at Rich's Department Store in the Lenox Square shopping center to work his extra job. After reporting to the security office, he began his routine of walking the floors and visiting the different departments. Mathis wore civilian clothes so it wasn't obvious that he was a cop working security. He chatted with store clerks and department managers as he made his rounds throughout the store, stopping in the security office from time to time. Just after eight PM, store employees said they saw Mathis entering the electronics/luggage stockroom.

Five minutes later, employees and customers adjacent to the stockroom heard loud voices, angry words (unintelligible), followed by what they thought sounded like gunshots. The door to the stockroom swung open. Officer Bruce Mathis staggered out and fell to the floor, bleeding from several gunshot wounds.

The phones in the APD 911 communications section lit up, followed promptly by the dreaded broadcast over all frequencies:
Police dispatcher: *"Any car near Rich's at Lenox Square, signal 63/50/4* [officer needs help/person shot/ambulance on the way]."

Two robbery detectives were at Lenox Square to have a robbery victim view a photo lineup. They were in the Rich's parking lot at the time of the broadcast and scrambled into the store, the first to get to Mathis. Mathis had no pulse and was not breathing. CPR did not help.

Detective unit: *"The 50 is on a police officer and he appears to be 48* [dead]. *We need Homicide and ID* [crime scene unit]."

Responding patrol cars from Zone 2, also special operations units—SWAT, Tactical Anti-Crime, Motorcycle Squad, Helicopter—and detective cars clogged the Rich's parking lots as cops left their cars and ran into the store. The crime scene was secured. All exit doors were locked to keep anyone who had not already left from leaving the store. A storewide search was conducted for anyone of "interest." That search ended with negative results.

Homicide detectives arrived and the investigation began. Witnesses were questioned at the scene; some witnesses were taken downtown to make written statements about what they had observed. Two witnesses who were near a down escalator saw a black male, tall and thin, within fifteen feet of them hurry past. They reported that he got on the down escalator. They gave a detailed description of him and said they could identify him if they saw him again. After completing their written statements, they assisted the police sketch artist with a composite drawing of the suspect.

The stockroom was the crime scene, and it was meticulously worked by all available homicide detectives and about a half dozen crime scene techs. Photos and measurements were taken, sketches drawn, and latent fingerprints were dusted to eliminate the prints of all employees and any others who had access to the stockroom. Eliminating prints allowed the police to concentrate on those that did not match and to compare those unidentified prints with any suspect. Other evidence, such as the bullet that missed Mathis and was removed from one of the walls, was collected, tagged, and bagged.

Florence Mathis was at home where she received several telephone calls from concerned friends and family who knew that Mathis worked at Rich's and that something was going on at Rich's-Lenox Square. She called Rich's and was promptly put on hold. After a time when no one came back on the line, Florence called the store again. This time she immediately said who she was and asked to speak to Bruce. Whoever was speaking from the store told Florence that Bruce was too busy to come to the phone. She accepted that, hung up, and decided to call again later.

It wasn't long after she hung up when her doorbell rang. When she opened the door, Major Worthy, the Zone 2 commander, the APD chaplain, and a department psychologist were standing there. Knowing why they were there, she let them in. They told Florence what had happened. Soon a Fulton County police chaplain arrived and then a female APD officer. Florence wanted to go to Rich's or to Grady Hospital, but they convinced her otherwise. She remained at home with members of her family. The female officer stayed with Florence for the next several days doing what she could to help her get through that very difficult time. (It is APD policy that whenever an officer is killed in the line of duty a police officer will be detailed to stay with the next of kin from the time of notification until the day of the funeral. That officer will be the same gender as the next of kin.)

About ninety minutes earlier that same evening, or about six thirty PM, Rick Vinson asked Bernard Williams a/k/a Fancy Dan and Elizabeth Scott a/k/a Queenie to drive him to Lenox Square so he could pick up a purchase that he had in layaway at Rich's. After parking the car, the three went into Rich's where they split up. Williams and Scott went to the women's department for ten or fifteen minutes and then returned to the car. A short time later, Vinson hurried into the car insisting, "Let's go!" The couple asked about the layaway package that Vinson didn't seem to have with him. Vinson replied, "I didn't have enough money on me to pick it up, but let's go, let's go!" As they were pulling out of the parking lot, they heard police sirens getting louder and they saw patrol cars, their blue lights flashing, converging in the parking lot. The three went to the 131 Club on North Avenue, had a few drinks, and then Vinson left.

During the next several days, the top story on the TV news and in the newspapers was about the killing of Atlanta police officer Philip Bruce Mathis at Rich's-Lenox Square. The police artist sketch of the suspect was shown in the media. When Williams and Scott saw it, they agreed that it could be Rick Vinson. Neither they nor anyone who knew Vinson saw him during the next week or so. When he returned to the clubs, everyone who knew him was amazed at how different he looked. Vinson had changed his appearance. He had shaved off his mustache and sideburns, he'd had his hair cut and a ponytail woven into it, and he wore a hat down low just above his eyes.

Walker Kemp became a suspect simply because he was a known booster. Several witnesses reported seeing a man fitting Kemp's description leaving Rich's immediately after the shooting, just as police were arriving. Kemp was picked up several days later. When he was searched he had in his possession a small quantity of cocaine, tools to commit a crime (bolt cutters in the possession of a known thief and burglar can be construed to be a tool for the purpose of committing a crime), and a knife large enough that it violated the City of Atlanta knife ordinance (a concealed blade over 4″ in length). Any one of those things found on Kemp was enough to hold him for questioning in the Mathis case. Holding him provided detectives enough time to contact witnesses. The state crime lab specialist who examined the bolt cutters against the lock cut from the stockroom was not certain that these same cutters were used to cut that lock. Because of the apparent damage to the bolt cutters, the specialist could not testify in court as an expert and say that they were the same ones used.

While being questioned by detectives about where he was at the time Mathis was shot and killed, Kemp became uncooperative and belligerent. "I wasn't at Rich's when the police got shot and don't remember where I was, so if you got something on me then lock me up. If not, then I'm out of here!" He did, however, tell someone, who told someone else, who in turn mentioned it to a detective's informant that he was in the Rich's stockroom "When the dude shot the police, but I thought he was a security guard, not a police." Witnesses were called in to view him in a lineup. None could identify him as the man they saw leaving Rich's. That vague talk on the street and detectives unable to find the original source was just that—talk! Lacking any evidence connecting Kemp to Mathis, detectives could only charge him with the three violations.

Meanwhile, the Georgia State Crime Lab was conducting ballistics tests on the recovered bullets and determined they were .38 calibers and had been fired from a Colt revolver. Trajectory tests showed those bullets were fired by a shooter who was at least 6′1″ to 6′2″ tall. The two witnesses who saw the hurrying man get on the escalator right after the shooting described him as tall and thin. Walker Kemp was 5′10″ and stocky.

The investigation continued throughout the summer. Homicide detectives Carl Price, Lou Moore, and Jerry Pendergrass followed up on leads and tips while putting the pressure on informants to get out on the street and find out what they could about the two suspects and anyone else that might know something about the Mathis killing.

During late August and early September some new information started to surface. Detective Carl Price received a call from an informant suggesting that he talk to Calvin Jackson who worked at the 131 Club because he had information about the shooter in the Mathis case. At about the same time, Fulton County police deputy chief Louis Graham heard about Calvin Jackson from a different informant. (Informants supply information for a variety of reasons—to get some help with their own criminal cases, money, revenge, jealousy, among other reasons.) Graham's informant was in federal prison and wanted to make a deal to lessen his sentence. Graham called APD homicide detective Sidney Dorsey and asked him to follow up on this new information.

Detectives from the APD and detectives from the Fulton County Police Department got together to speak with Jackson. Jackson told them that a man he knew only as Rick came into the 131 Club all the time selling stolen goods, and because of that, Rick might be the one they were looking for. He said the police sketch, provided through witnesses and shown on the news right after the killing, looked just like Rick. But he said that Rick had since cut his hair, shaved his face clean, and was now wearing a ponytail. Jackson said he was at the 131 Club on the night when Mathis was killed. And he told them that earlier that night he had heard Rick ask Fancy Dan (Williams) and Queenie (Scott) to drive him to Lenox Square. Jackson's description of how Rick appeared that night matched the description provided by the two witnesses who saw the man at Rich's hurrying onto the escalator after the shooting.

Rick was identified as Charles J. Edward. He used the aliases mentioned earlier when he was arrested in different jurisdictions. A fingerprint taken from a carton in the stockroom at the crime scene matched the corresponding fingerprint of Charles J. Edward a/k/a Rick Vinson. The state crime lab determined that the fingerprint from that carton was the spot where the shooter was standing when Mathis was killed.

Charles J. Edward was arrested and charged with the murder of Atlanta police officer Philip Bruce Mathis. He was tried in Fulton

County Superior Court and found guilty. He was sentenced to life in prison.

Some investigators feel that in this crime Walker Kemp had some level of culpability, either as a witness in the stockroom at the time of the shooting, which would make him an accessory, or possibly the shooter himself. Walker Kemp was never charged.

Bruce Mathis knew what "serve" meant in "to protect and serve," which is on patrol cars everywhere. One night, while patrolling the I-75 portion of his beat, he saw a large tour bus stopped in the emergency lane. Mathis stopped and learned the bus had mechanical trouble and needed repairs to continue. He saw that the bus was filled with passengers. Mathis got in touch with a church on his beat, arranged for the passengers to be transported to the church where they had some food, coffee, and access to restrooms until the bus was ready to go.

Bruce Mathis was always willing to help.

Florence Mathis became a widow after twelve years of marriage and was left alone with their five-year-old daughter, Amanda.

OFFICER
PHILIP B. MATHIS
"SHOT BY ASSAILANT"
APRIL 26, 1985

Atlanta Police Sergeant

James E. Richardson Jr.

He was not informed that the car he had stopped was stolen only a few minutes earlier

*P*olice unit: *"8003, hold me out at Peters and McDaniel Streets SW on a 1971 green Ford. Georgia tag number LOK 402, occupied by two black males."*

Police dispatcher: *"Received, 8003. Peters and McDaniel, a 1971 Ford. Georgia tag LOK 402."*

Those were the last radio transmissions between car 8003 (Sergeant Richardson) and APD Communications. That was shortly after four AM. A few minutes later, Sergeant James E. Richardson Jr. was down in the middle of the street. He'd been shot three times.

Then an unfamiliar voice was heard over Sergeant Richardson's police radio:

"A police been shot, a police been shot at Peters and McDaniel, need a ambulance right away, hurry!"

Police dispatcher: *"Any car near Peters and McDaniel Streets, signal 63/50/4* [officer needs help/person shot/ambulance on the way]. *Cars on the way to Peters and McDaniel, it's been reported that a police officer has been shot!"*

Within minutes at that location there were at least twenty police vehicles and more still arriving—patrol cars from three zones, cars with special operations units, and cars with detectives. Richardson was quickly loaded into an ambulance and escorted via a secure route that had been shut down to Grady Memorial Hospital; an ER trauma team was waiting there. He died several hours later in the operating room.

Sergeant James Richardson, a ten-year APD veteran, was assigned to the Flying Squad of the Special Operations Section. The mission of this special operations unit was to operate in the known high-crime areas, scouring for illegal activity. Sergeant Richardson was working the morning watch—the graveyard shift—on that oppressively hot Saturday morning, July 19, 1980. He was in plainclothes driving an unmarked car. He was alone.

Earlier that morning, Otis Lee Miller, a black male, twenty-two years old, and Glenn Lee Adams, a black male, twenty years old, both with criminal records, were looking for someone to rob. Miller and Adams roamed the dark streets on foot in search of a victim. They came upon a man and a woman sitting in a car in front of a closed liquor store at Pryor Road and Ridge Avenue. They approached the car, Miller on one side, Adams on the other, each pointing a gun at the couple. They ordered the man to climb into the backseat and the woman to slide across the front seat.

One of them, it's not clear whether Miller or Adams, moved into the driver's seat and drove the car around for a while. During that time, both victims were robbed of their money and valuables. The driver stopped on a desolate street where the kidnapped couple was ordered out. Miller and Adams started arguing over what gun to use and who was going to use it to eliminate the two witnesses. The couple had to die because they could identify who had robbed and kidnapped them. The two decided that before shooting their victims, they would "get some" of the woman. While they were arguing, the couple started to flee. As they were running away, they heard shots from behind them. One of the shots hit the fleeing man in his back. He stumbled several times but stayed on his feet. The shooting stopped, and the robbers sped away in the couple's car. On foot, the woman managed to get herself and her wounded boyfriend to the intersection of a busy street where she flagged down a passing taxi. The taxi driver stopped to pick them up and quickly drove them to Grady Hospital where their robbery and stolen car were reported to the police.

Sergeant Richardson was using the phone in the Jim Wallace gas station at Whitehall and McDaniel Streets when Miller and Adams drove the car they had stolen into the station to get gas. Rap music was blasting so loud from the car's stereo system that it could be heard two blocks away (the station attendant heard them coming from that distance). The two got out of the car, dancing, high-fiving, and demanding the attendant, "Hey motherfucker, fill it up. We ain't got time for that shit!" They were creating such a disturbance that the attendant told them there was no gas. Although he was on the phone, Richardson observed what was going on. When the two robbers sped out of the station with their tires squealing, Richardson jumped into his car and went after them. He caught up with them one block away at Peters and McDaniel Streets where they had stopped for a red light. Sergeant Richardson motioned to them to pull off the narrow two-lane street just beyond the railroad tracks and into the abandoned gas station on that corner.

The APD communications section was training a new group of radio dispatchers. One trainee, who was working the radio at the time, did not report information that was crucial to all cars—there was a stolen car, taken by two armed men who had shot one of the victims.

Sergeant Richardson was not warned that the car he had just stopped was stolen, taken in an armed robbery earlier that morning. The couple had reported that they were robbed, their car stolen, and that they were shot at by the two who had stolen their car. They reported this to police at Grady Hospital where the man's gunshot wounds were being attended.

The police dispatcher trainee did not tell Richardson that the occupants of the vehicle he had stopped should be considered armed and dangerous.

Jimmy Richardson was too street-smart, too savvy, to walk up to those two by himself if he had had that information. Richardson asked the driver (Adams) to step out of the car and told the passenger (Miller) to stay put inside the car. Richardson was standing at the rear of the car attempting to get the driver's license and registration from Adams, when Miller suddenly got out of the car and started shooting. Sergeant Richardson turned and ran to find cover but was shot in the back and went down. Miller stood over the wounded Richardson with his gun pointed down at him. Ignoring the sergeant's choked pleading, "Please don't shoot me no more," Miller shot Richardson two more times. Without waiting for Miller, Adams jumped back into the car and sped away heading westbound on McDaniel Street. Miller ran off in the opposite direction.

Some residents in the neighborhood who heard the shooting went to the intersection where they saw Sergeant Richardson lying in the street. One resident got on the police radio and tried to call for help. Another went to a telephone and called for an ambulance. Several calls to report what had happened came into 911.

The cops began arriving within minutes but not before a twelve-year-old in the crowd picked up the gun that lay next to the gravely wounded sergeant. It was Richardson's gun. (The twelve-year-old sold the gun to a third party later in the day for five dollars. Detectives eventually tracked down the gun through a network of informants. Several arrests were made in connection with that stolen gun.)

Adams and Miller met up with each other later that morning. (Adams had wrecked the stolen car, hitting parked cars several times, while trying to distance himself from the scene of the shooting. He finally abandoned it.) They decided to get rid of their guns. Wrapping each gun in his own shirt, they hid the shirt-covered guns in shrubs on a quiet street. One of those shirt-covered bundles was Miller's gun, the weapon used to shoot Sergeant Richardson. Miller quickly got rid of his gun in the bushes and left. Adams hadn't yet left the hiding place when a patrol car rounded the corner and spotted him. By this time, police throughout Atlanta were stopping all black males who fit the witnesses' descriptions. The cops searched through the shrubs and, without difficulty, found the guns wrapped in the shirts.

Adams was arrested on the spot at Windsor and Stephens Streets SW. Without much coaxing, he agreed to give up Miller, not wanting to take the fall himself for shooting a cop. Detectives obtained an arrest warrant for Miller, went to his house, and pulled him out of his bed where he was sound asleep.

James E. Richardson was born on April 10, 1946, in Birmingham, Alabama, where he lived until graduating from high school. During his high school years, he met Sheila Dowdell who was attending a rival high school, which did not get in their way of becoming good friends. After graduating from high school, James Richardson went north to attend the University of Buffalo in New York State. Within a year, he had had enough of the frequent snowstorms, enough of the snow that persisted after each snowstorm, and more than enough of the ice and bitter cold weather. In 1965, he returned to Birmingham and promptly joined the United States Marine Corps. While serving in the Marine Corps, Jimmy Richardson continued a correspondence with Sheila Dowdell. In 1967, halfway through his enlistment in the USMC, Sheila and James were married. During his four years in the U.S. Marines, James Richardson served two tours in Vietnam.

In 1969, after his honorable discharge from the Marine Corps, James and Sheila Richardson moved to Atlanta where James got a job with the Pinkerton Detective Agency. He wasn't happy with the job because it entailed investigating other Pinkerton employees. Doing that made him feel like he was spying on his co-workers. He left Pinkerton and took a job as an aircraft mechanic with Lockheed, a job where he worked when there was work and was laid off when there was not enough work. He had been laid off more total days than he had worked.

By 1970, Richardson had a job that he liked. He was then a police officer with the Atlanta Police Department. He knew right away that police work was what he wanted to do. But as time went on, he began to see things in the APD that disturbed him.

He saw the inequities between the white cops and the black cops. Some of the older white superior officers were seen by the black cops as still having the Jim Crow mentality, affecting who was promoted, who got what were considered favorable assignments and off days, and who got the unfavorable ones. He decided to get involved. The country was in the midst of the civil rights movement and so was Atlanta. Jimmy Richardson joined the Afro-American Patrolman's League where he spent a lot of time and effort as an advocate for the black cops of Atlanta. Eventually, James Richardson became the president of the AAPL.

During Richardson's term as AAPL president, the poor race relations within the Atlanta Police Department's black and white police officers progressively worsened. That began to change when Floyd Reeves, an individual black Atlanta police officer, filed a racial discrimination lawsuit in federal court against the City of Atlanta. This legal action by Reeves was joined by the AAPL. A counter lawsuit was immediately filed in that same court by the Fraternal Order of Police, which represented many white Atlanta police officers. The FOP claimed reverse discrimination, declaring that affirmative action caused preferences to equally or to less qualified black cops over white cops.

Federal judge Charles A. Moye put into effect a hiring and promotional freeze for the Atlanta Police Department. That meant that the APD could not fill any vacant positions or make any promotions. Judge Moye wanted a settlement rather than a trial. He ordered the parties—Floyd Reeves, the AAPL, the FOP, and the City of Atlanta—to negotiate an agreement that would result in a consent decree and resolve all the issues that were brought forth in the lawsuits. The judge also ordered federal mediators in to facilitate the negotiations. Five days a week, at least eight hours each day, for five weeks, Jimmy Richardson, along with the other parties, negotiated, discussed, bargained, haggled, bartered, dickered, met halfway, adjusted differences, came to terms, and settled. At times it became very emotional. But in the end, there was a consent decree. A decree that did not please everyone—but that's the way it is with compromise.

Jimmy Richardson continued his education. He attended Perimeter College in 1978, where he earned an associate's degree in sociology. Two years later, in 1980, Sergeant Richardson was selected to attend the Southern Police Institute in Louisville, Kentucky. The SPI is comparable to the FBI National Academy in Quantico, Virginia, but not as widely known by the general public.

Two months after graduating from SPI, Sergeant James E. Richardson was killed on a dark Atlanta street.

Adams and Miller were tried in Fulton County Superior Court for the murder of Sergeant James E. Richardson, plus aggravated assault, armed robbery, and kidnapping. Adams and Miller each claimed that the other one had shot Sergeant Richardson. Each was found guilty on all counts and sentenced to life in prison.

Sheila Richardson lives with the vivid memory of being awakened from a sound sleep by pounding on the front door, looking out into the darkness, seeing an Atlanta patrol car in the driveway, and a police officer at her door. "I'm sorry, ma'am, but Sergeant Richardson has been shot and I'm here to take you to Grady Hospital!"

The murder of Jimmy Richardson left Sheila a widow and their six-year-old daughter without a father.

SERGEANT
JAMES E. RICHARDSON
"SHOT INVESTIGATING TRAFFIC VIOLATION"
JULY 19, 1980

Atlanta Police Officer

Alfred M. Johnson Jr.

Thirty years later it remains an open homicide of an Atlanta police officer

*A*tlanta police officer Alfred M. Johnson Jr. worked the day watch out of the Zone 1 Precinct in the northwest quadrant of Atlanta. He had just completed his eight-hour tour. He then drove across into Zone 3 territory (which is in Zone 6 now) in the southeast section to the extra job he worked several evenings a week. It was a bitter cold February evening, and Alfred Johnson would have preferred going home after putting in his eight hours as a cop on the streets of Zone 1. But he did what most good men do—he worked an extra job because he wanted to provide better for his family.

The Big Buy Supermarket, an independent neighborhood grocery store that served a low-income neighborhood in Zone 3 (a high-crime area), needed a uniformed police presence to keep the wolves away from its doors.

Most times the uniformed presence succeeded in keeping the wolves at bay.

Sometimes it didn't.

It was a few minutes before seven thirty PM on Saturday, February 16, 1980. The last of the Big Buy customers had been served and gone. The store began closing up for the day. Most businesses in this neighborhood didn't stay open at night.

The doors had not yet closed when two robbers appeared. One stood just inside the front door. The other walked into the store, down an aisle to where Johnson was standing, and pointed a sawed-off shotgun at his chest.

"This is a hold up!"

Johnson attempted to bat the shotgun away. It fired, part of the blast striking him. Nevertheless, Johnson persisted, fighting for possession of the shotgun. The robber who was at the front door approached the scuffle and shot Johnson with a pistol, sending him to the floor. Although seriously wounded, Johnson was able to fire off two rounds from his revolver. His shots went wild, not hitting anyone. He remained where he was, on the floor, unable to move.

The robbers grabbed what was reported to be at least eight hundred dollars in cash and a large amount of food stamps then ran out the front door. They continued running outside, headed toward the rear of the Big Buy building. Half a block away, a car was waiting for them. The robbers jumped in and the car sped off into the darkness.

Zone 3 dispatcher: *"Car 3304, at the Big Buy Supermarket, 470 Flat Shoals Avenue SE, signal 65* [silent hold up alarm directly connected into the APD communications section]."

Car 3304: *"Big Buy Supermarket, 470 Flat Shoals, signal 65."*

Dispatcher: *"3304, it's coming up now signal 50/4* [person shot/ambulance on the way]."

Car 3304: *"Received, signal 50/4."*

Within two minutes, 3304 was back on the air:

Car 3304: *"It was a signal 44* [armed robbery] *and the 50 is to a police officer, give the 4* [ambulance] *a code 3* [rush call] *and start Homicide, ID* [crime scene unit], *and a supervisor."*

More than a dozen Zone 3 patrol cars and detective cars and an ambulance converged on the Big Buy Supermarket. Officer Johnson was quickly loaded into the ambulance and rushed with an escort via a secured route of blocked intersections to Grady Hospital. Upon arrival, he was feverishly tended to by the entire ER trauma team. After being stabilized, the seriously wounded officer was transferred to the operating room. The damage from the shotgun blast and the gunshot wound to his stomach were too severe.

Atlanta police officer Alfred Morris Johnson Jr. died two hours later.

The lookout was generic: two black males, mid to late twenties, one tall, the other short. The description of what they were wearing was bland except that the tall robber, armed with a sawed-off shotgun, was wearing a long dark coat and a white wool hat, cutouts for the eyes, pulled down over his face. The shorter subject, armed with a pistol, had on a leather waist-length jacket and rust-colored pants, no hat, no mask.

What seemed like it could be the first break in the case came within a few days. Atlanta homicide detectives were alerted that a woman living in Macon, Georgia (90 miles south of Atlanta) had received a telephone call from her twenty-three-year-old son, telling her that he was "in big trouble" and that he and a friend had held up a grocery store in Atlanta and "shot a cop." He told her that he needed a place to hide and left a telephone number where he could be reached. She gave the number to detectives who traced it to a bar in Chattanooga, Tennessee.

Atlanta detectives secured a murder warrant for Atlanta resident Clayborn Pounds, a black male, twenty-three years old. Then they notified detectives with the Chattanooga Police Department and asked for their assistance in locating and picking up the suspect. Within three hours, Clayborn Pounds was in the custody of the Chattanooga PD. Atlanta detectives drove to Chattanooga and returned Pounds to Atlanta.

After an intensive interrogation, it became apparent that Clayborn Pounds might not have been connected to the Johnson homicide. He said he told his mother that story because "I wanted her to feel sorry for me and send me some money." There was no evidence, nor were there any witnesses to tie Clayborn Pounds with Officer Johnson's murder. There was never anything more than the phone call to his mother. Nevertheless, Pounds's files with the APD and DeKalb County PD showed that he, Terry Sims, and Clarence McDaniel had committed armed robberies in Atlanta and DeKalb County. Pounds and the two others were promptly arrested by neighboring DeKalb County Police for those robberies and aggravated assaults.

Atlanta homicide detective P. D. Harris, the lead detective, along with other detectives spent more than four thousand hours investigating leads and interviewing hundreds of people for over a year on the Johnson case. They even had the benefit of fifteen thousand dollars in reward money offered, but all the leads were dead ends. Information dried up the longer the case remained open.

In April, 1981, fourteen months later, what appeared to be a promising lead surfaced. A Georgia prison inmate wanted to talk to detectives about the Atlanta police officer who was killed in a robbery over a year ago.

Samuel Carroll, who was doing time for several bank robberies, told Atlanta homicide detectives that his cellmate, Wayne Robinson, told him that he and his partner, Ricky Baker, had robbed a grocery store in Atlanta over a year ago and killed a cop. (Both Robinson and Baker fit the physical descriptions given by the witnesses at the time.)

Sam Carroll went on to say that Wayne Robinson told him that the plan for robbing the grocery store that February evening was for Ricky Baker to "take the police out with a shotgun, so we could rob the store." Carroll went on, "But Ricky fucked up and just half-assed shot him, and then they got to fighting over the shotgun, so I [Robinson] had to go down there and put the cop down with my pistol. We got a few hundred bucks and a whole bunch of food stamps, which we buried in Bowen Homes [a housing project on the other side of Atlanta from the grocery store], figuring we could sell them later when the heat died down."

Carroll continued and said that Robinson told him that he and Baker "holed up in a motel for a few days and watched the news about the police bring some guy back to Atlanta from Chattanooga for killing that cop."

Samuel Carroll was an informant for the Fulton County district attorney Lewis Slaton and would trade information about others' crimes in return for a lighter sentence. He was in prison serving time for bank robbery.

Wayne Robinson, also in prison for bank robbery, told Carroll that a dye bomb had exploded all over him from that bank robbery. A short time later, a woman who lived at the Eagan Homes housing projects observed a man putting a black plastic bag into the nearby dumpster. After the man left, she went to the dumpster and retrieved the bag, which contained some money, a pistol, and a pair of pants—all stained with red dye. She turned these items over to the Fulton County district attorney's office. Several hours later, she saw the same man take a sawed-off shotgun out of the dumpster.

The pistol retrieved from the dumpster was brought to the Georgia State Crime Lab where it was test fired and compared with the bullet taken from the body of Officer Johnson.

The bullets matched.

The match proved that the pistol the man put in the dumpster was the weapon that murdered Officer Johnson. That was significant because, although the shotgun blast did a lot of damage to Johnson's body, it was the pistol round that was fatal.

That pistol, stained with red dye, was the only physical evidence connected to the Johnson murder—but it could not be connected to any suspect. The woman who retrieved the pistol from the dumpster refused to identify the man she saw put it there.

And there were other handicaps to the investigation. The witness at the supermarket, who said she saw the face of one of the killers at the time of the killing, later could not identify him.

Any other evidence was what Samuel Carroll told the detectives. And he repeatedly told the detectives about the confessions Wayne Robinson made in their shared prison cell. In those same conversations, Carroll said Robinson told him that "Peaches," Wayne Robinson's girlfriend, drove the getaway car. When questioned by detectives, Peaches denied being with Robinson that night, insisting that she knew nothing about the robbery/murder except what she saw on the TV news. She said she only knew Wayne Robinson casually and was not his girlfriend.

Wayne Robinson and Ricky baker were questioned extensively, but refused to talk about the Johnson murder. Robinson denied having any conversations about it with Sam Carroll or anyone else.

The City of Atlanta is geographically within Fulton County, except for that area that protrudes like a bubble east of Moreland Avenue into DeKalb County. The Big Buy Supermarket located in that part of Atlanta was under the jurisdiction of DeKalb County. Therefore any criminal prosecution would have to be handled by the DeKalb County district attorney's office.

After several meetings among investigators from both the Fulton DA's and DeKalb DA's offices and APD's Detective Harris and his team, the DeKalb County district attorney declined to present the case to a grand jury for a murder indictment. The reasoning behind the DA's decision was that the murder weapon could not be placed in anyone's hands on the night of the robbery/murder and any potential witness refused to cooperate. All they had was the word of a career criminal wanting to make a "deal" to get his prison sentence reduced.

Thirty-year-old Alfred M. Johnson was a six-year APD veteran on the night he was shot and killed. A native of Decatur, in neighboring DeKalb County, he attended high school there. Following graduation, he joined the United States Marine Corps. During his four-year tour in the USMC, he saw combat in Vietnam. Upon his honorable discharge from the military, he applied for and was accepted by the Atlanta Police Department.

Alfred Johnson's wife, Mildred, was left a widow with two young daughters, Tanya, five, and Kessa, two.

Neither Wayne Robinson nor Ricky Baker, nor anyone else, was ever held accountable for the murder of Atlanta police officer Alfred M. Johnson. Thirty years later, his death still remains an open homicide of an Atlanta police officer.

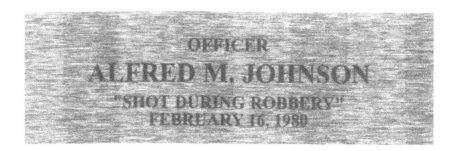

OFFICER
ALFRED M. JOHNSON
"SHOT DURING ROBBERY"
FEBRUARY 16, 1980

Atlanta Police Officer

Frank Robert Schlatt

It did not always work the way it was supposed to work

One-man patrol cars.

What was the City of Atlanta . . . what was the Atlanta Police Department . . . what were they expecting to gain from patrol cars with only one cop in each? The answers to those questions coming from the police Chief's office was, that with one officer in each car, twice the number of patrol cars would be on the streets for greater police visibility.

Neither the city nor the APD could have been considering the safety that one officer provides the other when two cops patrol in one car. Nor could they have been considering how vulnerable one cop alone can be when responding to an innocent call that can immediately turn violent. Nor the obviously dangerous call where backup is too far to arrive in time to be of help.

The decision to make this change, which was put into effect in the early 1960s, resulted in outrage and protest from police officers, their wives, the media, civic groups, and even from most of the general public. But none of that, nothing, deterred Police Chief Herbert T. Jenkins. "If you don't like it, go find a job somewhere else" was pretty much the chief's response to those cops who voiced their displeasure.

Chief Jenkins considered himself an innovator. "A man ahead of his time," he was reported to have said about himself. In 1948, he hired eight Negro Atlanta police officers to work in a very racially segregated South. This did not evoke happiness with the majority white population of Atlanta.

All this was happening against a deeply ingrained tradition in police departments around the country, at a time when the psychological makeup of police officers resisted change for tradition. However, changes did occur—slowly. Changes that provided the public with better law enforcement. The Atlanta Police Department decentralized. Instead of every function, every person, every piece of equipment operating out of one central headquarters building, precincts (zones) were established around the city to provide more localized police services. Radio communications improved as technology advanced, enabling quicker response time to calls for service.

But the APD's change from two officers to one per patrol car did not provide the public with better law enforcement. Some veteran cops were leaving the APD solely for that reason to join surrounding police departments where there were two cops per car. These veterans took their experience with them. Other cops grumbled, morale plummeted, adversely affecting "to protect and serve."

The consequences of the change were severe and tragic for several Atlanta police officers.

Officer Frank Schlatt was one of those police officers.

Frank Robert Schlatt, a five-year APD veteran, worked the day watch out of the Zone 1 Precinct, one of the larger zones covering the northwest quadrant of the City of Atlanta. Diversity characterized Zone 1, from some of the most violent housing projects in Atlanta to the fringes of the more affluent Buckhead section. Schlatt's regular assignment was beat 107, an area largely made up of modest homes, small businesses, light industry, and several housing projects. He worked car 107—and like all other Atlanta cops assigned to patrol cars—he worked it by himself.

The way the APD justified the soundness of one-cop patrol cars was this: If the dispatcher sensed something that didn't seem quite valid, that had some suspicious motive beyond the purported need of the 911 caller, or clearly could result in violence, then a second car from an adjoining beat would be dispatched as a backup. This policy appeared to the media and to the taxpaying citizens of Atlanta that it would work. But it did not always work the way it was supposed to work.

One problem with this policy was that it depended on the keenness of the dispatcher, as well as on other cars hearing a call, to sense the need for sending backup.

There were times when the backup car was already tied up on a call.

There were times when the backup car was too far away to respond fast enough to provide needed backup.

And there were times when a one-officer car on a routine patrol rounded a corner into an erupting violent situation that required immediate action, leaving no time to call for backup.

Each of these situations was real, they did occur. But not many were covered to any extent in the media. So taxpayers did not learn about them.

Warren McCleskey, Bernard Dupree, David Burney Jr., and Ben Wright Jr. were thieves. They were members of a crew that worked together robbing small businesses. This quartet of black males ranged from thirty-two to forty-four years of age. Each had served a number of years in prison for felony crimes, mostly armed robbery, plus a variety of other property and violent crimes. They were career criminals.

On the mild spring Saturday morning of May 13, 1978, Warren McCleskey drove his 1971 black Pontiac Grand Prix two-door hardtop around Atlanta picking up, one by one, Dupree, Burney, and Wright. When the fourth was in McCleskey's car, the crew was complete, ready to work. They cruised through the streets of Atlanta looking for a place to rob. After several hours of searching, discussing, and debating about what store would be the best target, they decided on the Dixie Furniture Company at 993 Marietta Street NW, a modest furniture store less than a mile from the fringe of the downtown area. They chose Dixie Furniture because it did a cash-only business, no credit cards, and therefore should have plenty of money on hand.

McCleskey walked into the store, appearing to be a prospective customer. He was really checking if the store had an armed security guard. The other three were waiting in the Grand Prix parked out of sight. McCleskey spoke to a woman employee about a bed he said he was considering purchasing. He left a few minutes later to rejoin the three in the car.

"It's okay, let's do it!" They gathered their equipment—guns, stocking masks to hide their faces, and tape to tie up the employees and customers. The plan was for McCleskey to go in through the front door, take control of anyone in the front of the store, and order them to lie down on the floor. The other three would enter the rear of the store through the loading dock and take control of anyone in the back, the same way as McCleskey would do in the front.

A secretary saw the start of what was going on. She hit the silent hold-up alarm button that registered at the Wells Fargo alarm company. Wells Fargo in turn notified Atlanta police. (Most times these alarm calls are "false alarms" due to accidental or unwarranted triggering, like lightning storms or technical malfunctions. Cops tend to treat these alarm calls too casually because too many turn out to be false alarms.)

Police radio: *"Car 107, 993 Marietta Street, signal 3* [silent alarm] *at the Dixie Furniture Company."*
Unit 107 (Schlatt): *"Okay."*
Radio: *"107, be advised this is a hold-up alarm, Wells Fargo is on the way."*
Unit 107 (Schlatt): *"Received."*
Unit 104: *"What is 7's call?"*
Radio: *"104, that will be signal 3 at 993 Marietta Street, Dixie Furniture Company."*
Unit 107 (Schlatt): *"I'm 26* [arrived on call].*"*

As the three robbers in the rear of the store were tying up the employees and taking the money from the manager, McCleskey was up front holding the customers on the floor at gunpoint and watching the front door. Less than two minutes later, Officer Frank Schlatt pulled up in car 107, got out, drew his service revolver, and came through the front door—alone!

At this point, the objections against the one-officer patrol car are obvious. Schlatt arrived on call in less than two minutes and decided to enter the store without backup. That backup—those adjacent beat cars—were either on call elsewhere or too far away to respond to the call to act as backup. Or they considered that Schlatt was likely only responding to another false alarm.

Having seen Schlatt pull up and enter with his gun drawn, McCleskey knelt behind a showroom sofa to get out of sight. Schlatt entered the store and started walking toward the rear. McCleskey jumped up from behind the sofa. He fired two close range shots at Schlatt—striking him in the eye. Schlatt went down. And McCleskey bolted out the front door to his car. The other three robbers heard the gunfire and ran out the back door. All four jumped into the car and sped away.

Unit 108: *"Ask 107 is there anything to it?"*
Radio: *"107."*
(No answer.)
Radio: *"107."*
(No answer.)
Radio: *"Calling car 107."*
(No answer.)
Radio: *"108, I am unable to raise 107."*
Unit 109: *"Is anybody with 107?"*
Radio: *"108?"*
Unit 108: *"Negative."*
Radio: *"Negative, 109."*
Radio: *"105, start for 993 Marietta Street, signal 3, hold up alarm. 107 is handling that call."*
Unit 105: *"Received, 993 Marietta Street. Is 107, 26 [arrived] on the call?"*
Radio: *"Affirmative."*
Radio: *"107."*
(No answer.)
Unit 104: *"107 still hasn't answered?"*
Radio: *"Negative, 104."*
Radio: *"107."*
Unit 105: *"Raise 104."*
Unit 104: *"Go ahead."*
Unit 105: *"105 to 104, I'm northbound behind Grady. If you can, go ahead and start to that location."*
Unit 104: *"I'm on the way."*
Radio: *"104."*
Unit 104: *"Go ahead."*
Radio: *"104, how far away from 993 Marietta are you?"*
Unit 104: *"Almost 26."*
Radio: *"Received, 104."*
Radio: *"104, be advised the call at 993 Marietta is coming up a 44/50 [robbery/person shot]."*
Radio: *"104, you receive?"*
Unit 150 (first sergeant to respond): *"Where is the 44/50?"*

Radio: *"993 Marietta Street."*

Unit 104: *"What is the name of the business?"*

Unit 155 (second sergeant to respond): *"Did 107 ever answer?"*

Radio: *"Negative."*

Unit 104: *"What is the name of the business at 993?"*

Radio: *"Dixie Furniture Company."*

Unit 155 (second sergeant): *"155 to radio."*

Radio: *"Go ahead."*

Unit 155 (second sergeant): *"If you can't raise him, put in a 63* [officer needs help]*."*

Unit 103: *"I'm on the way over there, what's the name of the business?"*

Radio: *"Dixie Furniture Company."*

Unit 108: *"I need an ambulance at Dixie Furniture, code 3, code 3* [rush call]*!"*

Radio: *"Received."*

Unit 108: *"Start Homicide out here and 104."*

Unit 115: *"I'm on the way."*

Unit 105: *"Give me some more cars, code 3."*

Radio: *"Received."*

Unit 105: *"Have 155* [second sergeant] *make a 59* [meet an officer] *over here right away."*

Unit 104: *"Call Fire Rescue. Get them out here as quick as you can."*

Radio: *"Received."*

Radio: *"155."*

Unit 155 (second sergeant): *"Is the officer okay?"* (Sirens in the background.)

Unit 155 (second sergeant): *"155 to radio!"*

Radio: *"Go ahead."*

Unit 155 (second sergeant): *"Advise on the police officer, is he okay?"*

Unit 105: *"It's gonna be a signal 50* [person shot] *on a police officer."*

Unit 155 (second sergeant): *"Have him repeat."* (Sirens in the background.)

Radio: *"155, signal 50 on a police officer."*

Unit 155 (second sergeant): *"Okay."*

Unit 160 (lieutenant): *"Received."*

Unit 104: *"104 with a 78 [lookout]."*

Radio: *"Go ahead."*

Unit 104: *"Tall black male, glasses, plaid shirt, dark pants, will be in the area. He'll be armed, wanted for a signal 50 on a police officer. He's gonna have a bumpy complexion."*

Radio: *"Received."*

Unit 160 (lieutenant): *"Ask him if the officer is serious?"*

Unit 108: *"That's affirmative . . . shot in the head."*

Unit 104: *"Have that ambulance come on!"* (Sirens in the background.)

Unit 155 (second sergeant): *"Get me some Zone 5 cars up there in the area also, there's enough cars on the scene. Have them circle the area."*

Unit 104: *"Have that 4 [ambulance] come on."*

Radio: *"Okay, 104."*

Unit 114: *"Can you have the officer repeat the lookout?"*

Radio: *"Cars around 993 Marietta Street, be on the lookout for a tall black male, subject will be wearing glasses, plaid shirt, dark pants, and have a bumpy complexion. Signal 69 [person armed], wanted for signal 50 [person shot] on a police officer."*

Unit 160 (lieutenant): *"Does he have a direction of travel?"*

Unit 104: *"They didn't see him leave."*

Radio: *"Be advised, no direction of travel."*

Radio: *"150 [first sergeant], do you want to pull in Zone 5 cars?"*

Unit 150 (first sergeant): *"Affirmative, pull in everything you got around there."*

Unit 104: *"See if you can get the cars to open the road for the ambulance. Get them to block the road so the ambulance can come on through."*

Unit 155 (second sergeant): *"Deploy some cars all from here to keep the intersections open. Tell the ambulance to come on!"*

Unit 103: *"Check on that 4 [ambulance], tell them to hurry it up."*

Radio: *"Okay, they advised it's Metro [private contract ambulance] going code 3 [rush call]."*

Unit 155 (second sergeant): *"Have the Zone 5 cars and other units to check in the area for the perpetrator. We got everything we need here."*

Unit 113: *"Which way you got Metro ambulance coming from?"*

Radio: *"Standby. We're trying to locate them."*

Unit 155 (second sergeant): *"Radio, give me the lookout that you have now."*

Radio: *"Tall black male, glasses, plaid shirt, dark pants, bumpy complexion."*

Unit 155 (second sergeant): *"Also, lookout on a black male, 200 pounds, brown shirt, white—correction, brown pants, white T-shirt. Subject ran west on, I believe it's west on Jefferson Street, from this location."*

Radio: *"Okay, 155."*

Unit 116: *"I'm on Jefferson, what's the lookout on Jefferson?"*

Radio: *"Okay, black male, 200 pounds, brown pants, white T-shirt, west on Jefferson."*

Unit 155 (second sergeant): *"Continue both lookouts. We don't know which subject is which."*

Unit 150 (first sergeant): *"You can cancel that Metro ambulance. The officer is on the way to Grady now in the Fire Rescue unit. Advise the units working the intersections that they are coming now, leaving the location now!"*

Unit 110: *"I am going to block Northside Drive and Marietta."*

Unit 113: *"I got Bankhead and Marietta . . ."*

The fire and police vehicles, a screaming motorcade, went down Marietta Street and through the heart of downtown, racing toward Grady Memorial Hospital. Everything and everyone froze as the vehicles rushed by. Was it a bad wreck? A heart attack? A fireman injured? Or maybe a police officer wounded? The hospital had been notified that a wounded police officer was being transported, and the emergency team was waiting on the ambulance ramp. They would, in a few minutes, be engaged in medical combat in a fight to save a gravely wounded cop's life. The doctors lost the battle. Frank Schlatt died in the operating room about three hours after he had been shot in the right eye. The bullet caused irreparable damage to his brain.

The public would learn on the six o'clock news that day who had been transported by the screaming emergency vehicles. Atlanta police officer Frank Schlatt had answered a silent hold-up alarm. He walked in on an armed robbery in progress at a local furniture store. He was shot by one of four robbers as he entered the store—alone. There had been no time to call for backup.

As always, whenever a police officer is killed, all available resources are employed to identify and apprehend the killer(s). There would be no peace in the underbelly of society—informants, pimps, prostitutes, dopers, gangbangers, and the rest of the sludge on the streets were being hassled, harassed, and hounded by the Atlanta police. There was no business as usual on the streets until names were provided in the murder of Officer Frank Schlatt.

The same quartet continued to rob businesses around the Atlanta metro area during the months that followed Officer Schlatt's murder. Warren McCleskey and Bernard Dupree robbed a convenience store and were apprehended as they were attempting to leave. Apprehended because what was supposed to work—and often didn't—worked this time.

A silent alarm had signaled APD Communications that a robbery might be in progress at the convenience store. The dispatcher gave the call to the beat car. Two of the adjacent beat cars heard the call and reacted promptly. They arrived as backup and were there to assist the first beat car to apprehend McCleskey and Dupree. Three patrol cars responded and arrived simultaneously, putting an end to any thoughts by the two robbers of a shoot-out with the cops. (The memory of Frank Schlatt arriving alone to a silent alarm was still fresh in the minds of most cops. Surely it was fresh in the minds of these cops who arrived promptly as backup.)

McCleskey and Dupree were placed in the Fulton County Jail until their cases could be heard by the court. They were put in separate cells on different floors, one cell directly above the other.

As in many jails and prisons, inmates will find a way to communicate with one another. In the Fulton County Jail,

McCleskey stood on the sink in his cell and talked into the vent in the ceiling. It was connected to the vent in the floor of Dupree's cell above. Their conversations centered on the Dixie Furniture robbery and the killing of Officer Schlatt three months prior.

Meanwhile, the pressure being applied to the streets by detectives for the identities of those involved in the Schlatt killing had started to bring results. The same four names—McCleskey, Dupree, Burney, and Wright—were being whispered, over and over, first by the streets' underbelly and then by detectives' informants. After McCleskey and Dupree were arrested for the convenience store robbery, they were questioned separately by detectives. The detectives told both of them the names of the four who had robbed Dixie Furniture when Officer Schlatt was shot and killed. Dupree denied knowing anything about it.

When McCleskey was questioned by police, he was confronted with the names of the four, including his own, in the furniture store robbery and killing. He admitted to being with the others at the store at that time. But he denied shooting the officer. He said, "I seen the police pull up outside and then come in the front door. I was hiding down behind a couch and watched him walk past me going to the back. I bolted. And when I got to the front door, I heard two shots and I kept running till I got to the car. The others got there and we hauled ass out of there."

When Dupree was questioned a second time, the detectives informed Dupree that McCleskey made a written statement admitting to taking part in the Dixie Furniture robbery. He named Dupree, Burney, and Wright as the other three. They told Dupree that McCleskey said he didn't know which of the three shot the police officer.

Dupree was angry with McCleskey for admitting to the detectives that the four were robbing the store when Officer Schlatt was killed.

"You know damn well you shot the police and now you are putting it on us," Dupree hissed at McCleskey down through the vent. "When it's my turn again, I'm damn sure let the police know you was the triggerman."

McCleskey answered, "I was scared man. It's one thing to do time for robbery, but you get the chair for killing a police."

These vent conversations were heard by McCleskey's cellmate, Offie Gene Evans, who later gave a twenty-one page written statement detailing what he had heard. In that statement, Evans related what McCleskey had told him (Evans):

McCleskey said that about that time the police walked in the store. But the police didn't act like he was coming in for no robbery. But he said that he did see the police put the hand on his gun. And he said that he knowed right then that it was going to have to be him or McCleskey, one. 'Cause the police was headed toward where Ben was back there. And McCleskey said that he panicked, he just shot. McCleskey did not say how many times he shot or nothing.

Warren McCleskey, Bernard Dupree, David Burney, and Ben Wright were arrested and charged with at least six armed robberies, including the Dixie Furniture robbery, and for the murder of Atlanta police officer Frank Schlatt.

The murder weapon, the .38 caliber Rossi revolver, was never found. McCleskey admitted to throwing it in the Chattahoochee River shortly after the robbery/murder. McCleskey had stolen the revolver in a previous robbery and kept it as his weapon. The victim of that robbery had reported that one of the robbers had stolen his .38 caliber Rossi revolver. The bullet taken from the body of Frank Schlatt was fired from a .38 caliber Rossi revolver.

Three of the four robbers were given lengthy prison sentences for several counts of armed robbery, plus being accomplices to murder.

Dupree, Burney, and Wright each named Warren McCleskey as the triggerman in the murder of Officer Frank Schlatt.

McCleskey was found guilty of murder and sentenced to death in the electric chair.

Warren McCleskey was executed in the electric chair. That was shortly before the courts ruled that death by electrocution was cruel and unusual punishment.

Frank Schlatt left behind a wife and a young daughter. He is buried in his native Allegheny County, Pennsylvania, near Pittsburgh.

OFFICER
FRANK SCHLATT
"SHOT INVESTIGATING ROBBERY"
MAY 13, 1978

Atlanta Police Officer

Barry Dean Melear

The sergeant agreed, "One hour—no more!"

The shattered glass on the ground beside the car reflected the lights of the city like a mosaic of the section of downtown Atlanta where people went to enjoy an evening out. Shattered glass was scattered over the interior. It was on the seats, over the floor. What was once a car window was now an open space that allowed uninvited admission for anyone with a mind to enter.

The couple returned to their car after an evening of dinner and entertainment. Their car had been broken into. Some of their possessions were gone.

They called the police and told the operator what had happened. They were switched to another faceless voice. That faceless voice took the information for the report over the telephone. The crimes of "entering an auto" and "theft by taking" did not warrant the response of a patrol car. Those crimes are not as serious as murder, rape, armed robbery, and aggravated assault—all crimes where life is threatened or bodily injury suffered.

However, their lives are now turned upside down having lost their wallet and purse and everything inside them: driver's licenses, credit cards, checkbook, cash. Gone. The more severe losses will be their social security cards, ATM pin numbers, irreplaceable personal papers, items of monetary value, and any personal items of sentimental value. All gone.

It wasn't only at nighttime in Atlanta's restaurant and entertainment districts where cars were being broken into and contents stolen. It also occurred during the daytime. Downtown office workers returning to their cars after work also suffered the anxieties that came with the sight of shattered glass that had once been a car window.

It was infuriating, and it was frustrating, not only for victims but to all those who considered themselves vulnerable to this kind of crime. They felt, not unreasonably, "Where were the police when this was happening?"

The Atlanta Police Department, aware that this kind of crime was increasing, was also aware that this kind of crime was a growing problem for the City of Atlanta and all its citizens and visitors. In response, the APD dedicated a unit of the Special Operations Section to deal with it.

Two members of that unit were Atlanta police officers B. D. Melear and W. C. Stalcup.

Barry Melear and Bill Stalcup were partners. Partners who did not wear the traditional blue APD police uniform. They wore jeans, sneakers, T-shirts, and sweatshirts. They did not patrol in a marked patrol car. They patrolled in an unmarked utility-type van. They were two white males in their mid to late twenties. Two unremarkable, "vanilla" looking guys who blended into the cityscape.

Melear, Stalcup, and other cops in plainclothes and plain vehicles were out day and night keeping surveillance on the many parking lots and decks throughout downtown and midtown. Their mission was to stop the hemorrhaging of stolen items from parked cars. The objective of this special operations unit was to apprehend the thieves, and in doing so, to discourage other thieves from thinking they could continue to get away with these crimes. This ongoing effort was draining the resources of an already understaffed police department.

It became clear to Melear and Stalcup that the parking lots they had under surveillance were being checked out by three young black males: George Will Hunter, age nineteen, Arthur James Swackard, age nineteen, and his cousin Marvin Luther Swackard, a sixteen-year-old juvenile. These three had been breaking into parked cars and taking such items as laptops, purses, cell phones, cameras, and whatever other valuable-looking items that had been left in the cars and were easily visible through the windows. It was common for thieves like Hunter and the Swackards to roam the parking lots "window shopping" for such easy takings.

The three had come downtown to rob someone, not to break into a parked car and steal its contents. That's why Hunter and the older Swackard were armed with handguns. They were following a potential victim, a middle-aged white male, down one of the dark side streets. He entered the YMCA before they could get to him. That opportunity to rob gone, Hunter and the Swackards decided to see what they could steal from the cars in the parking lots.

Officers Barry Melear and Bill Stalcup had apprehended their share of car burglars, either in the act or not long after, with the stolen items still in the thieves' possessions. But that was little comfort to targets of the thieves who got away. Being able to provide some degree of comfort to potential targets was the only motivation Melear and Stalcup needed to apprehend as many car burglars as they could.

It was September 23, 1977, Friday morning, about one thirty AM, when Melear and Stalcup were cruising through the downtown streets in their van. They were near the Omni Coliseum looking for any type of illegal activity. Their focus was on the parking lots for signs of thieves breaking into cars, when they spotted George Hunter and the cousins Arthur and Marvin Swackard walking slowly between the cars through the parking lot at Walton Street and Techwood Drive. The two veteran plainclothes cops, experienced and street savvy, were able to read the body language of the window shoppers and concluded that these three were potential car burglars.

Lacking any probable cause to detain and question them, Melear and Stalcup decided to play the cat-and-mouse game, so they followed the trio undetected, waiting for them to attempt to break into a car. After roaming through several parking lots, the three stopped at a car in a parking lot at Marietta Street and International Boulevard.

Officers Melear and Stalcup observed them as they started to break into a car. The cops drove their van into the lot and directly toward the three thieves. The trio bolted. They ran from the lot through alleyways, down city streets, and across other parking lots. They could not outrun the van chasing them. They stopped running at the corner of Techwood Drive and Nassau Street. Melear and Stalcup were able to keep them in sight during their short-lived flight and confronted them at the intersection.

Melear, who was riding in the passenger seat, jumped out of the van with his gun in one hand and his badge in the other and identified himself as a police officer. He ordered the three to put their hands up and to lean against the side of the van. Bill Stalcup came around from the driver's side and started to search the first of the three as Melear stood back. Stalcup removed a plastic bag of marijuana from the pants pocket of Arthur Swackard and handed it back to Melear. As Stalcup handed it backward, George Hunter turned, pistol in hand, and started shooting.

Barry Melear was hit in the temple and went down. Hunter turned the gun on Stalcup. Stalcup grabbed Arthur Swackard and fell backward into the doorway of the van, pulling Swackard on top of him. Hunter fired but didn't hit Stalcup. Swackard broke free of Stalcup's grasp, and the thieves took off running. As Hunter ran, he turned back to shoot at Stalcup. Stalcup chased after them and returned fire.

In all the chaos, Stalcup realized that his partner was not running alongside him. He paused, looked back, and saw Melear lying on the ground next to the van. He hurried back to the van and got on his radio:

Stalcup: *"My partner's been shot in the head, need an ambulance code 3* [rush call]! *We're at Techwood and Nassau and start some cars this way!"*

Dispatcher: *"Cars around Techwood Drive and Nassau Street, signal 63/50/4* [officer needs help/person shot/ambulance on the way]."

Detective unit: *"We're at Marietta and Williams and hear signal 25s* [gunshots]."

Dispatcher (on all frequencies): *"Cars en route to the 63, be advised there are 25s in the area."*

Stalcup: *"Three teenage black males running on Nassau towards Spring Street, signal 69* [person armed] *handgun, wanted for signal 50* [person shot] *on a police officer."*

Police unit: *"I have a young black male on the ground in the parking lot at Spring and Luckie. It looks like he's bleeding from a gunshot wound, start a signal 4* [ambulance]. *I've also recovered a handgun."*

George Hunter had been hit in the side by one of Stalcup's bullets and could run no farther than the parking lot where police found him. (The gun found with Hunter, a Llama .380 caliber semi-automatic pistol, was later determined by ballistics to be the same gun that fired the bullet that struck Melear.)

Hunter was transported to Grady Hospital and pronounced DOA. A short time afterward, a police officer found the Swackard cousins hiding in the alley of a parking lot at Poplar and Cone Streets. When the cop's flashlight lit them up, the older Swackard pleaded, "Please don't shoot, we didn't do anything!" Arthur Swackard's gun, a .22 caliber RG 14, commonly referred to as a "Saturday night special," was later found on Nassau Street where it was dropped as he was running. It had not been fired. (The RG 14 was the cheapest and most easily available gun and most often used in street corner or barroom shootings on Saturday nights.)

Officer Barry Melear was rushed by ambulance with a police escort to Grady Hospital where he was pronounced DOA.

Notifying the family fell to Sergeant J. W. Hagin, Melear's immediate supervisor, who made the call to his parents. Sergeant Hagin informed them that Barry had been shot and was at Grady Hospital. He offered to send a car to pick them up at their residence some fifty miles west of Atlanta. They declined, saying that they would drive themselves. When Mr. and Mrs. Melear arrived at the hospital, they were met by the police chaplain who took them to the family room. There they learned what they might not have wanted to anticipate during those fifty miles—that their son had been shot and killed while performing his duty as an Atlanta police officer.

Barry Dean Melear was twenty-nine years old when he was killed. He was originally from Carrollton and later from Bremen, both small Georgia towns west of Atlanta near the Georgia-Alabama state line. Prior to his six years with the Atlanta police, Barry Melear attended college, did a hitch in the United States Army, and followed that with work as a lab tech in Chattanooga for a short time. When he returned to Atlanta, he joined the Atlanta Police Department.

Melear's personality was what some people referred to as "introverted." He came across as standoffish, aloof, and cold. There were those who called him the "Iceman." He chose to have a close circle of good friends. The closest of them was fellow police officer Bill Dawkins. They worked patrol cars in adjacent beats for a long time, answering calls together, forming that special bond known only to partners. More than once, Melear confided to Dawkins, "Bill, I don't think I'll ever see my thirtieth birthday!"

For working Southside cars, a regular break stop for them was the Dunkin' Donuts on Stewart Avenue and Fair Street. Melear would stop several times during a shift for another jolt of caffeine— he was a coffee addict. Not only did Melear and Dawkins respond to each other's calls, they also spent a lot of down time together. At times they got on each other's nerves. One night during a coffee break while standing outside their patrol cars in the Dunkin' Donuts' parking lot, they argued about something. They usually had different opinions and outlooks on issues. Sometimes the issues were unimportant, sometimes they were major. This time, whatever the issue was, they were on different sides of it and each got angry with the other. They agreed to settle their differences about whatever it was they were arguing about "like men." Each got into his car, drove across the street from the Dunkin' Donuts to a large dirt field, jumped out of their cars, took off their Sam Brown belts with all their equipment, and started fighting.

The fighting was not so much slugging each other as it was grabbing, pushing, and shoving. Melear and Dawkins fell to the ground in each other's grasp where their fighting turned into wrestling around in the red Georgia dirt, muddy from an earlier rain shower. Because each was not wrestling or apprehending a criminal, a thug, neither one's bloodstream was pumping the adrenaline that would have kept them going, going until such a thug was completely restrained. Melear and Dawkins were professional colleagues who had disagreed. There was no adrenaline. Within a few minutes, each was out of breath. Pushing away from the other and still on the ground, sitting now, they started laughing at themselves. They were covered with red mud.

Dawkins said, "We can't answer calls looking like this."

Melear, still chuckling, said, "What about that Grady nurse who lives near here? She shouldn't be working now. Let's call and see if she's at home."

They called her. She answered the phone. They explained their need, and she told them that they could come over to clean up. Then they telephoned the communications sergeant and explained the situation to him—although they didn't go into too much detail about it—and asked if their calls could be diverted to the other cars in their vicinity for one hour. The sergeant agreed, "One hour, no more!"

Most police officers have had these kinds of experiences, embarrassing experiences, mostly on the job, involving themselves, a partner, or both. Sharing experiences like this among cops evokes laughter from everyone who hears them. It's cop humor. That's what it is. It's part of the fabric that clothes cops. It can't be seen, like the cop's uniform, but it's there.

Now Barry Melear can no longer join in the laughter, whether about himself or about some other cop. That ended for him one night on a downtown Atlanta street corner.

OFFICER
BARRY MELEAR
"SHOT DURING ROBBERY"
SEPTEMBER 23, 1977

Atlanta Police Detective

Ernest L. Wilson

Working auto theft kept him distant from the fray

Atlanta police detective Ernest L. Wilson was an auto theft detective—the perfect assignment for him.

Working auto theft was like working a white-collar job—not quite a desk job, but a desk was where an auto theft detective spent a lot of time doing his job. That desk was away from the streets, away from the dangers of the streets, the dangers that every police officer faces during his or her first few years in the APD.

Auto theft detectives, like other detectives, don't wear police uniforms, nor do they experience the excitement of driving a patrol car from one call to another. They do not experience the adrenaline rush that comes from the unexpected that often occurs when responding to a call. Some cops don't want to give up any of that—they are content to remain cops on the streets their entire careers.

Officer E. L. Wilson worked on the streets like other cops during his early years. He welcomed the change of pace the day he got his gold detective shield. He had an easy-going, quiet, mild-mannered personality. He never raised his voice, never displayed anger. Some of his colleagues considered Wilson a loner. He was satisfied working auto theft because it kept him distant from the fray that, in one way or another, entangled most cops during the days, sometimes all day long.

But, like most cops, Detective Wilson had to work an extra job. That approved extra job was at Gold's Antiques Auction on Lee Street in southwest Atlanta. He worked there every Tuesday evening, which was one of his off days from the APD. He worked that extra job in his police uniform, directing vehicular and pedestrian traffic in and around the auction area. He also maintained some semblance of an orderly flow of traffic within the adjacent parking lot. Wilson's uniformed presence also served as a deterrent to car break-ins and muggings. This extra job was uneventful. Wilson liked it that way.

Ernest Walls, a twenty-five-year-old black male, and Erwin Charles Crenshaw, a twenty-eight-year-old black male, were both career criminals with records indicating a lengthy history of crime. Ernest Walls was wanted in Detroit, Michigan, for several armed robberies. Erwin Crenshaw's record was with Atlanta, primarily for armed robbery. Both had committed a string of gas station robberies in Atlanta.

On Tuesday evening, April 27, 1976, Walls and Crenshaw were driving around looking for a gas station to rob.

On Tuesday evening, April 27, 1976, Detective E. L. Wilson was working his extra job at Gold's Antiques Auction.

It was about seven PM when Wilson realized that the parking lot was filling up quickly. He went to the adjacent Gulf service station to ask someone there if it would be okay for the overflow cars to park on the service station's lot for a few hours.

It was about seven PM when Walls and Crenshaw, in Crenshaw's 1966 dark blue Ford Fairlane, the right front fender missing, decided to rob the Gulf station at the corner of Lee Street and White Oak Avenue. They chose it for two reasons: only one attendant was on duty in the office and they could park their Fairlane, motor still running, on the side street that boarded the Gulf station where they could easily getaway.

Walls told Crenshaw to park the car facing away from Lee Street, which was busy with traffic going to Gold's Auction. He instructed Crenshaw to wait at the curb, behind the wheel, with the engine running.

Walls got out of the car. He walked around the corner and across the Gulf station's lot. Jeffery Parker, the nineteen-year-old attendant, was in the small office at the front of the station when Walls walked in and asked to use the restroom. Parker directed him outside and to the side of the building where the restrooms were located. A few minutes later, Walls returned and asked Parker for a pack of cigarettes. Parker went to the cigarette rack behind the counter. When Parker turned back toward Walls, Walls was pointing a gun at him. He demanded the money in the cash register. Parker complied and took all the bills from the register.

At that moment, Detective Wilson, who was in his police uniform, walked toward the Gulf station's small office to ask for the okay to park the overflow cars in the Gulf's lot. Walls and Parker saw Wilson approaching the office. Walls told Parker, "Be cool."

Wilson entered the office and stood directly behind Walls, expecting an opportunity to ask for the okay to park the cars. Wilson saw that Parker was staring at him. He saw that Parker had a handful of cash. Maybe Parker was staring at him because he was afraid to say something about the money and the man who was standing before him.

Wilson started to step aside so he could see Walls's front better. That was when Wilson saw the gun in Walls's hand. Walls spun around and shot Wilson in the neck. Wilson went down. Walls shot Wilson again. This time in the back.

Walls grabbed the money from Parker and ran out the front door and around the corner to the waiting Fairlane. Walls jumped in. Crenshaw sped down White Oak Avenue away from Lee Street and the Gulf station.

A patrol car and a paddy wagon were one block away at Lee and Tucker Streets when a car pulled up to them. The driver told the two cops that someone had just been shot at the Gulf station down the street at White Oak. It took those two cops thirty seconds to get to the Gulf station. They saw a police officer on the ground. From the waist down, he was lying out of the gas station office; from the waist up, he was lying inside the office.

Car 3403: *"Signal 63/50* [officer needs help/person shot] *at the Gulf station, Lee and White Oak. Need a 4* [ambulance] *code 3* [rush call], *a police officer has been shot!"*
Dispatcher: *"Any car near Lee Street and White Oak Avenue at the Gulf service station, signal 63/50/4. The 50 is on a police officer!"*

Arriving patrol cars and detective cars jammed in and around the Gulf station. The ambulance soon followed. Wilson was quickly loaded into the ambulance and rushed to Grady Hospital, patrol cars and motorcycles clearing the way.

Detective E. L. Wilson was pronounced DOA at Grady Hospital.

Jeffery Parker, the Gulf station attendant, provided a detailed description of the shooter. The description was broadcast over all police radio frequencies, while police officers and detectives canvassed the immediate area seeking any additional information that might help locate and apprehend the robbers.

Residents of a house on White Oak Avenue, around the corner from the Gulf station, told police that they had observed a car pull into their driveway, back out to turn around, and park at the curb in front of their house. They saw Walls get out and walk in the direction of Lee Street while Crenshaw remained in the car behind the wheel. A short time later, they said they observed Walls run toward the car, jump in, and then the car sped away. They described the car as a dark blue 1965-66 Ford Fairlane missing the right front fender, a brown baby seat in the backseat. This information was added to the lookout.

They were still racing away from the Gulf station when Walls said to Crenshaw, "I fucked up! I shot a cop! I had no choice! I had to kill him!" He told Crenshaw to drive to 82 Moreland Avenue where Walls's wife, Sylvia Heard, lived. After arriving at the house, Crenshaw parked the car in the rear. They both went in through the back door. Sylvia was home. Walls gave her ten dollars and told her to go out and buy some liquor. (That was ten dollars of the sixty-one dollars taken in the Gulf station robbery.) Crenshaw gave Sylvia the keys to his car. She drove to the liquor store at Moreland Avenue and Wylie Street and pulled into the store's parking lot.

An alert cop in a passing patrol car spotted the car wanted in the killing of Detective Wilson. The cop reported its location while Sylvia was in the store purchasing the liquor. She returned to the car. As she was leaving the parking lot, she was stopped and surrounded by several patrol cars. She was taken out of the car and questioned. In the backseat was a brown baby seat.

Sylvia Heard informed the police that Ernest Walls and Erwin Crenshaw had arrived at her house a short time earlier. That they sent her out for liquor in the same car they had arrived in. She said that they should still be at her house.

Arrest and search warrants were issued for 82 Moreland Avenue SE where detectives found Ernest Walls and Erwin Crenshaw asleep. Both were placed under arrest for armed robbery and the murder of Detective Ernest L. Wilson.

Ernest Walls told Crenshaw to take the detectives to where he had hidden the gun. Crenshaw and several detectives went to the abandoned house next door and retrieved a .32 caliber Beretta semi-automatic pistol wrapped in newspaper that had been placed up inside the flue of a fireplace. Ballistics tests later conducted at the Georgia State Crime Lab determined that this was the pistol that had killed Wilson. During a search of the house at 82 Moreland Avenue, detectives found a .38 caliber Smith & Wesson revolver that had been taken in an armed robbery in Detroit.

Jeffery Parker, the gas station attendant, identified Ernest Walls in a lineup as the robber who shot and killed Detective Ernest L. Wilson. Other witnesses viewed lineups and picked out both Walls and Crenshaw as the ones they saw in the getaway car.

Ernest Walls pleaded guilty in Fulton County Superior Court to the murder of Detective Wilson and armed robbery of the Gulf station. He was sentenced to life in prison for murder, plus twenty years for armed robbery. The Detroit Police Department requested a "hold" be placed on Ernest Walls in the event that he was ever released from prison. If that ever happened, the Detroit PD must be notified so that they could return him to Detroit for prosecution on armed robbery charges there.

Erwin Crenshaw was sentenced to ten years as an accessory.

Detective Ernest Wilson's family—his wife, twelve-year-old son, and fourteen-year-old daughter—were told of his death by Lieutenant W. W. Gable, who was in charge of the auto theft squad then. Lieutenant Gable said, "Telling the children their father was dead was hard."

Auto Theft Detective Ernest Wilson managed to stay above the fray working at his desk in the confines of the squad room for the major portion of the week. However, for that one evening a week, he wore his uniform for his extra job, and became an unwitting target when he walked in during an armed robbery.

DETECTIVE
ERNEST L. WILSON
"SHOT DURING ROBBERY"
APRIL 27, 1976

Atlanta Police Officer

Cled Neal Wingo

"I guess I've done enough for today"

Atlanta police officer Cled Neal Wingo, who worked the day watch out of the Zone 2 Precinct, had been a cop for over thirty years, and this would be his last week to wear the badge before retiring. On Wednesday morning, July 23, 1975, he received a radio call from his precinct to deliver some paperwork to 1933 Kilburn Drive NE as a courtesy. That paperwork was an "emergency admission physician's certificate," a document signed by a doctor authorizing the commitment of a mentally disturbed young man to the Psychiatric Ward at Grady Hospital.

Dan Alben Allison, a twenty-year-old white male, lived with his parents in a quiet middle-class Atlanta neighborhood at 1933 Kilburn Drive NE in a modest brick ranch house. Neighbors regarded him as a boy who was different, kind of slow, a boy who did not do much more than mow lawns in the neighborhood.

Dan Allison had been suffering for several years from what doctors diagnosed as paranoid schizophrenia. During those years, he was in and out of medical hospitals and psychiatric institutions from Atlanta to North Carolina and as far away as California. Jake and Lila Allison tried to get their son the treatment he needed that might improve his condition, but that treatment never seemed to be available; or when he got treatment, it didn't seem to do what they expected. The other problem was that he would leave the facility on his own shortly after being admitted.

His condition worsened.

On Tuesday, July 22, Mrs. Allison called the police to come to the house to take her son to Grady Hospital. The police officers who answered her call told her that they had to decline her request. They explained that unless her son was demonstrably violent or had commitment papers, APD police officers were not allowed to transport him. The police left, but not without first explaining to Mrs. Allison what she needed to do to get her son committed. She contacted Dan's latest doctor at Emory Hospital. The doctor agreed to draw up the documents needed to transport her son and to have him admitted to the Grady Hospital Psychiatric Ward.

According to Georgia State Law, only law enforcement officers are permitted to transport these kinds of documents. So DeKalb County Police sent a patrol car to Emory Hospital where the latest doctor to attend to Mrs. Allison's son drew up the documents to commit him to Grady Psychiatric.

The DeKalb County cops transported the documents to where the DeKalb and Atlanta jurisdictions met. That was where an APD patrol car waited for the transfer of the documents, to transport them farther into the Atlanta jurisdiction.

APD Officer J. D. Craig, working Zone 2 morning watch (after midnight) in car 1204, was instructed to go to the Allison residence to deliver the documents to Mr. or Mrs. Allison that would require the APD police to transport their son to Grady Hospital. Officer Craig rang the bell. No response. He knocked on the door. Again, no response. He was about to try again when he received an emergency call, a signal 36 (robbery in progress), so he left the Allison house without delivering the documents. He put them over the folded up sun visor on the passenger side of his patrol car. Responding to the robbery in progress call and to other calls throughout the night kept Craig so busy that he forgot about the documents in his car.

(For clarification, all patrol cars since 1973 have 4-digit radio numbers. The first number denotes the watch: morning is 1, day is 2, evening is 3. The second number denotes the zone. The last two numbers denote the beat or geographical area within that zone. Keep in mind that the same patrol car will be identified by different first numbers depending on which cycle of the day the car is being used. Prior to 1973, all police operations emerged from the APD headquarters building and patrol cars had 2-digit radio numbers.)

When Officer Craig's morning watch was over, he was relieved by Officer Cled Wingo, assigned to day watch car 2204. Wingo promptly headed for 204's beat.

Wingo, sixty years old and a thirty-year police veteran, was going to retire in a few days.

He had an on-again, off-again career with the Atlanta Police Department. He joined the APD in 1943, left in 1944 to serve in the military during the closing days of World War II, returned to duty with the APD in 1946, and left the APD again in 1953 to join the DeKalb County Police Department. He returned once again to the APD in 1957, where he remained an APD cop for the next eighteen years. Having accumulated enough years from previous time with the Atlanta PD, DeKalb County PD, and time credited for military service, Officer Wingo was going to retire in the summer of 1975.

On that terrible Wednesday morning, Mrs. Allison made several phone calls to the Zone 2 Precinct, wanting to know the whereabouts of the officer who was supposed to deliver the documents needed to transport and commit her son to Grady Psychiatric. Superior officers at the precinct called Craig at home. He told them what had happened, how he had gotten so busy with calls to attend to criminal activity that he had forgotten about the documents. He said that they were over the right sun visor in 204's car. The precinct then contacted Wingo by radio, instructing him that there were documents in the car he was driving, where to look for them, and to confirm that he had located them. When Wingo reported that he did have them, he was instructed to deliver the documents to the Allison residence, and to use his discretion to determine whether the subject of those documents, the son, Dan Allison, needed to be transported to Grady Hospital.

When Wingo arrived at the house, he was met outside the front door by Robert Lee Barnes, a neighbor and a good friend of the Allisons. Barnes gave Wingo some background on Dan Allison and advised him of what had occurred during the preceding few days. He explained that the latest in a bizarre series of strange behavior from Dan Allison had started when Dan asked his parents to take him to Grady Hospital where he committed himself to the Psychiatric Ward. A short time later, he left without saying anything to anyone. He then went to Crawford Long Hospital where they wouldn't admit him. He returned home, but his parents were not there. So he asked a neighbor, Mrs. Watkins, to take him to Piedmont Hospital, which she did. Dan checked himself into Piedmont, but, again, he did not stay long enough to see a doctor. As he was leaving, an orderly attempted to stop him. Dan ran out of the hospital with two orderlies in pursuit as he ran down Peachtree Street. Atlanta police stopped them, and Dan was taken back to Piedmont Hospital where he signed himself out.

Later that afternoon, Mr. Barnes saw Dan and Mr. Allison outside and went out to talk to them. Dan asked Barnes who the man standing next to him was. Barnes replied that the man was Dan's father. Dan shook his head and walked away. A few minutes later, Dan asked Barnes to take him to the bus station so he could visit his uncle in North Carolina. Barnes wanted to talk him out of going to North Carolina, so he suggested that they go get something to eat. Dan agreed to go to a restaurant with Barnes. Dan left the restaurant when Barnes went to the restroom. Barnes found Dan at the bus station and convinced him to return to his home.

Barnes told all this to Officer Wingo when he arrived. Together, Wingo and Barnes entered the house. They were greeted by Mr. and Mrs. Allison. Officer Wingo asked them where Dan was. They answered that he was back in the bathroom.

It was clear to Wingo that the Allisons were distraught. Wingo was the kind of person who could feel what someone in need was feeling. That empathy made him a police officer whose compassion led him to do whatever he could to make things easier for people. Wingo told the Allisons not to worry, that he would go back and talk to Dan, and then take him to Grady Hospital.

Wingo went to the bathroom door and called Dan's name three times. Dan did not respond. But then he suddenly walked out of the bathroom, and without saying a word, he went into his bedroom and attempted to close the door. Wingo told Dan to leave the door open. Dan said to him, "You don't want to come in here with me, do you?"

Wingo replied, "Well no, you've got your clothes on and the door will have to stay open." (Wingo implying that because Dan was dressed decently, they could talk from bedroom doorway).

Robert Barnes, who was still in the living room with Dan's parents, heard Wingo and Dan talking in low tones, neither of them raising his voice. Barnes had gotten to know the Allisons well enough to realize that they were very sensitive about their son, his problems, and what was going on. He felt that this was a family matter and being there made him feel uncomfortable. So he excused himself and left the house, feeling confident that Officer Wingo had the situation under control.

Within a minute or two of leaving the house, Barnes heard several gunshots. He immediately called the police.

(What follows is what homicide detectives believe happened in the house during those few minutes after Barnes left. Their conclusions were determined by the physical evidence collected at the scene and witnesses' statements.)

Officer Wingo then entered the bedroom. He got into a scuffle with Dan when Dan attempted to take Wingo's service revolver from its holster. During the scuffle, Wingo's revolver discharged, blowing a hole through his holster (bits of leather were found within the leg of Wingo's pants). A second round hit Wingo in the back, piercing his heart and exiting through his chest.

It was quite clear from the path of the bullet that Dan had fired that shot. Dan came out of the bedroom and saw his mother on the telephone in the hallway. He shot and killed her. Dan's father was attempting to leave through the front door when Dan shot and killed him.

Dan Allison left the house through the back door and went to the Locklin's house next door. There was a scuffle as Mr. Locklin tried to disarm him. During the scuffle, a round was fired but hit no one. The bullet hit the kitchen stove and ricocheted out through a window. Before any more shots were fired, Locklin was able to shove Dan out the front door and locked it, preventing Dan from reentering.

Dan Allison calmly walked away while other neighbors called the police.

Radio dispatcher: *"Any car near 1933 Kilburn Drive NE, signal 63/25* [officer needs help/ discharging firearms]. *Cars on the way be advised that 2204 is out at that location and we cannot raise him!"*

Police unit: *"Start a 4* [ambulance] *to Kilburn Drive, code 3* [rush call]. *2204 is signal 50* [person shot], *and there are two other*

50s in the house, all three look like they are signal 48 [person dead]*!"*

A lookout for Dan Allison was placed over all radio frequencies, fully describing him, and warning that he was armed with Officer Wingo's gun. A short time later, several police officers spotted Dan wandering the neighborhood not far from his house. He still had Wingo's gun in his pocket but was disarmed without any violence. As he was being handcuffed, Dan Allison looked at one of the cops and said, "I guess I've done enough for today."

He continued to mutter those words from the backseat of the patrol car all the way to the city jail.

Dan Allison was charged with three counts of murder.

It was determined that he was insane, therefore incompetent to stand trial. He was remanded to a mental institution.

At this writing, Dan Allison's whereabouts are unknown.

The irony of this tragedy is that Cled Wingo was four days away from retirement. If not for a mix-up in delivering some a legal documents, retired Officer Cled Wingo, might have lived out the rest of his life sitting on a beach somewhere.

OFFICER
C. N. WINGO
"SHOT BY DEMENTED PERSON"
JULY 23, 1975

Atlanta Police Detective

Sam Guy

Twenty-four years . . . an informant . . . back due child support . . . an anonymous phone call

Just before two AM on a cold January morning, an ambulance, its siren screaming in unison with the escorting patrol cars, raced through the dark city streets transporting the seriously wounded Detective Sam Guy to Grady Hospital. He had been shot twice: once in his shoulder and once in his right thigh. The bullet to his thigh severed his femoral artery, causing heavy blood loss.

Sam Guy was unconscious when they arrived at Grady Hospital. The trauma team was ready for him. They did everything they could about the blood loss. But they lost the battle. And Sam Guy lost his life.

"He was the best of us," murmured one detective, trying to control his emotions, "We've really been hit hard by this."

Police officers, detectives, and high ranking police brass crowded the entrance to Grady Memorial Hospital's emergency trauma section where Detective Sam Guy had just lost his life. They stood around, making awkward conversation to break the awkward silence that characterizes a state of collective shock in a situation like this. "One thing's for certain, if Sam was on your tail, sooner or later he'd get you," said a colleague who'd worked with him.

Samuel Milton Guy was born on February 15, 1925, in the tiny town of Lineville in East Central Alabama, no more than fifty miles from the Alabama-Georgia state line. His mother died when Sam was three years old; his father died a year later. There were eight Guy siblings. They were all separated and farmed out to foster homes throughout Alabama. Sam Guy's childhood and school years were patched together in different foster homes. When he reached his teens, he had to work part time doing manual labor, such as "skinning" pine trees to make telephones poles. He was forced to leave school before graduating to work full time until he turned eighteen.

In 1943, when he reached eighteen years of age, Sam Guy joined the United States Navy. That was during the Second World War.

Sam was on leave in Atlanta in late December of 1944. He went bowling on Christmas Day. For him, it was a great day in a great place. That was when and where he met Francine Harrington. When he was back at sea, Sam and Francine kept in touch as often as possible through the U.S. mail and the military mail services. When the war ended in 1945, Sam returned to Atlanta where he and Francine were married.

Sam was a happy man. He had three documents to prove it: his marriage license, his honorable discharge, and the GED (high school equivalency diploma) he earned while in the navy.

Sam and Francine settled in Atlanta where he went to work at the Fulton cotton mill. He worked there for almost ten years, until 1956, when he applied for and was accepted by the Atlanta Police Department.

Patrolman Sam Guy spent his first few years in uniform working a patrol car, answering radio calls, and convincing drunks—he often had to convince them with his fists—that he had to take them to jail. He was a big, powerful man who came out on the winning side of brawls in bars, usually with merely insolent drunks, as well as on the streets with vicious thugs. Sam Guy was the cop who evened the odds when he arrived at a scene where another cop was in trouble because he was outnumbered. Although Sam had brute strength and used it when needed, he wasn't a brutal man. He was a gentle, kind man, always with a smile on his face and a good word for all. Sam Guy was well-liked by everyone.

Sam was promoted to detective and assigned to the vice squad. That was back when drugs were not a widespread problem in Atlanta and when the biggest concerns for vice detectives were prostitution, gambling, and illegal whisky, commonly referred to by some as "moonshine."

Vice partners Sam Guy and Jerry Spicer knew that a moonshine bootlegger by the street name of "Badeye" was selling illegal whisky out of his house. They'd been trying for a long time to have sufficient cause to arrest Badeye. Not having had any success, they tried the following: Sam's grown son, David, a savvy young man (not yet an Atlanta police officer but in the process of becoming one), was entrusted by his father to play the role of a "go for." The detectives gave David some cash and sent him to Badeye's house where he was to say that he had come to buy some whisky on a tip from a bellhop at the Jefferson Hotel—a seedy flophouse in a rundown part of Atlanta. Badeye appeared at his front door, looked at David, and then said that if he wanted some really good moonshine he should "return to the Jefferson Hotel and ask for two other bellhops, Guy and Spicer." Badeye was a bit too street-smart for those two vice detectives . . . because they never did get him.

After a short time in Vice, Sam Guy was transferred to the robbery squad where he spent most of his investigative career. There are many robbers—mostly armed robbers—doing time in the various state and federal prisons because of Sam Guy's dogged determination "to get the bad guys"!

Like most cops everywhere, Sam had to work extra jobs. One he worked regularly was at the Howard Johnson Motor Lodge on Washington Street, several blocks from the Atlanta-Fulton County Stadium. This motel was in a high-crime area of Atlanta. Sam Guy had worked this approved extra job for several years as a deterrent to robberies, car burglaries, vandalism, disturbances, and any other illegal activities. He was usually there during the late night/early morning hours. In 1973, Sam Guy transferred to the APD North Precinct, but he continued to work the extra job at the Howard Johnson motel.

On January 7, 1975, about 1:50 AM, Sam Guy, working his extra job, was sitting in the motel lobby watching TV. The only other person there was the night desk clerk, Raymond Puhr, white male, age twenty-nine. It was quiet; the only sounds came from the low volume on the TV set. A black male entered the lobby and walked directly to the cigarette machine located in the alcove on the far side of the front desk. A few moments later, a second black male came through the front door armed with two handguns when, as Mr. Puhr reported later, "All hell broke loose!"

Raymond Puhr dropped to the floor behind the front desk counter. He heard a lot of shouting. Then he heard more gunfire than shouting. Sam Guy was in a gun battle with the two robbers who had him in a crossfire. Sam was hit in the shoulder. The force of the bullet knocked him down. When he fell, he lost his gun. One of the robbers shot Sam again while he was already wounded and down on the floor. Sam called out to Puhr, "I'm hit bad. I'm bleeding all over the place. Get me some help. Get me some help!" Still there, the two gunmen ignored the pleas of the badly wounded detective as they forced Puhr to open the money drawer. They grabbed what was inside, a little over two hundred and seventy-five dollars in cash, and ran out the front door.

Puhr got on the phone to call for an ambulance and the police. Then he went over to see if he could do anything to help Sam Guy.

Police dispatcher: *"Any car near 759 Washington Street SW at the Howard Johnson Motor Lodge, signal 63/4* [officer needs help/ambulance on the way]."

Police unit (less than one minute later): *"Have that ambulance come on, we've got a police officer shot, and he's bleeding badly!"*

Police unit: *"Two black males. Number one—about 6' tall, 175 pounds, about thirty-five years old, wearing a grey sport jacket; number two—about 5'7", twenty-five to thirty years old, big afro, wearing a blue tam-like cap with a bill on the front. Direction of travel unknown, both subjects armed with handguns, wanted for shooting a police officer and armed robbery."*

At the same time, Sam's son, David Guy, who had been an Atlanta police officer for three years, assigned to APD's North Precinct, was at the precinct doing some paperwork after coming off duty. David heard the help call over his radio. He jumped up and said to those around him, "Hey, that's where my dad works his extra job." David immediately left the precinct, got into his car, and rushed directly to Grady Hospital. On the way down, David kept hearing a lot of chatter over the police radio about Sam Guy's two gunshots—one in the shoulder and the other in the leg. He felt relieved that the wounds did not sound life-threatening. Arriving at the hospital, he made his way through a sea of cops and found Deputy Chief Chafin (chief of detectives), who looked into David's eyes, then slowly shook his head. David knew that his father hadn't made it.

Chafin said, "David, go get your mother." Sergeant Larry Peaden was authorized to drive him to Sam Guy's residence in the Atlanta suburb of Smyrna. They left immediately. When the three returned to Grady, Deputy Chief Chafin accompanied Francine and David to the family room where they were given the official notification of Sam Guy's death.

The manhunt was on. All available detectives were pressed into the search, every possible resource was being utilized—informants were being pressured, thugs were muscled, pimps and prostitutes were unable to make a living, neighborhood guys were hassled on the street corners, street drug sales dried up. The underbelly of society was being tossed like a garden salad. The drive was constant and fierce to achieve the number one Atlanta police priority—find the killers of Detective Sam Guy!

But they were not found. Nor were they identified, although scores of suspects were picked up, questioned, and placed in lineups for Raymond Puhr to view. And he viewed many lineups of possible suspects. Dozens of detectives worked thousands of hours during the months, and then the years, that followed. Despite all the work by so many, the results did not come close to finding the killers. As other crimes were being committed, detectives were slowly being pulled from the Sam Guy murder investigation. It ended up in a cold case file.

Seven years later, in 1982, FBI special agent Arthur Krinsky received information from a bondsman/bounty hunter informant. He told Krinsky that one of his clients was in the DeKalb County Jail charged with several felony crimes and that he wanted to make a deal. The bondsman/bounty hunter said that his man knew who killed the Atlanta detective a long time ago in the motel near Atlanta-Fulton County Stadium. Krinsky notified Sam's son, David Guy, and both went to the DeKalb County Jail where they interviewed the inmate. The inmate told Krinsky and David that several years ago, during the early morning hours on the same night of the Guy murder, he was driving in downtown Atlanta. He stopped for a traffic light at Edgewood Avenue and Decatur Street. A car pulled up alongside him occupied by two black males he knew by their street names, "Wolf" and "TJ." As they waited for the light to change, TJ had boasted through the open window, "We just shot the police at the Howard Johnson's by the stadium."

Krinsky and David Guy followed up and came up with one of the names—Terry Robert Jackson a/k/a TJ, an ex-convict with a lengthy record for violent crimes, including armed robbery.

Shortly after that, Special Agent Art Krinsky was transferred to the FBI's Cleveland field office, so he was officially off the Guy murder case.

In a way, David Guy was no longer officially involved in the search for his father's killers either. Here's what happened: Fulton County had formed its own police department and assumed the law enforcement duties previously done by the Atlanta PD in the unincorporated areas of Fulton County. Atlanta police deputy chief Chafin had transferred and become the police chief of the new Fulton County Police Department. David Guy transferred from the APD to the FCPD. Chafin called David into his office and told him that he was too emotionally involved to continue work on the search for his father's killers. Besides that, Chafin said it was Atlanta's case, not Fulton County's case. Chafin instructed David Guy to turn everything he had over to the Atlanta detectives to let them handle the case from then on.

David Guy did just that. But, for reasons that are not clear, Atlanta homicide detective J. T. Sweeney, who received all that David turned over and was assigned to Sam Guy's case, along with other homicide detectives who followed Sweeney, never followed up or were unable to proceed any further.

This murder of an Atlanta police officer was poorly handled and sadly mismanaged, given that there were new leads to follow. Because of ineptitude or carelessness or sloppiness or whatever the cause, some portions of this case file were missing. There was nothing to show that any additional investigative activity had been done. What was not missing remained lying dormant in the cold case file for seventeen years beyond the time when the informant identified Terry Robert Jackson a/k/a TJ as the one who boasted through the open window at the traffic light, "We shot the police at the Howard Johnson's."

In 1998, Detective Sergeant Scott Bennett in the APD homicide squad room received an anonymous telephone call. The caller was a female who stated that her husband, Abner Wilkerson a/k/a Wolf, and his friend TJ had shot and killed a detective some years ago during a robbery at the motel near the Atlanta-Fulton County Stadium. That was all she said, then hung up.

Bennett went to Major Mickey Lloyd, told him of the phone call, and was instructed to "pull the old Sam Guy case file, get one of the detectives to help you, and see where it leads." Bennett and Detective Jim Rose did just that. They were able to locate the original informant, the one who was interviewed by Special Agent Krinsky and David Guy in 1982 at the DeKalb County Jail. This informant was now living in Shreveport, Louisiana.

Bennett and Rose wanted to go to Shreveport to re-interview him, but the problem was that there was no money in the Homicide budget for the trip. Deputy Chief C. B. Jackson went to the narcotics squad and requisitioned the drug money that had been confiscated and kept on hand to buy drugs, pay informants, and finance official out of town trips. Bennett and Rose made the trip and returned from Shreveport with a written statement from Larry Gene Smith, the informant who told of his encounter with TJ and Wolf while stopped at a downtown traffic light on the night Detective Sam Guy was killed. Larry Gene Smith said that TJ told him that they had just held up the motel near the stadium, and that "Wolf froze up" and he (TJ) "came down on the police and shot him."

Detective Sergeant Bennett and Detective Rose pulled Abner Wilkerson's criminal record, commonly referred to as a "rap sheet," and found that he had been involved in previous armed robberies. His sheet listed Myrtle Wilkerson as Abner's wife. From that information, Bennett and Rose were able to locate her and not long after they showed up at her door. Myrtle told the detectives that she and Abner were divorced and that he had admitted to her many years ago that he and TJ had robbed the motel, but he said that it was TJ who killed the detective. Then she told the detectives where they could find her ex-husband, Abner.

Why did Myrtle turn Abner in? What made her make that phone call after all those years? It was money! And not a great deal of money. And not blackmail money. It was child support money for their two children. Abner had been behind on his child support payments for over a year. Myrtle did not have enough money for everyday expenses—groceries, rent, utilities, and other necessary bills. Each time Myrtle asked Abner for money, he would put her off, "I'll have some for you in a few days." She often had to beg him for money. Myrtle had finally had enough.

The detectives located Abner Wilkerson, but they lacked sufficient probable cause to have an arrest warrant issued. They told Wilkerson that the police knew that he and Terry Jackson had robbed the motel near the stadium so many years ago. The homicide detectives advised Wilkerson that they had information that Jackson was the triggerman who had shot and killed Detective Guy. They stressed that if this were true, it would be in Wilkerson's best interest to turn himself in voluntarily. Bennett and Rose talked while Wilkerson listened.

For three months, either Bennett or Rose, sometimes both together, would show up at some of Abner's hangouts. If he was not around, they would leave business cards for him, just to let him know they were there. After many conversations with the two detectives, Wilkerson agreed to turn himself in. Wilkerson was advised to bring his attorney with him. They met at APD Headquarters. After signing the waiver of Miranda rights ("You have the right to remain silent . . ."), Abner Wilkerson gave a written statement admitting to his part in the motel robbery. He named Terry Jackson as the triggerman in the murder of Detective Sam Guy.

An arrest warrant was issued for Terry Jackson. Detectives had information that he could be found at either of two locations. The most likely place was in downtown Atlanta. The other was in North Fulton County. Rose and a pair of fugitive detectives set up surveillance at the downtown location, while Bennett alone watched the house in North Fulton County.

It was Detective Sergeant Bennett who saw Jackson come out of the house, get in his car, and then drive to a gas station/convenience store. As Jackson was buying a lottery ticket, Bennett approached him, identified himself, and asked if he was Terry Robert Jackson. When a confused Jackson answered that he was, Bennett advised him that he was under arrest for the 1975 murder of Detective Sam Guy and then handcuffed him. Jackson offered no resistance. Bennett then called Rose.

In 1999, twenty-four years after Detective Sam Guy was shot and killed, Abner Wilkerson pleaded guilty in Fulton County Superior Court to armed robbery and agreed to testify that Terry Jackson had shot Detective Sam Guy during that robbery.

Abner Wilkerson was sentenced to eleven years in prison.

Terry Jackson pleaded not guilty and demanded a jury trial. He got his jury trial. The jury convicted him for the murder of Detective Sam Guy. He was sentenced to life in prison without parole. He was also convicted by the same jury for armed robbery and was given a sentence of an additional twenty years for that crime.

Over the years, Sam Guy's wife Francine and son, David, had been tormented by the fact that Sam's killer(s) were still roaming the streets free. The arrest and conviction of Jackson and Wilkerson gave them the satisfaction that justice was finally served.

David Guy had been promoted up through the ranks, retiring as a deputy chief from the Fulton County Police Department.

Detective Sergeant Scott Bennett and Detective Jim Rose received national recognition for their excellent police work in the arrest and conviction of the two responsible for the murder of Detective Sam Guy. A murder that had been a cold case for twenty-four years.

Atlanta Police Officer

Gregory R. White

The idea was for robbers to believe that stakeout cops were everywhere—always

In 1973, Maynard Jackson campaigned hard to be elected the next mayor of Atlanta, the first black mayor of Atlanta. His campaign was full of the typical political rhetoric and campaign promises.

Maynard Jackson was elected.

When he took office in early 1974, he delivered on two campaign promises: one, fire Police Chief John Inman; and the other, disband the APD stakeout squad.

But Chief Inman was not fired. Mayor Jackson could not fire him. The court intervened on Inman's behalf, ruling that legal contractual issues prohibited Jackson from firing Inman.

However, Mayor Maynard Jackson did disband the stakeout squad. Known for its aggressive tactics in combating armed robberies in small businesses, the stakeout squad consisted of fifty detectives under the supervision of a cadre of superior officers. A pair of detectives was placed out of sight, usually in the back room, where they could view the activity up front, such as at a convenience store, a liquor store, a fast food restaurant, a mom-and-pop store, or any similar small business that had been robbed or was in a vicinity where similar businesses had been robbed.

The detectives were staked out at a vulnerable location during the night or evening or day, whichever fit the pattern of robberies nearby. When the stakeout detectives witnessed, through a one-way mirror, armed robber(s) enter the front of a location, they would exit the back room, armed with shotguns, to confront the robber(s). In most cases, the robber(s) surrendered and were arrested without any problem.

But it was not always that way. There were instances when detectives identified themselves as police and the robber(s) had turned toward them, armed, and had shown no sign of releasing their gun(s). Failing to release their guns and pointing them at the detectives constituted a deadly threat to the detectives, resulting in a situation where the detectives had no other choice but to fire at the armed robber(s), usually with fatal results.

The stakeout squad had been operating for twenty-one months. During that time, nineteen felons were killed by members of the squad. Maynard Jackson referred to the stakeout squad as "the execution squad." He made it a racial issue during his campaign for mayor, calling to the attention of his constituency the statistic that the majority of the nineteen felons killed were black.

Michael Timothy Mack, James Matthew Smith, and Stanley Eugene Bradley were three eighteen-year-old black males who concentrated on robbing convenience stores—but not within the City of Atlanta. They knew about the stakeout squad and did not want to risk attempting to rob a store where detectives were staked out. There was no stakeout squad and no detectives in the back rooms of convenience stores in neighboring DeKalb County. These three robbers knew that in Atlanta it was not possible for stakeout detectives to be in every store all the time—but they did not know where they might be on any given day or night. Determining where the stakeout detectives would be was like the shell game or Russian roulette. These three robbers were smart enough not to play the game. For them, it was too risky not knowing where the stakeout detectives might be and not worth guessing knowing the reputation of the stakeout squad.

As he promised, Mayor Jackson dissolved the APD stakeout squad, proclaiming it a victory for the black community. But the black community was not going around with guns, robbing stores, and shooting people. Worse, a large number of robbery victims—some shot and wounded, some killed—were black citizens of Atlanta. The mayor did not say anything about these black victims in his campaign promises, nor later in his victory proclamation.

As soon as the stakeout squad was dissolved, Mack, Smith, Bradley, and other robbers like them had a shorter commute to work. They no longer had to travel to the surrounding counties to take money out of the tills of mom-and-pop convenience stores. They could work at home! The City of Atlanta had many convenience stores and other small businesses with cash on hand and no one but themselves—the owners, their employees, and their customers—to confront armed robbers.

Atlanta police officer Gregory R. White was a young twenty-two-year-old rookie with less than a year with the APD, having joined on September 17, 1973. He was a very religious Christian and had spent the previous two years in South America doing missionary work. His wife, Patricia, said that "Greg always felt that his calling was to serve mankind through law enforcement." He had attended Clayton Junior College in suburban Atlanta and was considering going to law school.

Officer Gregory White, during his brief ten-month career since completing the police academy, was first assigned to the High Crime Foot Patrol. It was a unit where he and other cops walked beats in areas of the city most susceptible to street crime. After that assignment, White was assigned to Zone 4 morning watch. His latest assignment was to the mayor's detail, also on the morning watch, guarding the mayor's house. Officer White's job was to sit in a marked patrol car in front of the mayor's house on Oak Crest Drive SW from eleven PM to seven AM, whether the mayor was at home or not. It was a boring assignment for a young cop and very difficult to stay awake, even though his sergeant would check on him every so often and a patrol car or two might stop by during the night.

Mack, Smith, and Bradley decided to rob the all-night 7-Eleven on Allison Court at Delowe Drive SW in Atlanta. No more stakeout detectives, so no need to go to DeKalb County. This 7-Eleven had been robbed three times within two years; the convenience store across the street had been robbed twice. Stakeout cops had been in place in both stores and arrests made in all five robberies.

But that was then.

Now was July 15, 1974, early Monday morning, just before two AM. Michael Mack and Stanley Bradley entered the 7-Eleven acting as customers; James Smith waited outside. The night clerk, William Harris, had run out of change and told the customers that if they did not have the exact amount they could not make a purchase. Harris had locked the door because of the problem of making change so there was no point in having other customers come in the store. James Smith knocked on the locked door; Harris opened it to tell him why no customers could be let in. Smith put a gun in Harris's face and forced him back inside. Mack and Bradley pulled out their guns and herded Harris and four customers who were still in the 7-Eleven toward the rear of the store. The robbers took the money and valuables from all five and then locked the four customers inside the walk-in cooler.

Harris was brought back to the front counter where he was told to open the cash register. The robbers took all the bills and the few coins left from the register and then demanded that Harris open the store's safe, threatening to shoot him if he didn't open it. He told them, repeatedly, that he couldn't open it by himself. Two keys were required to unlock the safe, and he only had one of the keys. He told them that a man would come around in the morning with the other key, and he would empty the safe of its cash, as he did every morning.

Officer Gregory White had been sitting in his patrol car in front of the mayor's house for almost three hours on that humid Monday morning. His eyes were weary and his butt was sore. Mayor Jackson was away from home, attending a conference at a beach resort on Jekyll Island off the Georgia coast. White decided he needed a break and headed for the all-night 7-Eleven nearby.

As White pulled his patrol car into the 7-Eleven parking lot, the robbers saw him. "There's 'the Man,'" warned Bradley.

"We're going to have to burn that pig!" Mack said to Smith and Bradley.

White knocked on the locked front door. Mack told Bradley to let him in and instructed everyone to "be cool." Mack walked to the back of the store. White entered the store, looked toward the two men at the counter, and said, "I need to get a 9-volt battery. But first I'll get a cold drink." He walked toward the soft drink cooler. As he walked past Mack, Mack pulled a gun from his pants and shot White in the back of the head.

Officer Gregory White fell to the floor.

The three robbers ran out the front door, but not before Mack grabbed the register cash that was on the counter.

Harris took White's service revolver from his holster and ran outside after the robbers, but they were gone. Harris got into the patrol car and attempted to call for help, but he did not know how to operate the police radio. He ran back into the store to use the pay phone, the only phone in the store. The robbers had not only cleaned out the store of money, but they had also taken all the pocket change from Harris and the four customers. Harris searched White's pockets, found a dime, and used it to call the police. He told the police operator that the store had just been robbed, a cop had been shot, and that an ambulance was needed immediately.

Next, Harris returned to the cooler to release the four customers who were locked inside. Three were soldiers from nearby Fort McPherson. One was an Atlanta fireman who tried to administer first aid to the wounded police officer. He grabbed some sterile gauze from one of the shelves and applied it to the wound to try to stop the bleeding. The bleeding would not stop.

Police dispatcher: *"Any cars near Allison Court and Delowe Drive. At the 7-Eleven store, signal 63/44/50/4* [officer needs help/ robbery/person shot/ambulance on the way]. *Cars on the way be advised a police officer has been shot!"*

Patrol cars arrived with blue lights flashing and sirens screaming. An Atlanta police helicopter hovered overhead, then notified the ground units by radio that it was going to land in a clearing adjacent to the 7-Eleven. Calls to learn when the ambulance was expected determined that it was going to be soon, but not immediately. That prompted the decision to load White into the helicopter, the fastest way to Grady Hospital.

Atlanta police officer Gregory R. White died several hours later.

Within less than twenty-four hours of the robbery, the shooting, and the killing at the 7-Eleven, homicide detectives received a phone call. It was from a man who said he had heard that there was a five thousand dollar reward for information leading to the arrest of those responsible for the murder of Officer White. The detectives confirmed the reward information. The caller told them that he knew where the three men they wanted were. He emphasized that he knew where they were "right now!" The caller said he would meet the detectives at the corner of Allison Court and Stanton Road.

A short while later, six detectives and two Zone 4 patrol cars met a man at that location. He said he was the caller and then directed them to the apartments at 1935 Allison Court, directly behind the 7-Eleven where Officer White was murdered. In apartment A-18, the police found five young black males, along with small amounts of crack cocaine and marijuana out in plain sight. The five men were detained on charges of drug possession and transported to the homicide office.

A search warrant was obtained and executed for the apartment on Allison Court where more drugs were found. More important than the drugs, much more important, was the .22 caliber revolver discovered in a nightstand in the bedroom. It was later determined that four of the five men being questioned had no part in the robbery/murder. They were booked into the city jail on drug charges.

The fifth man in the apartment was Michael Mack. He fit the description provided by the 7-Eleven clerk, William Harris, as the robber who shot Officer Gregory White. Mack's fingerprints were found on the underside of the cash drawer that fit inside the bottom of the cash register.

Harris, viewing a lineup, promptly picked out Michael Mack as one of the three robbers and identified Mack as the robber who had shot Officer White during the robbery. The .22 caliber revolver found in the bedroom nightstand in apartment A-18 belonged to Michael Mack. It was the gun that fired the bullet recovered from Gregory White's body.

Michael Mack was charged with murder and six counts of armed robbery. After intense questioning, he admitted to the allegations against him and identified Stanley Eugene Bradley and James Matthew Smith as the other two who were with him that morning robbing the 7-Eleven.

Within a few days, homicide and fugitive detectives located and apprehended Bradley and Smith. Harris identified them in line-ups as the other two robbers. Each was charged with six counts of armed robbery. Both gave written statements admitting their parts in the robbery and naming Michael Mack as the triggerman in the murder of Atlanta police officer Gregory White. All three entered guilty pleas.

Michael Mack was sentenced to life in prison plus twenty years on each of the six counts of armed robbery.

Stanley Bradley and James Smith were also sentenced to twenty years on each of the six counts of armed robbery.

Consider these events, perhaps aligning the path toward Officer White's murder:
- Mack, Bradley, and Smith were known robbers of similar stores and businesses not within the City of Atlanta.
- Maynard Jackson becomes mayor of Atlanta.
- Mayor Maynard Jackson disbands the stakeout squad.
- Mayor Maynard Jackson boasts to the media that he fulfilled a campaign promise to disband the stakeout squad.
- Mack, Bradley, and Smith do not fail to grasp the implications of that news.
- Owners, employees, and customers—white and black—become vulnerable to robbery, the least among other possible felony crimes accompanying a robbery.

- Mack, Bradley, and Smith, at one time not 100% certain there would be no cops waiting in the back room of the 7-Eleven, now 100% certain there would be no cops, enter to rob the store and customers.
- Officer White enters the 7-Eleven, not as a cop to thwart a robbery, but as someone who needs a cold drink.
- Officer White is shot and killed by one of the robbers in that store.

What do you think? If the stakeout squad had still been operating, might a pair of stakeout cops been in the back room of that 7-Eleven? Would it not have been enough for robbers to think that maybe the cops might be there? In either case, would Officer White not have been murdered when he went into the store?

One thing was for certain, most APD cops expressed anger, disgust, hate—an entire range of identical or similar emotions—toward Mayor Maynard Jackson for disbanding the stakeout squad.

You may have already realized the ugly irony in all this. Officer Gregory White was on the mayor's own detail, charged with guarding the mayor's house, when he took his break on that early, hot, humid morning and went for a cold drink at the 7-Eleven. That irony, if it could have been heard, would be deafening!

Officer Gregory White's death left his young wife, Patricia, a widow with an infant daughter who will never know her father.

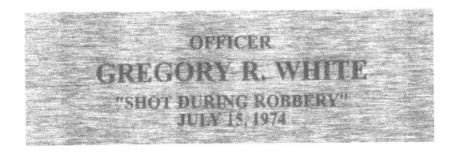

OFFICER
GREGORY R. WHITE
"SHOT DURING ROBBERY"
JULY 15, 1974

Atlanta Police Officer

Henry L. Jones

"This was the time I needed a radio!"

*A*tlanta police officer Henry L. Jones's body, with three gunshot wounds, was taken by ambulance to Grady Hospital from the parking lot outside the apartment where he lived. When the ambulance arrived at the hospital, Officer Jones was officially pronounced DOA.

Atlanta homicide detectives S. C. Dorsey and W. C. Meadows began their investigation into Jones's murder by entering Jones's apartment to search for the .38 caliber Smith & Wesson service revolver that had been issued to Atlanta police officer Jones.

As they stepped through the front door into the living room, Dorsey and Meadows tried not to get emotional about what they observed—an assortment of children's toys and packages wrapped in the colors of Christmas with Santa, reindeer, snowmen, and holly decorating the wrapping paper. It was only two weeks until Christmas. These were Christmas presents for Jones's five-year-old son who lived with his mother, Jones's estranged wife, Juliette. Henry Jones Sr. was going to make it a big Christmas for his son this year.

After the detectives got past their feeling that it was not going to be a big, happy Christmas, they moved on to Jones's bedroom. In the closet, the detectives observed several police uniforms neatly hanging together, perhaps unintentionally grouped to serve one purpose, distinct from the group of civilian clothes. In that same closet, on the top shelf above the police uniforms, there was a black leather Sam Brown belt. On the belt was each piece of the police paraphernalia a policeman like Officer Jones was required to have on his person when on duty. Snapped securely in a black leather holster on that belt was what the detectives were looking for—the .38 caliber Smith & Wesson service revolver issued to APD Officer Jones.

Having found the gun not discharged, undisturbed, and where it belonged was the first step in the process of eliminating the possible guns that had fired the bullets that had entered Jones's body and killed him. The detectives confirmed that Officer H. L. Jones was not shot and killed with his own service revolver.

Twenty-eight-year-old Henry L. Jones, a five-year APD veteran, worked an approved extra job as security for the Pace Setter Apartments off Harwell Road near Bankhead Highway and I-285 in northwest Atlanta. In addition to the salary he earned from this extra job, Jones lived on the premises in a rent-free apartment in exchange for being available to respond to any security problem whenever he was at home. He also had at his disposal a company security car to patrol the sizeable apartment complex.

Because the premises of his extra job was also his home, Jones was usually wearing plainclothes, although armed with a small .38 caliber snub-nose revolver carried in a holster clipped to his belt. This was Jones's second gun. It was also eliminated as the weapon that had fired the three bullets into him. On examining his body when it was still on the ground of the parking lot where he'd been shot, this snub-nose revolver was found undisturbed, fully loaded, in its holster.

Nathaniel Way and Frank Jerome Lee, black males, both in their early twenties, were burglars. Each had a criminal history to prove it. They preferred burglarizing residencies rather than businesses. Therefore, they operated during the daytime hours when most people were at work, not home in their apartments or houses.

On this cloudy, cool Wednesday, December 12, 1973, Way and Lee decided to hit the Pace Setter Apartments. It was sometime during late morning when Nathaniel Way backed his 1964 white Chevrolet onto the grass in front of a cluster of apartments at 211 Harwell Road NW.

A short time later, just before noon, Officer H. L. Jones was routinely patrolling the complex in the Pace Setter Apartments' security car. He observed that white car backed up on the grass—quite an unusual place for a car to be parked. Jones stopped to find out why the car was where it was. Before he had stopped to investigate, Way and Lee had already burglarized two apartments and were in the process of cleaning out a third when they saw Jones. Lee escaped out a rear window. Way ran out the front door where he was caught and held by Jones.

In that situation, at that moment, several things were not in Jones's favor:
- his uniform and all his police paraphernalia on his Sam Brown belt were back in his apartment (Jones did not have a pair of handcuffs with him);
- after he quickly patted down Nathaniel Way, Jones put the burglar in the security car (this car, unlike a police patrol car, did

not have disconnected interior door handles in the backseat);

- without his police radio, Jones could not call directly for backup; and

- because most of the people who lived there were not around (they were at work) there was no one to ask to call the APD to report that Jones needed a patrol car to come take and arrest the burglar.

What all that meant for Officer Jones was that he had to drive the security car, with an un- handcuffed burglar, through the streets of the complex to the Pace Setter Apartments' office on Skipper Place, a distance of about half a mile. When he arrived, and while standing outside of the security patrol car, Jones was able to attract the attention of Ms. Washington who worked in the office. He shouted to her to call the police and to have them respond.

Meanwhile, Willie Varnado, the assistant manager of the Pace Setter Apartments, was driving around, showing the complex and facilities to some prospective residents. Varnado noticed that same white car backed up on the grass on Harwell Road. He made a mental note to report the car to Officer Jones when he returned to the office. When Varnado got to the office, he saw the parked security car and Jones standing alongside it. As Varnado got out of his car, Jones walked over to him and said, "This was the time in which I needed a radio. I just caught one burglarizing and one got away."

Jones then told Varnado that the police were on the way. Just as he said that, the door of the security car opened and Nathaniel Way, the unrestrained burglar, got out. Jones ran back to the car to try to restrain him. Three gunshots were fired. Jones fell to the ground. Nathaniel Way jumped back into the security car on the driver's side and sped away.

Zone 1 dispatcher: *"Car 2113, at 314 Skipper Place NW in the Pace Setter Apartments, signal 50/4 [person shot/ambulance on the way]."*

Zone 1 unit: *"2113 received, 314 Skipper Place signal 50/4."*

Varnado later told detectives, "I shouted to Ms. Washington in the office to call the police again and tell them to send an ambulance, that a police officer had been shot. I ran to where Officer Jones was down on the ground and saw blood everywhere; he was not talking or moving. I then jumped in my car and raced to where I had seen that white car, but it was gone. Officer Jones's security car was parked there, unoccupied, the motor still running." He said that he could identify the man who shot Officer Jones if he saw him again.

Dispatcher: *"2113, the call on Skipper Place is coming up now signal 48* [person dead] *possibly a police officer."*
Car 2113: *"2113 received signal 50/48, possible police officer."*
Car 2110: *"2110 received the 50/48. On the way to Skipper Place with 2113."*

Mr. Robert King, a mailman with the U.S. Postal Service, was delivering mail to the Pace Setter Apartments. He also noticed the white car suspiciously backed up on the grass on Harwell Road. He identified it as a 1964 Chevrolet with a DeKalb County sticker on the Georgia tag, the first number he believed was "four." He said there was an Atlanta Falcons decal on the front bumper. He also told police, "I started to leave when I noticed Officer Jones coming up in the security car, and he drove down to check it out."

King later told detectives that "He [Jones] caught the fellow who had come out and was walking around the car, I saw Jones shake him down and place him in the security car." King continued, "I saw a man with a long black coat running away from this building across the street into some woods. Officer Jones also saw this subject running, but he couldn't chase him because he had the other subject in custody."

Police unit: *"2113 with a 78* [lookout]. *It'll be a 1964 white Chevrolet, Georgia tag with a DeKalb County sticker. One of the tag numbers might be four, and have an Atlanta Falcons decal on the front bumper. Occupied by one black male, midtwenties, 5'10", 160 pounds, dark complexion, wearing a blue flop-type cap, light brown leather jacket, blue pants, and blue shirt. Subject 69 [person armed] with a handgun, wanted for a signal 50/48 on a police officer. Start a superior officer, Homicide, and ID [crime scene unit]."*

Dispatcher: *"Received 2113, signal 78 broadcast on all channels. Superior officer, Homicide, and ID on the way."*

Where did the gun come from that Nathaniel Way used to shoot and kill Officer H. L. Jones? Both of Jones's guns were accounted for. It seems that Jones missed it during his cursory pat down of Way.

Jones was shot three times: one bullet went into his forehead, another into his chest, and the third bullet went through his upper left arm and into his side. Ballistics tests indicated that the bullets recovered from the body of H. L. Jones were .38 calibers, fired from a Colt revolver rather than from a Smith & Wesson. That gun, the murder weapon, was never recovered. But it was learned that Nathaniel Way sold the gun to a drug dealer known as "Blue" in the Carver Homes housing project; that drug dealer then sold it to another drug dealer. The known reliable trace of the gun went no further. Beyond that, unsubstantiated reporting indicated that the gun changed several anonymous hands once disappearing into the underbelly of Atlanta's dangerous streets.

The most promising lead that detectives had was the 1964 white Chevrolet, the DeKalb County Georgia tag with the number four, and an Atlanta Falcons decal on the front bumper. Pictures of a similar car were broadcast on TV and appeared in the Atlanta newspapers. Soon after, homicide detectives received a telephone call from a woman who lived in the Carver Homes housing project on the other side of Atlanta from the Pace Setter Apartments. The caller said that a car like the one she saw on the TV news was parked outside her apartment. When detectives arrived a short time later, the car was there, but the tag had been removed. The woman said that she happened to be looking out her window when the car pulled into the parking lot and that three black men in their early twenties got out and walked hurriedly down Pryor Road.

The car was impounded for processing and through the VIN number was traced to a used car lot on Stewart Avenue. The owner of the lot produced paperwork showing that that car, bearing Georgia tag EGI 412, was sold a month before to Nathaniel Way, home address 135 Davage Street SE. Detectives went to that address, picked up Nathaniel Way, and brought him to the homicide office for questioning.

During the questioning, Nathaniel Way denied knowing anything about the murder of Officer H. L. Jones and about the burglaries at the Pace Setter Apartments. He insisted that he had never been there; he said he didn't even know where they were. There were four detectives and a supervisor in the room where Way was being questioned. Way shocked them all by requesting that everyone leave the room except Detective S. C. Dorsey. (Way was familiar with Dorsey from a previous case the detective had investigated. Way had been a witness.) He said he would tell Dorsey what happened, but he would only tell him.

The others left the room. When only Dorsey and Way remained, Way said, "I'm going to tell you like it was, but I'm not going to make a written statement, and I won't sign anything." Dorsey told him to continue.

Way said that he and two others, Frank Lee a/k/a Dooley and Albert Harris, went to the Pace Setter Apartments for the purpose of burglarizing. They drove there in Way's 1964 Chevrolet. They had broken into three apartments and were still taking things when they saw the security car pull up to where Way had backed up his car. They all ran. Harris went out a back window of the apartment they were in. He (Way) and Dooley (Lee) ran out the front door of the apartment and were caught by the police. Way told Dorsey that "He [Jones] said that he was a police but he had on plainclothes. He put me and Dooley in the security car and as he was driving, I jumped out of the car and ran into some woods and hid for a while."

Way said he went back to where his car was and drove off.

Detectives checked with several witnesses who said there were only two burglars, not three, and Officer Jones had put only one of the burglars in the security car. Frank Lee and Albert Harris were picked up and questioned about the incident.

Lee admitted being there with Nathaniel Way and to burglarizing the three apartments. He said when he saw the security car, he jumped out of a rear window of the apartment (these apartments did not have back doors and they were ground level apartments) and ran into some woods, then took several buses to get home. Lee said that it was only him and Nathaniel Way at the Pace Setter Apartments on the day that Officer Jones was killed. Lee said that Albert Harris was not with them.

Harris insisted that he did not see Way or Lee until later that afternoon in Carver Homes. He had a good alibi to back it up.

Later, Willie Varnado, the assistant manager of the Pace Setter Apartments picked Nathaniel Way out of a police lineup and positively identified him as the man who shot and killed Officer H. L. Jones.

Nathaniel Way pleaded not guilty to murder in Fulton County Superior Court. The jury found Nathaniel Way guilty of the murder of Atlanta police officer Henry L. Jones. He was sentenced to life in prison.

Frank Lee pleaded guilty to the burglaries and was given a lighter sentence in exchange for his testimony against Way.

Jones's mother, Rosie Jones, told a newspaper reporter not long after the shooting that "He [Jones] seemed to be happy as a police officer, but I wasn't happy with it." Ms. Jones, a widow whose only child was Henry, also said, "I worried about him all the time. I hated [that] he ever got on the police force. He told me I worried too much, but I knew something like this was going to happen. Now I don't know if I'll ever get over it."

Several colleagues of Officer Jones delivered those Christmas presents to a grieving Henry Jones, Jr. at his home, but they were bitter-sweet.

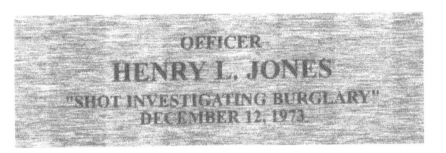

OFFICER
HENRY L. JONES
"SHOT INVESTIGATING BURGLARY"
DECEMBER 12, 1973

Atlanta Police Detective

Clarence E. Harris

A bag of popcorn

Not a robbery. Not a madman. Not a fanatic. Not a grudge. Not a drug mob hit. But a simple bag of popcorn.

Atlanta police narcotics detective Clarence Edward Harris was down on the stairs adjacent to the concession stand in the lobby of the Atlanta Theater. He was gravely injured by a gunshot wound to the stomach from his own .357 magnum revolver, which he carried when in plainclothes.

The Atlanta Theater movie house was located on Peachtree Street, N.E. between downtown and midtown. Harris worked his approved extra job at the Atlanta Theater. He worked this job in plainclothes rather than in his Atlanta police blue uniform. His function was to maintain general security, such as what might arise from ordinary disturbances by patrons or from illegal activities—robbery, drug sales, drug use, or theft.

It was a chilly autumn Saturday night on October 20, 1973, at 11:40 PM, just before the start of the midnight show, when a minor disturbance escalated into tragedy.

Two nineteen-year-old black males paid their admission and went straight to the concession stand. A few minutes later, they were joined by two young black females. They had come to the theater as a foursome.

The concession stand appeared to be closed, although a female attendant was behind the counter. One of the young men asked for a bag of popcorn. The attendant responded that she was on her break and that the counter would reopen in ten minutes.

"Just let me buy some popcorn now, girl. I won't tell nobody," said the young man. He was wearing white pants, a white jacket, and a white shirt. And he would not take "no" for an answer.

"I told him no again, that I was on my break," she said. "I told him flatly, no!"

He became loud and belligerent, saying, "Give me some damn popcorn."

That's when Detective Harris walked up to the concession stand. "You won't get anything talking and acting like that," Harris told him.

"Yeah, well I want some damn popcorn," the young man answered, getting louder and more belligerent.

The other man with him intervened, got in Harris's face, and said to Harris, "We just want some damn popcorn."

With that, Harris told them both to leave the theater.

They said they would not leave without their money back, and the man in white reached into his pocket.

Harris demanded that he take his hand out of his pocket. When the guy in white did not comply, Harris punched him, starting a fight between the two. The other guy got behind Harris and held him around the neck so that the guy in white could more easily hit Harris in the front.

Tony Turner, a sixteen-year-old employee of the theater, rushed in to help Harris. Turner pulled off the guy who was holding Harris around the neck. At that time, the guy in white, fighting in front of Harris, saw the gun in the shoulder holster beneath Harris's sport jacket. The guy in white pulled out the gun, backed up a couple of steps, and shot Harris in the stomach. Then he fired twice more, hitting Tony Turner once in the arm.

The two guys and their girlfriends ran out of the theater, the shooter still holding Harris's gun in his hand.

Police dispatcher: *"Cars near the Atlanta Theater, at 583 Peachtree Street NE, signal 63/50/4* [officer needs help/person shot/ambulance on the way]. *The caller stated that the 50 is on a police detective. First car advise radio."*

First police unit: *"Let the 4 come on to the Atlanta Theater, narcotics detective Harris has been shot!"*

Second police unit: *"The 78* [lookout] *from the Atlanta Theater will be two young black males. Number one: average height, slim build, dark skin, dressed in all white and 69* [person armed] *with a handgun. Number two: same height and build, dark skin, and wearing braids in his hair. Last seen on foot running east on North Avenue from Peachtree Street. Be advised two young black females are with them."*

Police units that were not at the scene of the shooting quickly set up at the downtown intersections on a direct route between the theater and Grady Hospital. The ambulance, with Harris aboard and patrol cars in front and behind it, sped to the hospital through the blocked intersections.

Atlanta police detective Clarence E. Harris, one gunshot wound to his stomach, was DOA at Grady Hospital.

All available detectives worked the Harris murder. They contacted informants and talked to those on the streets, anyone who might identify or lead police to identifying the two perpetrators. Detectives in the narcotics squad reviewed Detective Harris's recent history of arrests, searching for a possible motive for murdering him. Atlanta police issued a press release to the media that said in part:

> *At this point in our investigation, we wish to advise the two females who were with the male suspects that they will not be charged with the homicide if they cooperate in identifying their male companions. However, if the two females continue to conceal the identity of the male suspects, they become accessories to the homicide and can be charged and tried along with the male suspect who actually pulled the trigger. We urge the two females to contact their parents, their attorney, or their minister, and along with the person of their choice, come to the homicide office and identify their male companions.*

The first break came three days after Harris's murder, when a telephone call was received in the homicide squad—not from anyone representing either of the girls—but from the TV station Channel 11 in Atlanta. Their *Secret Witness* program received a call identifying James Carter and Kenneth Smith as the two who were at the Atlanta Theater on the night that Detective Harris was shot and killed. The caller said that after he heard gunshots, he saw James Carter, dressed in all white clothing, run out of the theater with a gun in his hand. The caller said Kenneth Smith and two young girls were running with Carter. The caller said he recognized Carter because he and Carter had attended high school together.

That tip led APD homicide detectives to adjoining DeKalb County where Carter and Smith had previously been arrested on burglary charges. From the DeKalb County police, Atlanta detectives obtained mug shots and fingerprints of both Carter and Smith. Additional investigation revealed that James Carter was a soldier in the U.S. Army and currently stationed at Fort Bragg, North Carolina, but was reported to be AWOL.

The two young females responded a couple of days after the notice in the media and met with APD homicide detectives. They confirmed that they were at the Atlanta Theater with James Carter and Kenneth Smith the night the detective was shot and that they saw James Carter shoot Harris. They also identified Carter and Smith from the DeKalb County PD photos.

Carter and Smith saw themselves on the TV news and in the newspapers. The media was reporting that the two had gone into the Atlanta Theater to rob it, when a gun battle ensued, and Detective Harris, who was working his extra job at the time, was shot and killed. Carter, knowing that was not true, sent a letter to the newspaper telling his side of the story. James Carter's letter appeared the next day in the *Atlanta Journal* (the letter is reproduced exactly as it was printed; all errors were kept to preserve its authenticity):

> *We walked in the show to the concession stand to get some popcorn, the girl said she would not open until 10 min. so I talk to her in a nice way, until she replied you want butter. At the same time my friend said something fresh to her about getting the popcorn she replied I am not talking to you but to him you want butter she said again? I said yes. That's when this man came up and said alright let's go. So I turned around and (hey man who is you?) is what I said. He said take your hands out of your pocket i'll blow your brains out. I saw him slide his hand in his coat. I questioned his action. That's when he hit me. I questioned his action again.*

He struck me again. So my friend said let's go man. So I asked the man to let me get my hat, he then grab me by my coat and threw me over to the stairs. He told my friend to go, so my friend said let's go man. So, that when I saw him going for his gun. So, I went to disarm him because I knew my friend didn't know he had a gun. When I snatch the . . . it went off. That when this other guy jumped my friend and throw him into me the gun went off again. I jumped back thinking he was shot. That's when the man charged me. When he got up to me and snatch me by my arms I remember the gun going off and him falling to the floor. That's when we ran.

THE GIRL AT THE CONCESSSION STAND SEEN EVERYTHING AND KNOWS WE WERE NOT THERE TO START TROUBLE. BECAUSE SHE AGREED TO GIVE ME THE POPCORN. WE ARE SORRY HE DIED, FOR WE WANTED TO SEE THE SHOW WITH THE GIRLS WE WERE WITH. WE DIDN'T WANT TO START TROUBLE.

PLEASE LET THE GIRL AT THE STAND READ THIS LETTER.

PLEASE BELIEVE THIS LETTER IT'S NOT A PRANK, SHE CAN TELL YOU, PLEASE THIS IS THE TRUTH, DIDN'T WANT THIS JUST SOME POPCORN.

After seeing that his letter was in the newspaper, James Carter, accompanied by his mother, went to Atlanta Police Headquarters where he turned himself over to homicide detectives. He revealed where they could find Kenneth Smith.

A short time later, fugitive squad detectives arrested Smith.

Both admitted to their versions of the events that occurred that night at the Atlanta Theater.

Carter and Smith said they got rid of Detective Harris's gun, tossing it into a heavily weeded area in the Kirkwood section of Atlanta. They led police to the weed patch in Kirkwood where they disposed of the gun, but the underbrush was too dense for the six city prisoners searching for it with swing blades to find it. It was not recovered at that time. (However, the gun was turned over to a beat patrolman four months later when a ten-year-old kid found it while playing in those weeds. He gave it to his father who called police. Unfortunately, the gun was too rusted for ballistics tests.)

James Carter admitted to shooting Detective Harris, although he insisted it was accidental. The following are the points he made to the detectives during his questioning:

1. He did not go to the Atlanta Theater to rob it but to watch the show with his friend Kenneth Smith and the two girls.

2. He and Smith were exchanging some words with the girl behind the concession stand over the sale of popcorn, when a man (Harris), wearing dress slacks, a sport shirt, and a sport coat, intervened. Carter said that Harris did not, at any time during the confrontation, identify himself as a police officer. (None of the witnesses at the theater, including the girl working the concession stand could say that they heard Detective Harris identify himself as a police officer.)

3. Carter said that during the fight, he saw a gun in the shoulder holster under the man's (Harris's) coat. Carter said he took the gun from Harris's holster, and while he was getting bumped and knocked around in the scuffle, the gun accidentally went off three times. One of those fired bullets hit Harris, another struck the guy (Tony Turner) that jumped on Smith, and the third did not hit anyone.

James Carter was charged with the murder of Detective C. E. Harris, robbery of Harris's gun, and aggravated assault on Tony Turner. Kenneth Smith was charged as an accessory. Carter and Smith pleaded not guilty to the charges and had a jury trial in Fulton County Superior Court.

James Carter was found guilty of voluntary manslaughter and sentenced to ten years in prison, with an additional one year for aggravated assault. He was likely released from prison sooner than those eleven years.

Kenneth Smith was found guilty and given two twelve-month sentences, which were suspended. So he was released immediately after the trial.

Twenty-six-year-old Atlanta narcotics detective Clarence E. Harris was killed in the line of duty over a simple bag of popcorn, while working an approved extra job.

Atlanta Police Officer

Larry Barkwell

Sometimes a killer wins and walks away after he's killed a cop . . . sometimes a killer loses when he gets killed by a cop

Mohammed Speaks.

That was the name of the publication some would say was extremely focused. Others would say it was highly bigoted. It was sold on the downtown streets of major cities by Black Muslims, the followers of the Nation of Islam. Targeting mainly black pedestrians, the publication was sold aggressively, quite aggressively, including what amounted to threat and intimidation.

Black Muslims were easily identifiable by what could be considered their uniform. They wore neatly pressed suits, not a wrinkle anywhere on their pants or jackets, mostly in solid black, maybe some pastels with thin stripes or faint plaid. There were no wrinkles in their starched white shirts and across their stiff white collars they'd wear a stark black bow tie. Although not part of their dress uniform, but still a component of their identity, was the shaven bald head; if not bald, very closely cropped hair. The bald head made Black Muslim men easily recognizable during an era when most black men wore afro hairstyles.

Every day, any time during the day, downtown office workers and shoppers would direct angry complaints to the Atlanta Police Department and to the mayor's office, such as:

> Each day, when I leave my office building to go to lunch, I don't walk a block when some Black Muslim-looking guy shoves a newspaper in my face, telling me that I have to buy it. When I say that I'm not interested, two or three more appear and block my way so I cannot leave; they then want to tell me about the white devils and all these bad things about my white boss. I have to go into the street, with all the cars, to get around them.

This complaint was from a black woman who walked downtown at lunchtime each working day. Tourists and conventioneers were also making their displeasure known to the Atlanta police. Most of the complaints amounted to the same problem: Black Muslims were intimidating the pedestrians walking the downtown sidewalks, trying to force them to buy what the Nation of Islam published!

The Atlanta Police Department reacted to these complaints by forming a new unit—the Downtown Foot Patrol, commanded by Captain Gary Shepherd. This was a highly visible unit of uniformed cops who walked beats on the downtown streets for several miles along the Peachtree corridor, from Memorial Drive below downtown to Fourteenth Street in midtown. The visibility of these cops on foot resulted in a clear decrease in street crime. Nevertheless, the increased visibility of the cops did not deter the Black Muslims from harassing black pedestrians to buy their publications.

Larry Barkwell had been an Atlanta police officer for four years when he was assigned to the new foot patrol, walking the Peachtree and Tenth Streets beat in midtown. He asked Captain Shepherd to reassign him to Broad Street. "He said he had personal reasons but also wanted to be where the action was and wanted to stay busy," recalled Shepherd about Barkwell's request to be reassigned. He also said, "I transferred him the next day. He was the kind of officer who was needed there, muscular and very strong. He could not be intimidated or bullied. Larry Barkwell went about his duties in a very professional manner."

Captain Shepherd went on to say that in his opinion, "Broad Street during that time was the most dangerous street in the City of Atlanta. And, in addition to the problem of the Black Muslims and their newspapers, we also had to keep a wary eye on the Black Panthers who occupied a small storefront office on Broad Street."

This new police unit had been operating only two weeks when it was tested by the Black Muslims. In the early afternoon on the warm summer day of June 19, 1973, eight, maybe ten, Black Muslims appeared on Broad Street in the heart of downtown. Each had an armful of newspapers. Each shoved a newspaper at any pedestrian who attempted to walk by. Any pedestrian who walked on, making it clear that he or she refused to accept the newspaper, was followed by the seller, closer than an arm's length, who shouted threats and insults at him or her.

One pedestrian who was targeted by a couple of Black Muslims was the street preacher, a black man, mid-fifties, a regular on the downtown streets, who was known to the police and everyone who frequented downtown. He would stand on the corner of one intersection, then move on to another, bible in hand, preaching religious rhetoric to all within the sound of his voice but to no one in particular.

The preacher walked down Broad Street on that June afternoon and was stopped by two Black Muslims. One shoved a *Mohammed Speaks* newspaper in his face, demanding that the preacher buy it. The preacher refused.

"I am a Baptist minister, and I don't believe in the Muslim religion," he told them.

He was immediately surrounded by all the Black Muslims who were there. They shouted threats and insults at him. One saying, "Your religion is the white man's religion; you need to join the Nation of Islam!"

They blocked the sidewalk, preventing the preacher from walking away.

Atlanta police sergeants C. W. Johnson and Julius Derico, both black, were standing nearby on Broad Street in front of Woolworth's Five and Ten Cent store. Both sergeants walked over to see what was going on. The preacher asked the sergeants if there was anything they could do to stop these men from bothering him. Sergeant Johnson told the group of Black Muslims that they could not force their papers on people and that they were not allowed to harass people who refused to buy them. The leader of the group (later identified as Lee Anderson) got loud and belligerent in response to Johnson's warning. He said, "We will sell our papers anywhere we wish and in any manner. Go tell your white boss the same."

Sergeant Johnson told them that they were violating the Safe Streets and Sidewalks ordinance, and if they did not disperse, they would be arrested.

Anderson got in Sergeant Johnson's face and said, "We're not going anywhere until the police leave."

Johnson then declared that all the Black Muslims present were under arrest. Anderson just smirked at Johnson. He said, "You must not know who you are talking to. We don't give a damn about you or going to jail!"

Officers Larry Barkwell and R. C. Simmons, far enough away not to be able to hear the substance of what was being said but close enough to observe that it was a confrontation that could benefit by additional police presence, moved in to join the two sergeants. Just about when they got there, Anderson started to shout and bellow a string of obscenities at all four cops. Then, as if by some prearranged signal, all the Black Muslims (no one was quite sure if there were eight, nine, or ten of them) attacked the four police officers.

The first blow was a fist to the face of Sergeant Johnson, who went down. Then two Black Muslims grabbed Barkwell, the only white cop among the four, when the melee started in full. One of the Black Muslims took the gun from Barkwell's holster. Johnson heard someone yell, "Kill the pigs!"

Hearing that, Johnson shot at the Black Muslim who was attacking him. After firing his revolver, it was wrested from his hand.

There were more gunshots. It was bedlam on Broad Street. People were screaming and running for cover.

Two foot patrol officers, L. R. Moore and M. L. Moon, part of the new Downtown Foot Patrol unit, were taking their lunch break at a small sandwich shop on Broad Street across from Woolworth's. They heard the gunshots, looked out, and observed people running. Officers Moore and Moon rushed out the front door and saw the fighting in front of Woolworth's. Moore observed one of the Black Muslims crouched down beside a police three-wheel motorcycle, firing a revolver at a police officer down on the ground. Seeing that he had a clear shot, Moore braced against the restaurant doorway and fired twice, hitting the shooter both times and killing him. This shooter was later identified as the Black Muslim Kenneth Dozier.

Police radio dispatcher: *"Any cars near number one Broad Street SW in front of Woolworth's, signal 63/25/50/4* [officer needs help/gunshots/person shot/ambulance on the way]. *Cars be advised that several people have been shot including police officers, also be advised the 25s* [gunshots] *are still up on the call!"*

Patrol cars, detective cars, undercover vehicles, paddy wagons, motorcycles—all types of APD rolling stock went screaming to Broad Street at the location of the Woolworth's store. Chaos pervaded and persisted. Civilians were running and screaming. Gunshots were fired from different locations toward various targets. And cops were engaged in hand-to-hand combat with Black Muslims. At the same time, several Black Muslims were attempting to drag Sergeant Johnson to the Black Muslims' van parked farther down Broad Street. Officer Simmons ran toward them to help Sergeant Johnson escape from the grasp of the Black Muslims. He started to beat the Black Muslims off Sergeant Johnson with his nightstick. Several other cops arrived, enough to overpower and handcuff those Black Muslims.

It was never determined why Sergeant Johnson was being forcibly taken by the Black Muslims toward their van. But there was no shortage of speculation by the APD cops. The two popular theories were that the Black Muslims wanted to hold Sergeant Johnson hostage as a bargaining chip in demand for something or someone the Black Muslims might have wanted or would want, and the other theory was that maybe the Black Muslims wanted to video his execution.

Injured during the melee, Sergeant Derico was down and hurt, but not wounded. He was pulled out of the line of fire by a Newberry's security guard, Robert Watson. To take cover from the shooting, Derico hobbled toward the parking garage next to Woolworth's. As he was seeking cover, he was shot in the back of his upper leg and went down between two parked cars.

Officer Larry Barkwell was shot twice: once in his chest and once in his back. He was shot with his own gun. His gun was taken by one of the three Black Muslims who had overpowered him. Barkwell had customized the gun, his service revolver, by replacing the brown wooden grips with white bone grips. Officer L. R. Moore said he saw the gun on the ground next to Kenneth Dozier, the Black Muslim he'd shot and killed. Instead of taking a few seconds to retrieve the gun, Moore had gone directly to where Barkwell lay on the ground to see if he could help him. The gun was gone when he returned a short time later to look for it. Officer Moore said it looked like the gun that Officer Barkwell always carried. After days of collecting evidence from the crime scene, Officer Larry Barkwell's service revolver was not found.

Officer Moore retrieved Sergeant Johnson's service revolver from a wounded Black Muslim lying in the street. He returned it to Johnson. No ambulance had arrived yet. Barkwell was placed in the backseat of a patrol car and transported to Grady Hospital, where he was officially pronounced DOA.

The ambulance had still not arrived, so Sergeant Derico was taken to Grady in another patrol car.

Robert Watson, the black security guard for J.J. Newberry's (a department store near Woolworth's) saw what was happening in the street between the Atlanta police and the Black Muslims. When Watson observed a Black Muslim shooting at a police officer, he drew his gun and shot the Black Muslim. In the melee, someone, somewhere, shot Watson in the leg. He stumbled back into Woolworth's and fell to the floor. When the first ambulance finally arrived, it took Watson to Grady Hospital.

Not long after it was over and safe to be on Broad Street again, what had happened was quickly reported on radio and television. The first reports indicated that there was shooting, several men had been shot and killed, even an Atlanta police officer had been shot. The Barkwell family, aware that that was where Larry was working, called the police department to learn if he was okay. Captain J. F. Johnson was at police headquarters when they phoned. When an officer is killed or seriously injured, the policy of the Atlanta Police Department is to notify the family in person. When Barkwell's wife, Linda, got Captain Johnson on the phone and asked if Larry was okay, he had no choice but to tell her the truth over the phone.

Homicide detective W. F. Perkins was the lead detective in the murder of Officer Larry Barkwell and all those shot that day on

Broad Street. Perkins was assisted by homicide detective sergeant Berlyn Compton. Their investigation concluded that six people had been shot and taken to Grady Hospital:

1. Atlanta police officer Larry Barkwell (deceased) received two gunshot wounds to the chest and back.
2. Atlanta police sergeant Julius Derico received a gunshot wound to his rear upper leg.
3. Black Muslim Kenneth Dozier (deceased) was shot twice in the small of his back.
4. Black Muslim John 5X Chambliss received one gunshot wound to the stomach.
5. Black Muslim Perry X Shirley received one gunshot wound to the right hip.
6. Private security guard Robert Watson received one gunshot wound to his left upper leg.

In the midst of all the chaos, Lee Anderson, the apparent leader of this group of Black Muslims, and several other Black Muslims left the scene in their easily identifiable van—painted blue and white—that was parked farther down Broad Street. A citywide lookout was placed on the van. And an arrest warrant was issued for Lee Anderson, charging him with the murder of Officer Larry Barkwell. Sergeants Johnson and Derico identified Anderson as the man who had shot and killed Officer Larry Barkwell and who had shot Sergeant Derico in the leg.

At eight thirty the evening of the brawl and shootings, Lee Anderson, at the wheel of that blue and white van, was apprehended at Simpson and Chappell Roads NW. Three other Black Muslim men, passengers in the van, were also arrested. By the end of the day, seven Black Muslims were in the city jail or in Grady Hospital, all facing one or more charges of murder, aggravated assault, simple battery, and obstructing an officer.

An eighth Black Muslim, Kenneth Dozier, was dead.

What was not found was the one crucial piece of evidence—Officer Barkwell's service revolver. It was determined that Officer

L. R. Moore was the last person to see the gun in the street next to the body of Kenneth Dozier. That was after Moore had shot Dozier and then had ran to Barkwell lying on the ground. During the investigation that followed, a witness stated that she had observed the entire incident from her fifth-floor office window. From that vantage point, she observed two teenage black males (not dressed in the Black Muslims' code) walk over to where the policeman was lying on the sidewalk in front of Woolworth's. She said she saw them pick up a small object from the ground and walk away toward Rich's Department Store.

Ballistics tests conducted at the Georgia State Crime Lab determined that the two bullets recovered from the body of Officer Barkwell were fired from the same gun and were consistent with being fired from an APD issued Smith & Wesson .38 caliber revolver, model 10, with a 4″ bull barrel. There were two other APD .38 caliber Smith & Wesson revolvers fired in the incident—one was Sergeant Johnson's and the other was Officer Moore's. The Georgia State Crime Lab eliminated their guns as the ones that had fired the bullets recovered from Barkwell's body. Security guard Watson's Rossi .38 caliber revolver was also eliminated.

The conclusion was that Officer Larry Barkwell was shot and killed with bullets fired from his own gun.

Two questions remained though: (1) Who fired Barkwell's gun? Lee Anderson? Or Kenneth Dozier? and (2) What happened to the gun?

Sergeants Johnson and Derico were convinced that Lee Anderson was the triggerman in the murder of Larry Barkwell and the one who wounded Derico. However, three civilian witnesses identified Kenneth Dozier as the shooter. Those three witnesses were in positions to have observed the entire incident independently of one another. Their observations were consistent with the physical, forensic, and ballistics evidence, including fragments of testimony from other witnesses pieced together to fit with the testimony of the three witnesses.

All the Black Muslim defendants were bound over to the Fulton County grand jury for murder. The grand jury heard all the witnesses' testimonies. It was their opinion that Officer Larry Barkwell was killed by Kenneth Dozier. Murder charges were no billed (not indicted), and charges on all the defendants were downgraded to misdemeanor simple battery.

Eventually all the charges against the Black Muslims in the Broad Street "disturbance" were dismissed. They walked out of the courtroom with smirks on their faces.

The cops were livid. The public—both black and white—was astounded. The media couldn't get enough of it.

How could the courts have allowed this to happen? The simple answer, the criminal justice system had failed, again!

Larry Barkwell graduated from Dallas High School in Dallas, Georgia. Following graduation, he joined the United States Air Force, serving from 1961 to 1965. When he completed his tour, he went to work at Lockheed Aircraft as a machine operator. But what he really wanted to do was to get into law enforcement. He worked for the Powder Springs Police Department and the Cartersville Police Department, both in suburban Atlanta. From those jobs, he was highly recommended to the Atlanta Police Department. Two years prior to being shot and killed on Broad Street, Atlanta police officer Larry Barkwell had been shot in the arm in an altercation with an assailant. He fully recovered from that wound and hardly mentioned it; most of the cops he worked with were unaware of it.

Larry and Linda Barkwell had moved into a new house one week prior to the tragedy on Broad Street.

Larry Barkwell was thirty-three years old when he was shot and killed.

The APD cops and cops in every city were not the only ones upset with the findings of the Fulton County grand jury.

The Barkwell family and many ordinary citizens everywhere were upset too. Especially with the Fulton County Court's action—or lack of action—in the murder of Larry Barkwell, and that Black Muslim Lee Anderson just walked away.

It wasn't justice, but some satisfaction came three-and-a-half years later while Anderson was still walking freely among the rest of us.

A house on Westwood Avenue near Cascade Avenue in southwest Atlanta was rented in the name of Al Muhamahim a/k/a Al Jashua a/k/a Lee X Anderson. It was occupied by a group of Black Muslims. The house had been sold. The new owner did not want to renew the rental agreement. He asked Anderson and the Black Muslims to leave. They refused, making it very clear that they would use force against anyone who tried to put them out. The new owner obtained an eviction order, giving the occupants thirty days to vacate the house. During those thirty days, Atlanta SWAT officers R. S. Johnson and P. M. Tovey were assigned to observe the house and to report on the comings and goings of the occupants. On several occasions, they even had conversations with Anderson.

On December 28, 1977, a bitterly cold day, the thirty-day period expired. A group of Fulton County marshals, supported by the Atlanta police SWAT team, arrived at the Westwood Avenue house to serve the eviction order. As the marshals were getting out of their cars, they were shot at from inside the house.

Marshal Larry Folds was shot at and killed instantly. Marshal James Broadwell was shot at and wounded.

Return fire from the SWAT team and the marshals killed one of the two Black Muslims inside the house. The one who was killed was identified as Lee X Anderson. The other one continued firing during an hour-long gun battle. He surrendered to police when the house caught fire from police tear gas canisters. He was Mujahid Jerubbabel Muhammad a/k/a Mickey Gore. He was charged with murder and aggravated assault.

213

This time, the fate of Lee Anderson was not up to the Fulton County Courts. His fate was up to himself . . . and the APD SWAT team!

OFFICER
LARRY BARKWELL
"KILLED WHILE QUELLING A DISTURBANCE"
JUNE 19, 1973

Atlanta Police Officer

James R. Greene

"Mayday, mayday, mayday . . . policeman shot . . . need an ambulance!"

The frantic words that bellowed from the police radio were strange, almost foreign, not the usual Atlanta police call for help. However, the dispatcher recognized the international distress signal, understood what the caller was trying to say, and got a location from the excited caller, a private security guard. He was driving by a police paddy wagon when he noticed that the passenger door was wide open. There was no activity and no one nearby. He pulled over, stopped, and looked to see if something was wrong.

Over all frequencies, the dispatcher promptly transmitted: "*Any car near Boulevard and Memorial Drive, signal 63/50/4* [officer needs help/person shot/ambulance on the way]*!*"

That chilling combination of signals —63/50/4—gets the immediate attention of the greatest number of cops who receive it. Every cop in the City of Atlanta heard those signals. The arriving patrol cars found Officer J. R. Greene slumped over the steering wheel of his assigned paddy wagon. It was clear that he'd been shot several times. He did not react to those who accompanied him in the ambulance to Grady Hospital. Not until the gurney was being rolled from the ambulance ramp to the emergency room did Greene attempt to speak. But he was unable to talk. He was unable to provide any information about the identity of his shooter(s).

Atlanta police officer James Richard Greene died in the ER a few minutes after he arrived.

James Richard Greene was born in Virginia on April 5, 1944, the son of a military family who settled in Florida when he was a baby. Jimmy's early years were in West Palm Beach and later Jacksonville. He was a quiet kid, a Huckleberry Finn, who loved the outdoors, fishing, and hunting. He earned a few dollars running a paper route and a few dollars more mowing lawns.

Larry King, the same age as Jimmy Greene, also mowed lawns in the same neighborhood. On one occasion, a property owner unwittingly engaged both Jimmy and Larry to mow his lawn, a job that could be done by either. Both showed up to cut the same grass in the same yard. Jimmy Greene was there first but was not yet mowing because of a problem with his lawnmower. Larry tinkered with the mower, got it started, and at the same time, started a friendship that would bring Jimmy and Larry as close as brothers for the rest of their lives.

James Greene went to high school in Jacksonville, but he wasn't interested in school. He quit before graduation. He spent a lot of time at Larry King's home where he got to know Larry's younger brother, Woody. (Woody later became an Atlanta police officer.)

James Greene was drafted into the United States Army in 1965, serving most of his two-year obligation in Okinawa, Japan, assigned to a heavy artillery unit. During that time, he received his GED, which is recognized everywhere as the equivalent of a high school diploma.

When Greene was discharged, he didn't know what he was going to do next. He did know that there was no future in civilian life for anyone experienced in heavy artillery. Woody King, then with the APD, suggested that Jimmy consider becoming a cop.

James Greene became an Atlanta police officer in August 1967. As a rookie, he worked a variety of duties, the same as any other rookie street cop. Three years later, assigned to the morning watch (midnight to eight AM, the graveyard shift), he drove a paddy wagon covering Atlanta's south side regularly.

James Greene was a quiet, unassuming guy, with a laid-back personality, and a pleasant word for everyone. People said of him, "If you can't get along with Jimmy Greene, you can't get along with anyone!" He was well-liked by all.

Greene was engaged to Samantha (Sam) Smith. They were having a house built, expecting it to be completed when they got married. He maintained a close relationship with Larry King, who was then living in Atlanta, and Woody King. He was very happy working the job he liked.

Greene loved to kid around when the opportunity presented itself. One morning, when he had just gotten off duty, he got a call from Larry. Larry asked him for a favor—to bring a motorcycle from the State Capital in downtown to Larry's service station in midtown, a distance of less than three miles. Larry had purchased the motorcycle for his son from a man who worked across from the State Capital building. It was a Suzuki 50, a child-sized motorcycle, the type that clowns rode at the circus. Greene was still in his APD uniform. He thought it would be fun to appear to onlookers as an Atlanta motorcycle cop riding on what was clearly a child's motorcycle. And that was how he brought it to his friend Larry King.

During the night of November 3, 1971, Freddie Hilton and Twyman Myers roamed the dark, wet Atlanta streets looking for a lone cop in a vulnerable position. Hilton and Myers were members of a group known as the Black Liberation Army, the BLA, an extremely violent, militant offshoot of the Black Panther Party. The BLA, which originated in New York City, broke away from Huey Newton's Black Panthers to become disciples of Eldridge Cleaver. Cleaver escaped to Algeria to avoid prosecution for his violent crimes in the United States. Cleaver and his followers wanted the Black Panther Party to engage in the random assassination of police officers everywhere. The Black Panther Party would not do that. The BLA had been identified as taking part in the assassinations of four New York City police officers and attacks on at least six other NYPD cops. After one of these attacks on two NYPD cops, the license plate number of the getaway car was identified and made public on TV and in the newspapers.

Two days later, the *New York Times* received a package that contained the license plates of the getaway car accompanied by the following message:

May 19, 1971
All power to the people.
Here are the license plates sort after by the fascist state pig police. We send them in order to exhibit the potential power of oppressed peoples to acquire revolutionary justice. The armed goods of this racist government will again meet the guns of third world peoples as long as they occupy our community and murder our brothers and sisters in the name of American law and order. Just as the fascist marines and army occupy Vietnam in the name of democracy, and murder Vietnamese people in the name of American imperialism are confronted with the guns of the Vietnamese Liberation Army, the domestic armed forces of racism and oppression will be confronted with the guns of the Black

Liberation Army, who will mete out, in the tradition of Malcolm and all true revolutionaries, real justice. We are revolutionary justice.

All power to the people.

On that rainy November night, Officer J. R. Greene left Atlanta Police Headquarters shortly after the midnight roll call and drove to his beat. He did not receive any calls requiring his paddy wagon. At 1:20 AM, he stopped at Grandma's Biscuits, a fast food restaurant located at Hill Street and Interstate 20. He purchased a take-out order of two sausage biscuits and a Coke, and then he drove a half dozen blocks to Boulevard and Memorial Drive SE. He pulled into a Gulf service station, closed for the night, and parked under the overhang between the building and the gas pumps. He sat in his wagon, out of the rain, eating his snack.

The Black Liberation Army had relocated its headquarters from New York City to Atlanta. The heat had become too intense for them in New York City. The NYPD, thirty-two thousand strong, had deployed all its resources in the massive manhunt for the killers and attackers of its cops. BLA leaders John Thomas, Andrew Jackson, and Joanne Chesimard led a series of bank robberies in the Metro Atlanta area, operating out of a house in the Kirkwood section of Atlanta. Robbing banks provided them with the cash for living and operating expenses. But robbing banks was not their number one priority—it was assassinating police officers because they were police officers. No other reason.

Freddie Hilton and Twyman Myers, the two least experienced BLA members, had screwed up their assignments on several jobs. John Thomas chewed them out for "some of the dumb shit" they had done. Joanne Chesimard told them to "go out, find a pig, and off the motherfucker." As soon as they did that, Thomas would be satisfied that they could successfully do what was asked of them.

Myers and Hilton went looking for a cop to kill. They saw a policeman sitting alone in a paddy wagon parked at a closed gas station. They approached the wagon on the passenger side, each with a gun in his hand. One of them opened the door and asked for directions. Greene had just finished eating his sandwiches and was about to put down what was left of his coke to oblige them. That was when explosions and flashes filled the interior of the wagon. Greene slumped over the steering wheel mortally wounded. The two BLA assassins grabbed Greene's service revolver, holster, and gun belt, then ripped his badge from his shirt and ran.

Freddie Hilton and Twyman Myers burst into the Kirkwood house where the others were waiting. They threw the dead officer's gun and badge on the table, displaying their trophies for all to admire, and exclaiming, "We did it! We did it!!"

Joanne Chesimard smiled approvingly.

Shortly after the Greene murder, members of the BLA split up and headed for different U.S. cities with the intention of killing police officers. In San Francisco, a police sergeant was stopped for a traffic light when a car occupied by two black males pulled up alongside him. One aimed a submachine gun out the window at the sergeant, but the gun jammed and they sped off. The chase was on. Other patrol units joined in. The chase ended when the fleeing car jumped a curb and crashed into a fire hydrant and several No Parking signs. Both occupants jumped from their wrecked car and started shooting. The cops returned fire, wounding and arresting both.

Found in the wrecked car were two guns that led to a break in the murders of the NYPD cops. One gun was the .38 caliber service revolver that belonged to one of the murdered NYPD cops. The other gun was the .45 caliber semi-automatic pistol—the murder weapon of that same NYPD cop.

The next day, three black males walked into a San Francisco police precinct. One pointed a shotgun at the desk sergeant and, without a word, murdered him. Pellets from the blast wounded a female clerk nearby.

About a year after James Greene was killed, a telephone call was directed into the APD homicide squad from a Miami police detective. He said, "We've got a guy in our jail on an armed robbery charge, says he knows something about an Atlanta police officer killing, and he wants to make a deal." That guy was BLA member Samuel Cooper.

APD Sergeant Louis Graham and Detective Don Lee flew to Miami to interview Samuel Cooper. Graham and Lee returned to Atlanta with a thirty-five page written statement in which Cooper identified the leaders of the BLA. He provided details on all the BLA crimes that he knew of, including the assassination of Officer James Greene. He named Freddie Hilton and Twyman Myers as his killers.

Several months prior to the Cooper interview in Miami, Greene's service revolver was recovered from a pond in the southwest section of Atlanta. A woman, while fishing, found it submerged in shallow water near the bank. She retrieved it and gave it to the man in charge of the pond. He brought it to the APD where it was turned over to Homicide. The revolver was corroded with rust and appeared to have been in the water for some time, but the APD serial number was still legible. The state crime lab was able to restore the manufacturer's serial number but could not provide any additional evidence. A diver searched the pond for Greene's belt, holster, and badge; they were never found.

Five members of the BLA appeared in St. Louis. A shoot-out with St. Louis police ended with the apprehension of three of them. Twyman Myers and Joanne Chesimard fled during that shoot-out, before they could be apprehended.

The next time Joanne Chesimard surfaced was in 1973. She was on the New Jersey Turnpike where a New Jersey State Police car stopped her for speeding. She pulled over, and as the trooper walked up to her car, she shot and killed him. She was apprehended in New Jersey in 1997, where she was tried and convicted for the murder of that trooper. She was sentenced to a life term at the New Jersey State Penitentiary. Two years later, she escaped with the help of four visitors who took a corrections officer hostage and commandeered his prison van as part of the getaway. Chesimard has been on the FBI's ten most-wanted list ever since, still at large, and reported to be living in Cuba under the name of Assata Shakur. (The U.S. has no extradition treaty with Cuba.)

In 1975, Freddie Hilton was apprehended for robbery in New York City, unrelated to any police killings. There was insufficient evidence to indict him or to try him for any of the police killings or attacks. He served time for robbery in the New York State Penitentiary.

From the 1970s to the early 1980s, most of the BLA leaders and members were killed in shoot-outs with police or were caught, served time, then released. Some are still serving various prison sentences.

In 1974, Twyman Myers returned to New York City. The FBI and the NYPD discovered that he was hiding out in the Bronx. They set up surveillance at his hideout and waited for him to come out. They wanted to take him on the street. Myers carelessly left his hiding place one night, and as soon as he was on the street, FBI agents and NYPD detectives surrounded him. As reported, he pulled his gun but did not have a chance to squeeze off a round. Because as soon as his weapon appeared, the agents and the detectives fired their shotguns, handguns, and automatic weapons at him. It was easy to imagine that his bullet-riddled body looked much like the bodies of Bonnie and Clyde in the last scene of the *Bonnie and Clyde* film.

The night Twyman Myers's body, oozing blood from many gunshot wounds, lay on the garbage-littered street in the Bronx, the APD dispatcher announced over all radio frequencies that Twyman Myers had been found, shot, and killed in New York City. Police sirens from patrol cars throughout Atlanta could be heard celebrating the delivery of justice to the BLA member who had murdered Atlanta police officer James R. Greene.

Freddie Hilton served his time for robbery at the New York State Penitentiary and was released. He found a legitimate job with a telephone company in New York. Atlanta police detective Jim

Rose, working cold cases, picked up the Greene file in 2001, thirty years after his assassination. He followed new leads, developed fresh information, and found several witnesses. Each witness was a former BLA member who had served time, was out of prison, working a regular job, and supporting a family. They each agreed to testify against Freddie Hilton for the murder of Officer James Greene. Detective Rose had sufficient cause to have a warrant issued. Hilton was arrested by the NYPD, extradited to Georgia, and held in the Fulton County Jail.

James Richard Greene was assassinated because he wore a blue uniform and carried a badge. He was murdered simply because he was a cop and happened to be in the wrong place at the wrong time.

In October 2003, thirty-two years after the murder, Freddie Hilton was tried in Fulton County Superior Court, found guilty, and sentenced to three life terms without the possibility of parole for a series of violent felonies and for the assassination of Atlanta police officer James Richard Greene.

Jimmy Greene is buried in the Atlanta suburb of Douglas County.

OFFICER
JAMES R. GREENE
"SHOT BY ASSAILANT"
NOVEMBER 3, 1971

Atlanta Police Officer

Billy M. Kaylor

Given the death penalty, a cop killer goes free thanks to the law and the Georgia Pardons and Parole Board

*A*tlanta police officer Billy M. Kaylor was working a one-man patrol car in one of Atlanta's inner-city high-crime areas during the darkness of the early morning on August 23, 1971. He had graduated from the police academy not more than twelve months before. Kaylor answered a silent alarm sent from a liquor store. When he arrived, he discovered and caught two thugs burglarizing the store. Both burglars were prison-hardened, street-savvy, and vicious.

Billy Kaylor was born on October 29, 1943, in Copperhill, a small town on the Tennessee side of the Tennessee-Georgia state line. On the other side of the state line was the small town of McCaysville, Georgia. Kaylor's childhood and adolescence were occupied with the various activities available in either of those towns in the foothills of the Smoky Mountains. He was a star athlete at West Fannin High School in McCaysville. Billy graduated in 1964 and then joined the United States Air Force. After basic training, he was stationed at Norton Air Force Base in California where he was assigned to an air police unit.

Anita Skomars, a young woman originally from California, worked at the base day care center. She was walking the children back to the center after an outing when a voice from a passing AP patrol car yelled, "Hey you!" in her direction.

She promptly turned to the car and indignantly retorted, "My name is not, 'Hey you'" and then turned back to shepherding the children to the day care center. The next day, air policeman Billy Kaylor went to the day care center to apologize to Miss Skomars for his rudeness. His apology was couched in an invitation to dinner. The apology was accepted and so was the invitation to dinner. They dated for several months and were married in 1968, shortly before the end of his four-year air force tour of duty.

After his discharge, Billy and Anita Kaylor moved to Pomona, California, where Billy went to work for General Dynamics.

However, Billy was restless in that job and told Anita of his desire to return to Georgia. His activities during his time as a policeman in the air force convinced him that law enforcement was for him. Billy Kaylor wanted to be a cop! While his focus was on Georgia, he looked in various cities and states for open positions with a police department. Despite negative results, he persisted with his search. Payoff came one day with good news from Atlanta, Georgia. The Atlanta Police Department was hiring. Billy and Anita moved to Atlanta where he went through the application, selection, and training processes.

Billy M. Kaylor became Atlanta patrolman Billy M. Kaylor in 1970. He was assigned to the morning watch (midnight to eight AM) in the Uniform (Patrol) Division.

As he worked the dark streets in the different areas of Atlanta, Billy Kaylor realized that police work on an air force base was one thing, the work of a cop in Atlanta was quite another. Experience accumulated during time on the job had helped him transition from small-town kid to air force AP. Now experience and time would help him transition from air force AP to big-city cop. Unfortunately, time and experience were in short supply for Atlanta police officer Billy Kaylor.

Among the routine functions of the morning watch are answering calls for service and attending to traffic accidents. A less routine responsibility is intervening during burglaries at businesses and apprehending the burglars in the act.

There are several different types of burglar alarm systems installed in businesses. The type depends on whether the business employs the services of a private alarm company or an Atlanta police burglar alarm, which is installed by Atlanta police technicians and connected directly to the APD communications section at police headquarters. Business burglaries often occur during the night when the business is closed and everyone is gone. An unauthorized entry is designed to trigger a signal that alerts the APD's communications alarm board. The alarm board identifies the location of the premises where the entry has occurred. There is no indication on the premises that an alarm has been sent. That's why it's considered a silent alarm. The burglar is unaware that an alarm has been tripped.

On August 23, 1971, at 2:20 AM on a Monday morning, two burglars forced open the front door of the Deluxe Liquor Store and set off the silent alarm.

APD dispatcher: *"Car 11, the liquor store at 22 Northside Drive SW at Mitchell Street, signal 65* [silent police burglar alarm]*."*
Kaylor: *"11 received, signal 65 at the liquor store, 22 Northside Drive."*

In less than two minutes, Kaylor came back on the radio: *"11. Start me another car, I've got two subjects."*

227

Police unit: *"10B, I'm close."*
Police unit: *"31, on the way."*
Police unit: *"32, on the way."*
Police unit: *"12, starting that way."*
Police unit: *"71 [lieutenant], 22 Northside Drive."*
Dispatcher: *"Car 11, several cars are en route."*

Kaylor had both burglars outside at gunpoint with their hands up against the wall in front of the liquor store. He approached them before his backup arrived. While he was searching one burglar, the other turned and grabbed Kaylor's gun. The two grabbed him and threw him to the ground. Instead of jumping into their car and getting the hell out of there, they kicked and stomped Kaylor into unconsciousness. These two were not just burglars, they were cold-blooded killers. The one holding the gun shot Kaylor three times in the head before he and his partner jumped into their car and sped away.

Officer D. B. Davis in car 10B was the first to arrive. He saw Kaylor's patrol car in the parking lot and Kaylor on the ground. Davis also observed a dark colored older model Ford Falcon speeding out of the parking lot. A taxi stopped at the curb not far from the liquor store. The driver pointed at the fleeing Falcon and shouted at Officer Davis, "Those two guys just shot the police!"

Davis went after the car. It was traveling south on Northside Drive and turned west on Fair Street. He attempted to advise the police dispatcher that he was in pursuit of the shooters, but he was unable to. The radio traffic from the arriving cars, from the other units trying to get medical help and an ambulance to the scene, and still others requesting a lookout on the shooters congested the radio airwaves, and Davis could not get through.

Police unit: *"Signal 50 [person shot] on a police officer, 22 Northside Drive, need an ambulance right away!"*
Dispatcher: *"Ambulance is on the way to 22 Northside Drive, code 3 [rush call]."*
Police unit: *"Do you have a lookout?"*
Dispatcher: *"No lookout at this time."*

Police unit: *"71 [lieutenant] to radio, have cars block intersections between 22 Northside and Grady Hospital."*

Dispatcher: *"Advise radio what cars have which intersections."*

When the ambulance arrived on the Grady emergency ramp, the trauma team was waiting to rush the wounded officer into emergency surgery. Billy Kaylor died a short time later.

Meanwhile, the Ford Falcon was speeding along Fair Street with Davis in pursuit. It was running red lights and not slowing down for stop signs. At Fair and Ashby, the Falcon stopped. Its doors flew open and both occupants jumped out shooting. Davis returned fire through the front windshield of his patrol car, blowing out the window. No one was hit by either fire. There was a break in radio traffic, and Davis was able to get on the air and advise of the shoot-out with the occupants of the Falcon. Patrol cars headed for Fair and Ashby. The two shooters fled on foot. A two-hour ground search conducted by more than a dozen cops was fruitless. But they had the car. It was a starting point for detectives.

Homicide detectives H. F. Pharr and L. F. New traced the Falcon to a middle-aged man whose son fit the general description of one of the shooters. Looking into the son's whereabouts, the detectives were informed by the father that his son had been in jail for the last several days. They went to the jail to verify. It checked out. He was in jail as his father had said. While speaking with the son, they got the names and the location of two of his friends who might have been using the Falcon. Pharr and New went to an apartment in the Grady Homes housing project and found Ronnie Franklin, black male, age twenty-one, and Matthew Callahan Jr., black male, age nineteen. One of them was feigning sleep on a couch downstairs, the other doing the same in a bed upstairs. Detective New pulled Callahan out of the bed fully clothed and still wearing sneakers that were wet from the early morning dew. He had blood on one pant leg. Callahan's mother, who was also in the apartment, insisted that both boys had been in all night and were sleeping for hours. Several items found in the trunk of the Falcon matched the items taken from the liquor store during the burglary. The fingerprints of both Callahan and Franklin were on the items.

It was determined that after Callahan and Franklin overpowered Officer Kaylor and stomped him into unconsciousness, it was Callahan who stood over him and shot him three times in the head.

Callahan and Franklin were tried in Fulton County Superior Court and found guilty of murder, aggravated assault, and burglary, among other charges.

Callahan received the death penalty.

Franklin was sentenced to life in prison.

Not long after his trial, Callahan's death penalty was declared unconstitutional. That was in 1972, when the death penalty was wholly banned in the United States. Callahan's death sentence was automatically reduced to life in prison.

Before there was the sentence of "life without parole," there was inherent in a "life sentence" in Georgia that prisoners were eligible for parole after seven years. The Georgia Pardons and Parole Board granted parole to both Callahan and Franklin after serving just thirteen years of their life sentences because they were "model prisoners"!

Consider this: If it weren't for the timing of the constitutional ban on death sentences, Callahan would have been dead and buried. As he deserved. Instead, a cop-killer was freed. He was as free to walk the streets as those of us who have never committed a crime of any kind.

Consider this, too: How is it possible to measure "model prisoner" against the murder of a cop, or anyone.

Consider this as well: Why doesn't the Georgia Pardons and Parole Board realize it is further diminishing the respect and confidence the public has in our criminal justice system?

Anita Kaylor lost her husband, "a caring, loving, kind, and

sweet man," to two vicious thugs who had no care for another's life.

The murder of her husband left Anita Kaylor a widow with a three-month-old infant son to raise alone. That son, Billy Kaylor Jr., who never knew his father, is now (at this writing) thirty-seven years old and a successful computer programmer.

Atlanta police officer Billy Kaylor is buried in McCaysville, Georgia.

OFFICER
BILLY M. KAYLOR
"SHOT INVESTIGATING BURGLARY"
AUGUST 23, 1971

Atlanta Police Officer

Donald D. Baty

Airports have police officers and federal security personnel and private security guards . . . A bus station in Atlanta had one police officer

*T*here remained the unmistakable odor of gunpowder and a thick layer of smoke made halos around the ceiling lights, much like in an indoor pistol range. This gunpowder odor and smoke was within the Greyhound bus station in the heart of downtown Atlanta. It was calm, quiet—now. The shooting had stopped. Yet people still huddled behind and beneath whatever they had found for cover when the shooting had started.

"What the hell happened?" That question, or the sense of it, was whispered throughout the bus station from person to person to anyone who heard it. Because it was more of an exclamation than a question, there were no replies—only shocked and frightened looks. Even the cops who were there, and there were many, all seemed dazed and unaware of the details of what had happened. The only certainty that the cops had was that an Atlanta police officer had been shot and killed.

Bus stations nationwide, likely worldwide, attract the underbelly of society—thieves, pickpockets, derelicts, winos, pimps, prostitutes, runaways, nickel-and-dime drug pushers, and street thugs—especially at nighttime. They all prey on unaware, unsuspecting travelers. Bus stations, unlike airports, don't have legions of police officers, federal security personnel, and private security guards maintaining order and dealing with illegal activities. In Atlanta, all that was handled by one lone Atlanta police officer, on each watch, who was assigned to the adjoining Greyhound and Trailways bus stations.

On Wednesday, June 3, 1970, on the morning watch, that one lone police officer was Donald D. Baty.

Shortly after four thirty AM, several people reported to Officer Baty that a man was pacing in the waiting room, and that he was intimidating and frightening the passengers whose buses were not ready for them to board.

One frightened young woman told Baty, "I was talking on a pay phone when this Negro man walked up to me and said, 'You must confess, confess.' I said, 'Confess to what?' He just looked at me with this wild look in his eyes." Then the frightened young woman said, "He got right in my face. That's when I saw that he had a gun."

Other passengers in the waiting room reported similar things to Officer Baty. They pointed to Wordell Brock, a twenty-seven-year-old Negro man, as the source of their complaints.

Wordell Brock Jr. of Tuscaloosa, Alabama, was discharged from the United States Air Force on a Section 8 (mental instability) in March of 1969. On June 3, 1970, he was traveling by bus from Tuscaloosa to somewhere in Kentucky. His bus from Tuscaloosa arrived at the Greyhound bus station in Atlanta during the early morning hours. His connecting bus to Kentucky was not going to depart until several hours later.

During that time, Brock walked around outside of the bus station where he met and befriended Charlie Woodard, a local thug. Brock had a pistol. And Woodard had a pistol. Together they robbed four people on the surrounding streets within less than an hour. The victims called the police. When the police arrived, Brock and Woodard were no longer on the street, they were inside the bus station where Brock continued to harass and frighten waiting passengers.

Officer Baty approached Wordell Brock in the bus station waiting room. He ordered Brock to turn around and to put his hands up against the bank of the public lockers. Brock complied. But then spun around and shot Baty once in the chest at point blank range. Severely wounded and going down, Baty drew his service revolver and fired six rounds, missing Brock and everyone else.

Someone called the police.

Police radio dispatcher: *"Any car near the Greyhound bus station, signal 63/50/4* [officer needs help/person shot/ambulance on the way]. *It's been reported that a police officer has been shot."*

Two patrol cars were a couple of blocks away. The officers were there taking reports from Brock's and Woodard's robbery victims. The two cops heard the call to the bus station and were there less than a minute later. As they entered the bus station, they heard shots fired from within the baggage room. The bullets splintered wooden benches, shattered windows, and ricocheted off metal lockers.

Police unit: *"Car 22, let those cars come on. Someone's shooting at us, and it looks like it's coming from the baggage room. And let that ambulance come on, too. We've got an officer shot."*

As more and more cops poured into the bus station, they saw that the cops who were already there were directing their fire into the baggage room. So the late arrivals did the same. All those police officers, with their adrenaline pumping, were letting their emotions superseded their training, their good judgment, and their common sense. They were all firing into the baggage room at an unknown target with an unknown location within the room.

The streets outside the bus station were thick with patrol cars. Some patrol cars butted against others. Some still had their blue lights flashing and sirens wailing. All of them had been left behind. Their drivers had rushed to join the shooting inside. Left where they were, those vacant patrol cars, and some civilian cars, created a traffic jam that extended blocks beyond the periphery of the bus station.

The ambulance that was dispatched to transport the wounded officer had difficulty reaching the bus station because of the police vehicles clogging the surrounding streets. The ambulance driver had to negotiate his way over sidewalks, down narrow alleys, and through empty parking lots to get as close as possible to the bus station. Once he arrived, the engine stalled and would not start again. A second ambulance was dispatched, got through the same obstacles in much the same way, and transported Officer D. D. Baty to Grady Hospital. He was pronounced DOA in the emergency room. The ER doctor said that the delay in getting Baty to the hospital did not contribute to his death. The bullet had pierced Baty's heart, and the probability was high that he had died within the first minute after he was hit.

Back at the bus station, the shots fired from within the baggage room stopped. But the cops still fired several more rounds into the baggage room. When all was quiet, the cops slowly and cautiously entered the baggage room. There they found two Negro males. One was dead. It was Charlie Woodard. His body was bleeding from multiple gunshot wounds, and his gun was still clutched in his hand. The other Negro was fifty-year-old Tony Plant, a Greyhound employee who worked the shoeshine stand. Plant had sustained two gunshot wounds and suffered additional injuries from one of the cops who beat him. Homicide detective Lee New recognized Plant, knew him to be a long-time worker at the bus station, and removed him from the baggage room to await medical help.

Having found Woodard dead, but still clutching his gun, it was easy for all the cops to conclude that he was the one who had shot and killed Officer Baty. But that conclusion evaporated when two of the many cops who were still milling around in the baggage room noticed another Negro male hiding on one of the shelves behind some luggage. One cop reached in and pulled out a gun; the other cop pulled the man out from behind the luggage and off of the shelf. This man was Wordell Brock. Witnesses still in the waiting room identified him as the man who shot Officer Baty.

A mob of out-of-control cops forcibly escorted Brock out of the baggage room, through the waiting room, and to a waiting paddy wagon outside the station. The cops beat him the entire way before literally throwing him into the wagon. Superior officers were able to establish some semblance of order among the cops once Brock was inside the wagon. They sent officers back to their assigned beats and only kept those police personnel who were needed to assist the homicide detectives in taking witnesses' testimonies and in processing the crime scene.

After the violence ended and the passengers began to walk cautiously back to the bus station, one man climbed aboard a bus and remarked over his shoulder, gesturing toward the luggage room, "My luggage is in there. They can have the damn stuff. I'm getting out of this town!"

Several robbery victims were brought to the Fulton County Morgue. They identified the body of Charlie Woodard as the one who had robbed them outside the Greyhound bus station earlier that morning when Officer D. D. Baty was killed.

Both Brock's and Woodard's guns were taken to the Georgia State Crime Lab for ballistics comparison with the bullet recovered from the body of Officer D. D. Baty. It was concluded that Brock's gun was the murder weapon. Woodard was listed on the APD incident report as "felon killed by police."

Wordell Brock was declared insane and sent to a mental hospital. He was never brought to trial.

Tony Plant, the shoeshine stand operator for Greyhound, did not sue the City of Atlanta for his injuries. He told Detective Lee New that he felt no anger toward the police for shooting and beating him, that he understood the feelings and actions of the officers. He was glad that they had gotten the one who had killed Officer Baty. Plant said that he had gotten to know Baty, after all, they both worked at the Greyhound bus station.

All that is known about twenty-three-year-old Atlanta police officer Donald D. Baty is that he was an APD cop for only eighteen months before he was shot and killed in the pre-dawn hours by a madman. And before becoming a cop, he served in the military in Vietnam.

All Atlanta police officers are now required to attend annual in-service training at the Police Academy where they must qualify on the pistol range in order to remain certified. Also, classroom training now includes subjects such as firearms discipline and professional conduct under stress. The incident at the bus station was the basis for this new training.

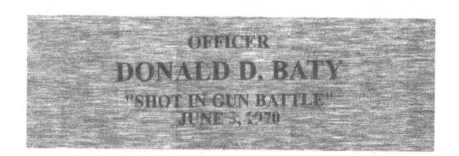

OFFICER
DONALD D. BATY
"SHOT IN GUN BATTLE"
JUNE 3, 1970

Atlanta Police Lieutenant

E. Bryson Mitchell Jr.

"Give me an ambulance . . . I've been shot . . . oh God . . . in the stomach!"

The plea for help was broadcast over every police radio in the City of Atlanta. No radio number was given to identify the caller. No location was given to identify where the call had come from. The call came in at 4:18 AM on Wednesday, May 17, 1967. All the cops on the morning watch froze, waiting for the caller, someone, anyone, to broadcast the location.

Waiting . . . waiting . . . then, "374, I've been shot!" That was Lieutenant Mitchell's radio number. But where was he? Where did the call come from?

A woman in her apartment was awakened from sleep by gunshots fired outside and nearby. The gunshots were followed by a man's voice, "Oh lord, someone help me!" She looked out her window and saw a patrol car in the driveway. She heard the voice again and realized it was coming from someone lying across the front seat of the patrol car. She rushed to the phone and called the police.

Police dispatcher: *"Any car near 256 Rawson Street SW, signal 63/50/4* [officer needs help/person shot/ambulance on the way]. *First car to arrive, advise."*

Police unit (less than a minute later): *"Car 40, Lieutenant Mitchell's been shot. We need that ambulance right away!"*

Lieutenant E. Bryson Mitchell Jr. was found slumped across the front seat of his patrol car with two gunshot wounds. The radio mike was still grasped tightly in his hand, although he was nonresponsive. Led by a police escort, the ambulance went as fast as it could to Grady Hospital. But the life left Lieutenant Mitchell before the ambulance had arrived. Mitchell was pronounced DOA by the doctors in the emergency room.

Bryson Mitchell was an Atlanta police lieutenant. He was only twenty-six years of age. And he was dead.

Bryson Mitchell was born in the small town of Elberton, Georgia, located east of Atlanta and near the Georgia-South Carolina state line. His family moved to Atlanta where he attended Bass High School. He was 6'2" and an athletic 200 pounds—an outstanding high school football player. He was awarded a football scholarship to Georgia Tech in 1959. While playing for Georgia Tech, Bryson sustained a career-ending injury. After completing his first year at Tech, he left to serve his two-year obligation in the United States Army. (This was back when the U.S. military was drafting eligible young men.) Bryson Mitchell was honorably discharged after fulfilling his service time. He joined the Atlanta Police Department shortly thereafter. The year was 1962.

Bryson Mitchell met Sally Stynchcombe. They dated, and in time, they were married. Sally was the daughter of Fulton County sheriff Leroy Stynchcombe.

It was apparent to all those Mitchell worked with and to those he reported to that he was quite bright. Not many Atlanta cops had college backgrounds to any extent in the '50s and '60s. He progressed up the ranks—detective, sergeant, and lieutenant—within five years. That was unprecedented—no other cop had moved up that fast. At the age of twenty-six, Bryson Mitchell was the youngest lieutenant in the APD, destined to move further up the ranks for sure!

But that path was not to be.

The events that led to Lieutenant E. B. Mitchell's death began during the early morning when a hardware store was broken into and merchandise was taken. A short time later, several Negro males were observed unloading merchandise from a car at a nearby Rawson Street apartment complex. Whoever had observed this activity called the police. A patrol car was dispatched. Car 40 got the call and was responding. Lieutenant Mitchell was also on the street at that time, so it was likely that he had heard the call. As the superior officer in that district, and apparently not far away, he decided to respond as backup. Lieutenant Mitchell arrived at the scene of the reported activity before car 40.

Mitchell opened the door of his patrol car, started to step out, and he was shot twice by one of the men unloading merchandise from the car. He fell back across the front seat, grabbed the radio mike, and tried to call for help. The men ran before car 40 arrived, abandoning their car. It was later learned that the car was stolen. The merchandise they had been unloading was identified as the stolen merchandise from the hardware store. None of the responding police units observed anyone running in the predawn darkness.

The hunt was on for the killers of the popular young lieutenant. Patrolmen, detectives, superior officers, and even those cops with inside desk jobs were working the streets, looking for the killer and those with him. It didn't take long to locate and apprehend them. Information was received from an informant that the man the police were looking for was hiding in the attic of 226 Rawson Street, a building within the same block as the murder scene.

In 1967, there were no SWAT or tactical teams in the APD. Police, when confronted with a tactical situation, used whomever and whatever was available at the time to apprehend the suspected criminals. When the police received the address of the Rawson building where the killer was hiding, several detectives and superior officers responded—together, they quickly collected themselves, and whether they realized it or not, they were the tactical team. They entered the building and proceeded to an unoccupied upstairs apartment. In the apartment's bathroom ceiling was an opening that provided access to the attic. In one of the rooms of that vacant apartment were a couple of old bedsprings. The makeshift tactical team brought the bedsprings into the bathroom, placed them against the wall, and used them as a ladder to climb to the opening and into the attic.

Lieutenant H. L. "Buddy" Whalen, Captain J. F. "Johnny" Johnson, along with Detectives J. F. Paschall and L. D. Howard climbed up through the hole in the ceiling and into the attic. They cautiously and quietly searched in the dark, expecting that somewhere in the maze of wooden beams was an armed cop killer.

From out of the quiet darkness, Lieutenant Whalen sharply commanded, "Drop that gun. Put your hands up where I can see them!" For a moment, none of the other three cops had any idea who Whalen was ordering to drop the gun. Whalen was standing alongside a chimney, looking down into a narrow opening in the attic floor that led to a very confined space nearly eight feet below. In the space was a Negro male holding a gun in his hand. The man complied with Whalen's command and dropped the gun where he stood. Either the man slipped and fell into that narrow space or he voluntarily took refuge in it, expecting to find his way out later. However, that was not possible as there was no way out of the space without the help of someone from above the opening in the attic. There and then, that help was the police. To get him out, the man raised both of his arms and Whalen, with Johnson's help, grabbed the man's arms and pulled him up and out.

While still in the attic, the police sent word to the cops waiting on the street that they needed a skinny and lanky teenager sent up. They needed a teenager to lower down into the narrow space to retrieve the gun. A sixteen-year-old boy volunteered to go up to the attic. He appeared to be just the right size to do what the police needed him to do. The boy was lowered headfirst into the space as Lieutenant Whalen and Captain Johnson held him by his ankles. The boy's arms reached downward and recovered the gun that the suspect had dropped there.

The gun, a .22 caliber pistol, was turned over to detectives, who took it to the Georgia State Crime Lab for ballistics tests.

The man found hiding in the attic was identified as Jesse Leon Jones, a twenty-four-year-old career criminal with a lengthy record dating back to when he was a juvenile. He had recently escaped from the Oglethorpe County Prison where he was serving a twenty-year sentence for multiple burglaries, larcenies, and auto thefts. He committed all these crimes in the City of Atlanta.

Detectives found two witnesses who said they saw Jones on the morning of May 17, soon after the murder of Lieutenant Mitchell. John Lucear, who lived at 226 Rawson Street, told detectives that Jesse Leon Jones had stopped by his apartment and had said that he had robbed somebody and shot a policeman.

"He said he thought the police was going for his gun, so he grabbed his own gun and shot twice," Lucear said.

Another resident of 226 Rawson Street, John Shanks, said that at about five AM, Jones came into his apartment and unloaded a pistol.

Shanks said that Jones told him, "I shot a police. I don't know if he's dead or not." Jones then asked Shanks to turn on the radio so he could listen to the news and find out how badly the officer was hurt.

Subsequent to his arrest, Jesse Leon Jones was turned over to homicide detectives. During the detectives' questioning, Jones denied any involvement in the murder of Lieutenant Mitchell. He also denied any knowledge of the hardware store burglary and the stolen car, a Pontiac. However, the bullets recovered from the body of Lieutenant Mitchell were determined to have been fired from the .22 caliber revolver that Jones had had in his hand in the attic when he was arrested. In addition, Jones's fingerprints were found in the burglarized hardware store and in the interior of the stolen Pontiac.

When homicide detectives G. E. Davis and F. L. Russell confronted Jones with this evidence, he admitted to the burglary and the stolen car. He said that he and four others were unloading the items taken in the burglary when Lieutenant Mitchell pulled up beside the Pontiac. Jones said that he ran and did not look back. He told Davis and Russell that the others must have run too, but he did not know which of the four shot the lieutenant.

The other four suspects, John Shanks, John Lucear, Charlie Berry, and Edgar Roberts were rounded up and brought in for questioning. When told that Jones had named them as partners in the burglary and implicated one of them in the murder of Lieutenant Mitchell, all four admitted to the burglary. The suspects were questioned separately. Each of the four, independent of the others, gave the same account of what had happened when Lieutenant Mitchell pulled into the driveway.

John Shanks set the record straight, "The four of us started running before the police car stopped, but not Jones. He was still standing beside the Pontiac when the police started opening his door. By that time, we was gone behind the buildings."

The next time they saw Jones was when he had come into the apartment where they were staying. He told them, "I shot a police. I don't know if he's dead or not."

Jesse Leon Jones pleaded not guilty in Fulton County Superior Court and was given a jury trial. Shanks, Lucear, Berry, and Roberts testified against Jones. With the weight of the forensic and ballistics evidence, the jury found Jones guilty of murder, burglary, and auto theft. Jesse Leon Jones was sentenced to death in the electric chair for the murder of Atlanta police lieutenant Edwin Bryson Mitchell Jr. The other four received lighter sentences for burglary in exchange for their testimony.

Bryson Mitchell's death left Sally Mitchell a widow with two young daughters, Gina and Pam.

LIEUTENANT
E. B. MITCHELL
"SHOT INVESTIGATING BURGLARY"
MAY 17, 1967

Atlanta Police Officer

Claude E. Mundy Jr.

When Atlanta awoke to see what was hard for anyone—white or colored—to imagine

Claude E. Mundy Jr. was the first black Atlanta police officer intentionally killed in the line of duty.

In 1948, Police Chief Herbert T. Jenkins decided that Atlanta needed "colored" police officers. (For at least 150 years, "colored" was the accepted way to refer to the Negro in the United States. It was not until the mid to late 1960s that "colored" was replaced by Negro, which was later replaced by black, then African American, and more recently, "of color.") There were increasing numbers of colored police officers in the northern cities of the United States in the late 1940s and 1950s.

But it remained a radical idea in the segregated Deep South. In Atlanta, there were strong objections from the segregated and extremely nervous white community about how colored police officers would affect the social order. Nevertheless, there were some forward-thinking leaders, newspaper writers and editors, and those within the religious communities who supported Chief Jenkins's recommendation, possibly because they recognized that it was inevitable. The proponents in Atlanta who supported the introduction of colored policemen realized that they had to be introduced to the community in a careful and deliberate way. All parties to this complex and emotional "first" reached a compromise with the support of Atlanta mayor William B. Hartsfield. The following are the agreed conditions:

- Colored policemen would have no authority or arrest powers over white citizens.
- Colored policemen would only work in colored areas.
- Colored policemen would be headquartered in and work out of the colored YMCA.
- Colored policemen would be led by a white commanding officer.
- Colored policemen would be completely segregated from white policemen.
- Colored policemen were not permitted to wear their uniforms or carry their equipment when off duty like the white policemen were allowed to do.

Despite these restrictions there came a day in 1948 when Atlanta awoke to see for the first time what was hard for anyone, white or colored, to imagine—eight colored men in Atlanta police uniforms, driving Atlanta police cars, and walking beats on the streets of Atlanta.

Inherent in the job of any police officer, in any city at any moment, are stress and danger. For that first group of colored police officers, in a racially segregated society, there was also the added stress and danger from external sources not related to their work as cops. The white cops shunned the colored policemen. They also had to endure the taunts and insults from many in the black community who accused them of being "Uncle Toms" (an insulting reference to their status in relation to the whites, prompted by Harriet Beecher Stowe's book, *Uncle Tom's Cabin*).

For those first colored cops, worse than being shunned by the white cops and worse than the insults from the colored community, was the incessant uncertainty that the white cops would not back them up in dangerous situations. Policemen depend on one another for their physical well-being and safety. The colored cops saw the white cops go to the aid of other white cops who were in danger, but the colored cops were never sure when or if they could count on their white counterparts in the same situations.

This is not an indictment of white policemen, but it is an honest attempt to understand and explain their reasoning when faced with this new and drastic change. World War II had ended just three years before with a racially segregated U.S. military. It was the way things were; it was the norm. (During that era most Atlanta police officers were southerners.) In 1948, all that changed for Atlanta and its police department, resulting in difficult times for both black and white police officers.

By 1961, colored cops still only worked in the colored areas. However, a few of those original restrictions were turned off: colored cops no longer operated out of the colored YMCA. They operated out of the police headquarters, although they were confined to a separate colored section where they had their own roll call room, locker room, and restroom. In 1961, their numbers had risen to thirty-five, and they were commanded by a colored sergeant, the first colored superior officer, Sergeant Howard Baugh. But they were still completely segregated from the white cops. Thirteen years had gone by, and although animosity and mistrust still remained, things had settled down with an uneasy peace between Atlanta's colored and white policemen.

As they had from the beginning, all the colored cops worked six PM to two AM. They were known as the "six o'clock watch." Some in the colored community still felt animosity toward the colored policemen. There were many times when someone from the colored community called the APD operator needing a police officer and then had insisted, "Don't send those colored police, send the white police!"

Officers Claude Mundy and H. H. Hooks, two of the original eight colored policemen recruited in 1948, were assigned to car 13. Their beat covered an area just east of downtown in the Fourth Ward, commonly referred to as "Buttermilk Bottoms."

On January 5, 1961, just after midnight, Mundy and Hooks received a signal 42 (burglary) to 572 Parkway Drive NE, apartment #6. It was a two-story building, and apartment #6 was on the second floor. When Mundy and Hooks arrived, they were met by the caller, Wilbert Ponder, who lived in apartment #5. He told them that he had heard someone break into apartment #6. Ponder cautioned the two cops that apartment #6 had a back door.

Officer Hooks went around to the rear of the building and then ran up the back stairs to cover the back door. He looked through the glass door and observed a man turning off a light inside the apartment. As Hooks looked through the glass door, Officer Mundy climbed the front stairs to the second floor and knocked on the main door of apartment #6.

In 1961, the only police radio available to all the officers, white and colored, was the radio mounted in the patrol cars. Hooks could not tell Mundy that he had just seen someone in the now-darkened apartment. A woman resident across from apartment #6 heard Officer Mundy knock on the door several times without any response. On the third attempt, she heard Mundy say, "Open the door please."

The door opened and a colored man stood there facing Mundy. Mundy stepped inside and started to search the suspected burglar.

In the next instant, the suspect jammed a .22 caliber pistol against Officer Mundy's chest and fired twice. Mundy drew his service revolver and fired all six rounds as he fell, hitting the shooter five times.

Officer Hooks, hearing the gunfire, tried and failed to break in the back glass door. He had to run around to the front of the building. Inside the front entrance, he found a man on the hallway floor bleeding from multiple gunshot wounds. He ordered Ponder to call the police and an ambulance. Hooks then ran up the stairs and entered apartment #6, where he found Mundy on the floor bleeding from the two gunshot wounds in his chest. Both guns, the suspect's .22 caliber and Mundy's .38 caliber, were on the floor next to Mundy.

The shooter, twenty-five-year-old Joe Louis Pass, was DOS (dead on the scene). Officer Claude Mundy still had a spark of life in his seriously wounded body. The cops at the scene, both colored and white, desperately pleaded for an ambulance. (Grady Hospital ambulances were one of the few entities that were not racially segregated.) A Grady ambulance arrived within minutes to transport Mundy to Grady Hospital through downtown streets and intersections blocked by white cops. The escorting patrol cars were driven by colored and white cops. By the time Claude Mundy was brought to the "Colored Clinic" of Grady Hospital (across the hall from the "White Clinic"), he was DOA.

That incident began to answer the questions of how the white cops would react when a colored cop was in dire need.

Homicide detectives investigating the murder of Officer Claude Mundy interviewed witnesses, including the estranged wife of Joe Louis Pass, her neighbors, and her friends. The detectives concluded that Pass broke into the apartment where his wife was living and was going to ambush her when she returned home. It was determined that the murder weapon, the .22 caliber pistol, was small enough for Pass to conceal in his hand and that he was likely holding it when Mundy entered the apartment.

Atlanta police officer Claude Mundy Jr. was one of the first eight colored police officers in the Atlanta Police Department.

But he will always be recognized singularly as the first black Atlanta police officer killed in the line of duty.

OFFICER
CLAUDE E. MUNDY JR.
"SHOT INVESTIGATING BURGLARY"
JANUARY 5, 1961

Atlanta Police Officer

Hoyle W. Dye

He asked me my name . . . and I shot him

It was "back in the day" when all Atlanta police officers reported for duty, regardless of assignment, at the same location: Atlanta Police Headquarters, 165 Decatur Street SE, in downtown Atlanta. Roll call for the Uniform (Patrol) Division was held in a large assembly room in the basement of the building.

Cops arrived early, some an hour or more before their reporting times, sat around with their colleagues, and did what cops everywhere did—told war stories. It became a social phenomenon. A ritual.

Officers H. W. Dye and J. R. Weldon were partners who enjoyed those light-hearted early morning moments before they had to take possession of their patrol car from the previous watch and head to their beat.

November 9, 1960, started out like any other day for the two veteran cops who were assigned to car 11, day watch. Dye and Weldon's beat covered a predominantly colored area west of downtown. Their first stop every morning was the Luckie Street Grill, a small rundown restaurant in the seedy part of the city. It was where they got coffee to go, coffee that got them going in the morning to face the day ahead. They usually returned several hours later for lunch. The Luckie Street Grill was rundown, but it was always crowded with other cops, detectives, and an assortment of blue-collar workers.

(Note: The Luckie Street Grill, a favorite cops' eatery, is no longer there. In its place is the Georgia Aquarium [the world's largest aquarium].)

That morning was uneventful. They answered three low-priority calls, took reports on minor thefts, and handled a fender-bender traffic accident. At 11:50 AM, they received the call that triggered the events that would end in tragedy:

Police dispatcher: *"Car 11, at 449 Northside Drive NW, apartment 217, signal 39/29* [information on a disturbance], *be advised a possible 69* [person armed] *pistol on call."*

Car 11: *"11 received, 449 Northside Drive #217, signal 39/29, possible 69 pistol."*

When Dye and Weldon arrived at the address, they were met by a woman who identified herself as the caller. She said she lived at the address with her two grown children, a son and a daughter. Earlier that morning, her thirty-five-year-old son had attacked his sister. He had knocked her down and had threatened her with a pistol. The mother told Dye and Weldon that she and her daughter had run out of the apartment and had called the police about an hour later.

The woman told the officers that she was afraid of her son, George Gray. She asked them to come into the apartment with her to make sure that he was not there. She told Dye and Weldon that her son had a history of mental illness. After searching and finding no one in the apartment, they assured her that he was not there. She gave the officers a description of George Gray. As the two were leaving, she said that if they found him, her daughter would press charges for assault from earlier that morning.

Dye and Weldon decided to check a few of the neighborhood hangouts for George Gray, then they would head to the Luckie Street Grill for lunch.

The first place they checked was the Wiener Wonder Bar, a popular colored bar and grill, at Northside Drive and Simpson Street NW. Once inside, Weldon went up to the bar to ask the manager if he was familiar with George Gray. At the same time, Dye walked toward the rear, along a row of booths that were opposite the long bar, to the last booth where a man was sitting alone. Dye probably recognized Gray from the description his mother had given them. Dye asked him his name. Without answering, Gray stood up, gun in hand, and shot Dye in the chest, killing him instantly.

Gray never spoke a word.

Dye's last words were either "What's your name?" or "Are you George Gray?"

Weldon heard the shot, turned, and saw his partner fall to the floor. Gray fired a second shot at Weldon. It missed. Weldon returned fire. He didn't miss, hitting Gray once in the stomach.

Weldon said, "I looked down at Dye on the floor and then looked back at the subject, who was still standing with the gun in his hand, and I fired two more shots, at which time the subject then fell to the floor."

Weldon then ran outside to his patrol car, got on the police radio, and called for assistance, an ambulance, a superior officer, Homicide, and several patrol cars (to protect the crime scene and to detain the people in the bar who had witnessed the entire incident). When Weldon returned to the bar, Gray was gone. The manager pointed to an exit door and told Weldon that the man had gotten up from the floor and had stumbled through the door. Weldon went out and found Gray, wounded, leaning up against the building. Weldon brought Gray back inside. He was still able to walk despite having been shot three times.

Northside Drive and Simpson Street, a major intersection, was clogged with police cars and emergency vehicles. Motorcycle cops had to be dispatched to get traffic moving again at the intersection and the surrounding streets.

George Gray was turned over to homicide detectives H. Baugh and C. J. Perry (the first two black detectives; Baugh later became the first black superior officer) to investigate the murder of Atlanta police officer Hoyle W. Dye. Gray needed medical treatment for his gunshot wounds, but he said he didn't need to be transported in an ambulance (that had not yet arrived). He insisted that the backseat of their detective car would be fine; he walked to their car with very little assistance.

En route to Grady Hospital, the detective car burst into flames at Simpson and Marietta Streets. The three occupants quickly got out, although Gray needed some help. Once out of the car, they had no radio. So they flagged down a passing taxi and instructed the driver to call his taxi dispatcher. They told the taxi dispatcher to call the fire and police departments to report that a detective car was on fire at Simpson and Marietta Streets. After a short delay, Gray and the two detectives were transported to Grady in another detective car.

(Each year the APD acquired new cars for its fleet. Some of the older cars were passed on to the colored cops. The cause of the fire in the car assigned to Detectives Baugh and Perry was later determined to be gasoline leaking from a faulty connection under the hood.)

At Grady Hospital, while being prepped for the operating room, Gray told homicide detectives Baugh and Perry, "I was on my side of town, and I wasn't bothering nobody. He come up and asked my name, and I shot him. He had no right to bother me."

The detectives said Gray showed no remorse over the shooting.

George Gray had been in the military for seventeen years. When his behavior became erratic and bizarre, he was given a Section 8 discharge (mentally incompetent). This was less than one year before the shooting. He survived his gunshot wounds. When his mental health was evaluated, he was declared insane and not competent to stand trial.

George Gray was sent to the state hospital for the criminally insane in Milledgeville, Georgia, with orders from the court that if he was ever released from Milledgeville, he must be remanded to the Fulton County sheriff.

Forty-one-year-old Atlanta police officer Hoyle W. Dye, a fourteen-year APD veteran, left behind a widow, Julia Ellen Dye, and a son, Robert Hoyle Dye.

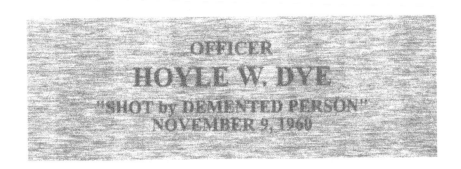

OFFICER
HOYLE W. DYE
"SHOT by DEMENTED PERSON"
NOVEMBER 9, 1960

A Word from the Author

I am sitting in the middle of a pew, somewhere in the middle row of pews. I have been here before. Not seated in the same place, not exactly. But for the same reason, exactly the same reason. Most things in life get easier to do each time you do them . . . but not this. This gets more difficult. For the others who have been here before . . . it gets more difficult. The others, in their blue uniforms, sitting sternly in the pew beside me, in front of me, behind me. I can see a deeper layer of heartbreak in the faces of those who have been here before. Not in this place, exactly. But for the same reason, exactly. I think those who have been here before see the same in my face.

When all is in place. And all are assembled. There is silence . . . From somewhere in the nearby pews I hear breathing. Someone attempting to cover a cough. Or clearing a throat. I know what happens next to the silence. I have been here before. The first time I was here, I was startled when it happened. I hear what seems like a growl. A faint growl. Those around me who have never been here are startled. The growl becomes a moan. It grows deeper . . . grows louder . . . louder . . . then that one long syllable . . . pleading . . . nooo-o-o-o!!!

I know that sound. It comes from the front pew. From the young widow. There's no suppressing her grief. Her young children, hearing her wail, begin to sob. They cling to each other. They are small children. I can't see them from where I sit. But I know they are holding each other . . . I have been here before.

They are in the first pew. Closest to the flag-draped casket and nearest to the altar. Within is the Atlanta police officer—their father, her husband. He left for work, what seems to them an eternity ago, but it was only a brief day or two before. To do his job as an Atlanta cop or his extra job, which he did, not as a cop,

259

but because he was a cop. He did not return home. He was killed because he was a cop.

The church seems larger than it really is . . . I have been here before. Larger perhaps because the aisles and the back are swollen with people. Silent. Still. Only their eyes flickering. From the front pew. To the casket. To the chaplain at the altar.

The chaplain will say what he says. I wonder about what he says. I have been here before. I wonder if what he says could provide comfort for my own wife and my kids if I were in that casket. I wonder. Each time I have been here, I have wondered. I am an Atlanta police officer. So I wonder about that.

A police officer steps slowly toward the head of the casket. He is going to say a few words about the officer inside it. He is the partner of the officer who has been killed. He begins. Words start. Pause. A sob . . . the next few words come in a voice different from the first few words . . . another sob . . . pause. The partner steps down. No more words. More words are unnecessary. I have been here before.

Pallbearers from the Atlanta Police Honor Guard assemble. Even spaces separate each officer on each side of the casket. Together. Precisely. They lift the casket. They move forward. Carrying it down the main aisle. Their steps are as though locked together . . . precisely . . . slowly . . . reverently. To the hearse waiting outside. Its door open. I am still where I was sitting when I came into the church. I can't see the hearse. But it's there. I have been here before.

The family and close friends follow behind the casket. Followed by APD ranking superiors. Followed by officials from the government of Atlanta. Followed by a shuffling wave of blue, Atlanta police officers—hundreds—exiting the church and assembling in an order beside the hearse with uniformed police officers from the Metro Atlanta area, from throughout Georgia, from other parts of the United States, from Canada. A kaleidoscope of respect and mourning from colleagues near and not so near.

A black stripe rests horizontally across the police badge on every uniform. I wear that black stripe across my badge. I have worn it before. The black stripe is on every badge on every uniform of every police officer from the time of the death notification until the day after internment.

I assemble with the other Atlanta police officers. I know where to be. I have been here before.

The honor guard team leader commands—sharply— ATTENTION! All police officers, from near and not so near, stand more firmly erect. Their faces frozen, facing forward. All eyes are fixed on the horizon—PRESENT ARMS. We respond immediately. Snapping as one a crisp military salute as the casket is slid, slowly, into the hearse. A lone bagpiper plays "Going Home." I have heard it before. I choke back a sob. But I can't withhold the watery film that fills my eyes.

The piper presses a long slowly diminishing note. The hearse quietly begins to move. We all break from our assembly. I look for the patrol car. I know where it is. It will take me to the cemetery. Motorcycles roar to life. Car doors open. Car doors close. Engines start. The motorcade forms, without requiring direction. The drivers have been here before. They know what to do, where to be, how to go, the way to drive, so do the cops leading the Atlanta police motorcycle escort, followed by the police motorcycles from the other agencies. A double line of one hundred motorcycles leads the hearse and limousines with family members.

Following behind those limos are APD patrol cars, APD unmarked cars, patrol cars from other police agencies, and civilian cars. I'm in one of the APD patrol cars. I have been here before.

The motorcycles give a coarse hum as they lead the hearse. I think to myself how remarkable it is that they don't tip over going so slowly. The funeral procession makes its way to the cemetery. Through surface streets, then through the interstate freeway. It stretches ahead farther than I can see . . . but I know it is about three miles in length. I have been here before. Traffic is disrupted all along the way to the cemetery. Motorists are delayed. But it's okay. They're aware from the media that this is the police officer who was killed recently. As the hearse passes the disrupted motorists, many get out of their cars. Place their hands over their hearts. I have seen this before.

Patience and emotional endurance enter us as we arrive at the cemetery. Atlanta cops in blue. Cops from near and not so near in the colors of their uniforms. Shoulder to shoulder. Eyes forward. On both sides of the path from where the limo with the family stops. Up to the gravesite we form this aisle of honor and respect. It's what we do. For one of us who was working one day, as we work every work day, but did not return home. We are here because we returned home from work the day that officer was killed.

I am here this day. I have been here before.

It takes awhile for the mourners to proceed from their cars to their places at the gravesite. The immediate family is escorted by the honor guard from the limo to the gravesite. Since the death notification, two members of the honor guard have been with the family. The family is seated at the gravesite under a canvas canopy. The mayor, the police chief, other high-ranking police officials, and dignitaries flank the family. I have seen this before.

When all is ready and everyone is in place—there is quiet. The kind of quiet that signals all is ready and everyone is in place. The honor guard team leader speaks. ATTENTION . . . PRESENT ARMS. The right arm of every cop moves upward, open palm facing downward at the forehead. A mass salute—frozen— from the moment the flag-draped casket is taken from the hearse. Slowly it is carried through our aisle of honor and respect.

The bagpiper follows the casket. Behind him is a riderless horse. In the stirrups are riding boots facing backward, representing the slain officer facing the rear, reviewing the procession for the final time.

"Amazing Grace" plays from the pipes. I feel myself trembling, but I hold my salute. The casket and piper pass where I am standing. I am unable to stop the tears from sliding down my cheeks, nor the sobs that escape from my throat. I have been here before. It gets harder . . . each time I am here.

The casket arrives at the gravesite and is placed atop the grave. We break our salute. We break from our places. The only sound is of the grass yielding under our footsteps. We proceed toward the gravesite, assembling there in no prearranged order. We are now just people—not cops—silently saying goodbye to another. A friend. Someone we knew. Or could have easily known as a friend. The chaplain says what he says . . . as he has said before . . . and has said before . . . and as he has said before . . . and before.

The honor guard lifts the flag, holds it taut, and starts to fold it above the casket. Folded, it is delivered to the Atlanta chief of police. The seven-member Atlanta Police Firing Team fires three volleys, the twenty-one gun salute, into the sky above the casket. I have been here before. A lone bugler plays "Taps" as the casket is lowered into the grave. I try again not to tremble. The chief of police presents the folded flag to the widow.

An increasing whup-whup of engines comes from overhead. Six police helicopters from Atlanta and other agencies appear in the sky heading directly toward the cemetery. They approach together. Then one of the Atlanta police helicopters breaks formation, peels off from the other five. The missing man formation—representing and saluting the slain Atlanta police officer.

The casket is in the ground. The ceremonies are done. We return to the cars that brought us here. We return to our work. We return to our daily lives. We try to.

I have been here before. Others have been here before. Some were here today but not before. We will be here again. One of us will be among us . . . but not with us.

Epilogue

I was an Atlanta police officer. After thirty years, I retired. That was in 1992. But I still think of myself as an Atlanta police officer.

When I was an active police officer, I thought about the realities of the job every moment of every day. All cops face these realities. The most difficult reality to face—the risk. All cops think about the risks.

We are aware of the risks but not deterred by them. Instead, the awareness of those risks stimulates our alertness and motivates our need for caution as we enforce the law and protect the public. We maintain order—on the streets, other public places, everywhere.

We wear a distinct blue uniform, and we respect the badge pinned to it. Take off that uniform. We are the neighbor next door or someone from down the street. While not in uniform, we are special to special people. We are husbands, fathers, sons, brothers, friends. We are mothers, wives, sisters, daughters.

We are a brotherhood and a sisterhood. We are male and female. We are white, black, Hispanic, Asian. We are Protestant, Catholic, Jewish. We are straight; we are gay. There are many other differences—qualities, attributes, characteristics—that make us who we are.

But as Atlanta police officers we are all the same. There is only one thing that makes one of us different from the others. Some paid the ultimate price in taking those risks.

After thirty years of working on the streets of Atlanta as a police officer, facing those risks, I am alive today. I am alive and have written about twenty-eight police officers who were distinguished from the rest of us because they were intentionally killed in the line of duty.

Why did I make it? Why didn't they? It could have been luck or the difference of an instant. It could have been not being in the wrong place at the wrong time. It could have been an instinct that kicked in, in the right place and the right time. It could have been the backup that arrived exactly when I needed it. To this day, I don't know. Not for certain.

But I did make it!

With thoughts of and respect for those who didn't.

With the sorrow that all of them could have made it too.

With the realization that if they did, this book would not have been written.

But this book had to be written, written to remind us all how fragile life is for those who wear the badge, how their lives can end in an instant, and for their families who must bear the grief.

This book was written as a memorial to the twenty-eight featured on these pages, and to all the other Atlanta police officers who were killed in the line of duty by other means. They must never be forgotten!

Acknowledgements

I would like to acknowledge and thank so many people for their help in putting this book together, but doing so would almost be a book in itself. However, it would be remiss of me not to identify some individuals who went "above and beyond."

I want to thank former Atlanta Police Chief Richard Pennington for giving me authorization to research the files in the central records section and the homicide squad. Also, my thanks to APD Assistant Chief Pete Andresen and APD Major Lane Hagin for opening so many doors for me to walk through, without having to jump through hoops.

Many thanks to Ray Braswell, Mary Pealor, Lou Arcangeli, Patricia Cocciolone, Floyd Reeves, B.C. Williams, Lou Moore, Gary Shepherd, Steve Johnson, Stan Williams, Berlyn Compton, Mike Greene, and Donald Hannah who gave me interesting and valuable insights that were not in the files. Some of these same people enabled me to contact family members, partners, and friends of the twenty-eight slain police officers who graciously offered personal and poignant memories.

And to my ad hoc editorial staff of Alex Goldhagen, David Deutchman, and Hannah Silvers who, more than once, pulled me out of the grammatical ditch and put me back on the correct road, I say thanks.

As for my very good friend of fifty years, Michael Elia, it is hard for me to express the deep feeling of gratitude that I have for him. Mike is a retired editor, a veteran of two major publishers in New York. Interrupting his lucrative freelance work, he has once again used his editing skills, giving me his time, his energy, and his interest to help me put my manuscript in order, as he did for my previous book, *"Signal 63"... Officer Needs Help!* It has been my good fortune to have this good friend who happened to be an editor. Mike is enormously talented, a master of the written word, using those words like an artist uses a brush and palette; the sculptor uses a mallet and chisel. With those words, he takes my prose to a higher level. Mike's influence can be felt in the raw, deep emotions, and astonishing clarity found on many pages of this book. He is a thorough professional, and I say that with admiration and respect.

Quoting the late Mario Scimeme—a good friend to Mike and me—*"To thank a true friend for a kindness is not only unnecessary, but might be insulting."* There is nothing more for me to say to my pal, Mike Elia.

And as always, to my wife Betty; my best pal.

CPSIA information can be obtained
at www.ICGtesting.com
Printed in the USA
BVHW092357181122
652278BV00021B/1913

9 781665 305051